True Tales of the
Paranormal

True Tales of the

Paranormal

Hauntings, Poltergeists, Near-Death Experiences, and Other Mysterious Events

Kimberly Molto

A HOUNSLOW BOOK
A MEMBER OF THE DUNDURN GROUP
TORONTO · OXFORD

Publisher: Anthony Hawke
Copy-Editor: Jennifer Bergeron
Design: Jennifer Scott
Printer: Transcontinental

National Library of Canada Cataloguing in Publication Data

Molto, Kimberly
    True tales of the paranormal : hauntings, poltergeists, near-death experiences, and other mysterious events / Kimberly Molto.

ISBN 1-55002-410-8

1. Parapsychology. 2. Parapsychology and science. I. Title.

BF1031.M64 2002   130   C2002-902290-8

1   2   3   4   5   06   05   04   03   02

THE CANADA COUNCIL | LE CONSEIL DES ARTS
FOR THE ARTS | DU CANADA
SINCE 1957 | DEPUIS 1957

Canada

ONTARIO ARTS COUNCIL
CONSEIL DES ARTS DE L'ONTARIO

We acknowledge the support of the **Canada Council for the Arts** and the **Ontario Arts Council** for our publishing program. We also acknowledge the financial support of the **Government of Canada** through the **Book Publishing Industry Development Program** and **The Association for the Export of Canadian Books**, and the **Government of Ontario** through the **Ontario Book Publishers Tax Credit** program.

Dundurn Press
8 Market Street
Suite 200
Toronto, Ontario, Canada
M5E 1M6

Dundurn Press
73 Lime Walk
Headington, Oxford,
England
OX3 7AD

Dundurn Press
2250 Military Road
Tonawanda NY
U.S.A. 14150

This book is lovingly dedicated to my brother Robert Mitchell LeDuc. Also in the memory of my sister Sharlene Catherine and her husband, my dear lost friend, Ronald Pollard, who remain *"Together Forever."*

Millions of spiritual creatures walk the earth
Unseen, both when we wake, and when we sleep.
— Milton, *Paradise Lost*

The names and locations represented within this book have been changed or altered to protect the people, their survivors, and the properties involved.

Table of Contents

Acknowledgements

The author wishes to acknowledge following sources. I am greatly indebted to these people and organizations for their valuable contributions and permissions to quote from some of their material to enhance vital points. Please refer to the list of suggested readings for further resources, many of which enhanced this book.

Thanks to: Tony Hawke and the team at Hounslow Press, one of the best little parapsychology publishers, amongst many of the other subjects they cover (I still say that with a name like Hounslow, there must be a good ghost story there); also from Dundurn, Jennifer Bergeron for her careful and exceptional editing skills, not to mention the overtime; Paul Stevens, Koelster Parapsychology Unit, University of Edinburgh; Eberhard Bauer at the Institut für Grenzgebiete der Psychologie und Psychohygiene; Richard Shoup at the Boundary Institute; Dawn Elizabeth Hunt, RN with the Division of Personality Studies at the University of Virginia Health Science Center; Dr. Darryll Walsh at the Centre for Parapsychological Studies in Canada; Sue Darroch at the OPRC; Daniel Cumerlato at Haunted Hamilton; Matthew Didier at the Toronto Ghost Hauntings and Research Society; Heather Anderson of the British Columbia Ghost Research Society; Dale Kaczmarek of the Ghost Research Society; the Institute of Noetic Science; Sally Rhine Feather at the Rhine Research Center; Grady Hedrix at the American Society of Psychical Research; Arnold Lettieri, Ph.D. of the PEAR research team at Princeton; University of Virginia Personality Studies team; Dr. Eric Anderson; Ronald Pond, M.D.; Raymond L. Braida, M.D.; Michael A. Briggs, M.D.; and Mark Cuddy, Reference Clerk at the City of Toronto Archives.

Finally, and at the risk of this turning into an Academy Award speech, I would like to thank the following individuals for their personal support: Paul Taylor Papandreou, who has reread the manuscript so many times, he has it memorized; Terry "it needs a comma" Clayton, who is close to having it memorized; Kelly Zaâcharüs; Carol M. Pederson, for her excellent and patient editing assistance; Darien Papandreou for his technical support; Edgar "I'm not a copyright lawyer" Lavour; Liz and Dave Vogt (patron saint of the Macs) for their computer (when no less than two of mine blew up — the writing of this book is a book in and of itself!); Scout Vogt for her help with the typing; Dr. Deni Diejen, M.D. Ph.D.; my brother Bob for whom thanks does not begin to cover it; and Sharon Stock Feren for her artistic skills. To the book's mascot, Dusty; to Brett for his piano, ghost and all, which kept me grounded; to Madeline Kinney, Jon Ainsworth, Steve Patterson, Ian Godfrey, Dr. Michelle Douglas, Chris Howard, Alex Cooper, Kim Darely, and the other occasional members of the psychic research team. It was an arduous, uncomfortable and at times even dangerous endeavour, but was it ever worth it! I owe you all big time and look forward working with you all again. I'll bring the coffee this time. Also many thanks to Tony Arpa for helping me reopen the connecting door and entering the vortex; to Wendy Connor-Darmon, a friend whose enthusiasm was uplifting during the most stressful of times; and to Kathy Pezzack, caretaker of the magical Merlin, and John Costello for their tremendous personal support.

Those who find some tales of the paranormal difficult to believe at times would find the process involved in the creation of this book even more unbelievable. It was done against incredible odds (one of the reasons I became reinvigorated by Jung's synchronicity theory). Were it not for some of the people credited herein, this book would probably not have found its way into the world.

Most of all, my heartfelt thanks to all those people who took the time and sometimes even courage to share their stories. In the majority of cases, they did so in hopes it would become a beacon of like to others as well as an assurance to those readers experiencing such phenomena, or to those who may yet share in such experiences. They are not alone or "crazy." As is evident throughout this book, quite the contrary, they are in excellent company. There would be no book without their generosity of time, spirit, and conviction to, as one interviewee put it so eloquently, finally bring the boogeyman out of the closet!

Introduction

The title of this book was originally going to be *Rubicon: True Tales of the Paranormal*. The name came to me in a flash of inspiration one day (naming a book is much harder than one would suppose). Its historical reference is to that of Caesar crossing the river Rubicon with his army. This was tantamount to a declaration of war. Once he embarked on this endeavour, there was no turning back. The experiences shared in this book are like crossing a personal Rubicon; once your life has been touched by these extraordinary events, you are changed and things will never be the same. Fortunately, in most cases these changes are for the better, enriching people's experience and perception of life.

Since I was a child, I have been enthralled with tales of the supernatural. I read everything I could find on the subject of reincarnation, psychokinesis, telepathy, and especially ghosts. When my family moved into a seemingly innocuous three-bedroom bungalow on quiet residential street, I had my first personal encounter with the paranormal. This in turn led to my meeting others who had shared similar experiences, but we would always discuss it in hushed tones lest someone find out and think we were crazy.

Things have not changed much since the seventies. I have even been cautioned that writing a book on a so-called pseudo science could have negative repercussions on my reputation as a "serious" scientist, perhaps even affecting research grants. As there are many "serious," well-respected scientists from many disciplines who research the paranormal, I am not too concerned about negative repercussions. In fact, as you will read, much of the research findings and methodology in this unconventional field often find their way into the mainstream. As for those not researching but actually having paranormal experiences, not only did many of them wish to be anonymous, in some cases not even their close friends or family members knew of their experiences. Consequently, names were changed and the locations disguised to protect property values. A parapsychologist joked with me that at one time anything around the topic of sex was secretive; now you can't get away from it — people even reveal all on television! How odd that it is the subject of the paranormal, a rather common experience, that is kept secret.

Such experiences are more common than most people realize, probably because very few talk about it. Tales of the mysterious or supernatural date back to the time humans first began to share their stories, in part to help make sense of it all. These experiences, then and now, have a great effect on our lives, altering the way we view life, death, ourselves, and those around us. In effect it causes a paradigm shift in our basic sense of reality. The world at once becomes both smaller and infinitely larger. The old adage about things not being what they seem takes on a whole new meaning and import. It seems like there are other realities operating just under or beside the one we all inhabit. Some highly sensitive individuals are able to tune into alternate states, while others become aware of them during times of crisis or even in a dream, when the lines between reality structures are blurred.

It is important to recognize that paranormal experiences are a shared human phenomena, traversing all religions and cultures, the only difference being a matter of interpretation and, in some cases, the consequences of sharing such experiences. In some cultures, these events were accepted and the people who experienced them were often revered or considered blessed. In other cultures, you would be considered in league with the devil and burnt at the stake. These days you may be looked upon as being a bit odd or perhaps sent off to be assessed by a psychiatrist and put on some medication to help cure your delusions.[1]

When I became older, I felt compelled to examine these experiences and their meaning under a more scientific light. Most of the books I read did a marvellous job of relating the stories and they were quite entertaining, but I felt there was a lot more to it than that. Maybe it was the scientist in me, but I felt like the stories had only been half told with the ending omitted. They always left me with particular questions. What does it all mean? Why does it happen to some and not others? Why does it happen at all?

I examine these questions throughout this book. In some instances, I was left with more questions than answers, but nevertheless, I trust this book will offer you an alternative view of reality and life and perhaps offer you some food for thought that may help you uncover your own answers. In addition to providing you with reading pleasure, I hope it also serves to remind you that even in our darkest moments we are never alone on this journey through life. It may often feel that way, but as this book makes abundantly clear, things are rarely what they seem.

The Crimson Angel.

Chapter One

Rubicon 13

Charge and strict watch
that to this happy place...
No evil thing approach
or enter in.
— Milton, *Paradise Lost*

The first thing that struck my brother Gary about the house on Highgate Street was its street number: the infamous number thirteen.[1] It would prove to be an omen.

It was a pleasant three-bedroom bungalow on a large lot on a quiet, old residential street. It is one of the older houses in Guelph, Ontario, dating back to 1870, and constructed from local limestone. Though there was nothing outwardly exceptional in the architecture of the little bungalow, appearances can be deceiving. It would have exceptional effects on the lives of many touched by the house. For those more susceptible, it would alter their lives forever.

For reasons of space, I will focus on the events that occurred to the family — my family — that lived at number thirteen from the early to late seventies. This is by no means the entire story of this house.

Most of the actual physical things that happened were minor curiosities that we almost grew accustomed to. For instance, my eldest sister, Sharlene, and I were having dinner in the living room one evening when the teakettle began to whistle from the kitchen. As neither of us had put the kettle on the stove, we just looked at one another as if to say, "What else is new?"

This particular ghost, for lack of a better designation, had a penchant for water, hot water in particular. It always seemed to be turning on hot water taps in the kitchen and the bathroom, and, of course, the kettle.

Other little nuisances would often occur, such as the time a very heavy glass fruit bowl that sat atop a shelf of the kitchen hutch went crashing to the floor, startling both myself and Sharlene. Though the crash was exceptionally loud, the bowl did not sustain so much as a scratch.

My mother shared one touching event with me. "Whitey," an old and dear friend of hers, had died. She awoke one night to find him at the foot of her bed, clear as could be, assuring her that he was all right.

As I stated earlier, we became almost accustomed to these sorts of things. Other things happened that I would never get used to or, for that matter, get over. One such event has even left me with a physical scar.

I was watering a Christmas cactus in the living room window. I had an eerie sensation that someone was watching me. I turned around to see if my sister Chris was there, but as I already knew, no one was in the house. Some rattling sounds coming from the top right corner of the Venetian blinds caught my attention. At first I thought I had imagined it, but then it resumed and I not only heard it but saw it as well. The top right portion of the blind was moving in such a way as to suggest someone was parting the blades of the blind a bit in order to peek out. I just stood there, mesmerized by this oddity; then the other side of the of the heavy blind came crashing down on my right hand and arm. Understand that these were the old-fashioned blinds that were made of metal and quite heavy. They were suspended by sturdy metal brackets, which they locked into on either side. They have to be unlocked and lifted out of place, so I have no idea how this blind came crashing down. But down it came, opening up the side of my hand from the thumb to the wrist, deep enough to reveal a glint of white bone.

It was bleeding profusely, and as both my parents were at work, I had to dash over to the neighbours' house to procure emergency transport to the hospital, where I received just more than twenty stitches. I was left with a permanent scar and an unsolved mystery. What or who was parting the blades of that blind, and how did it come free from the wall brace?

The second incident that left a psychological mark on me happened one evening while I had a girlfriend staying overnight. We retired fairly early, she in the bed and me on the floor beside it. There was a small night light on so she would not trip over me if she needed to get up in the night. Or at least that is the reason I gave her for the nightlight. The truth was that the house was getting to me and I didn't like to be in the dark.

I was having trouble getting to sleep and was just lying there, thinking. One can often make out different shapes in the semidarkness, and I happened to be watching a peculiar one in the far-left corner of the room. At the time, I was a fan of the telly series *Kung Fu* and thought that this shadow formation looked just like one of the hooded monks on that program. That's when it began to move! It slowly made its way across the room, gliding in a sideways motion. I called out to my girlfriend. I felt transfixed by this spectre; it was not just some abstract shadow configuration. It was a clearly defined figure, tall in stature and wearing a hooded robe more solidly black than the semidarkness that surrounded us. Worse, it was moving with a purposeful volition.

I repeated my attempt to get my girlfriend's attention, but must have attracted "his" instead, because he immediately paused and took notice of me. I decided to shut up. When he resumed his progress, his course was toward me! This was no optical illusion, and I had had enough. I grabbed for the light beside the bed, finally arousing my friend. The hooded figure did not evaporate in the sudden illumination but rather receded slowly into the corner from whence it had emerged, much to our horror, until it finally disappeared. If either of us were able to get back to sleep that night, it would have been with the lights on, not that that necessarily would have made a difference!

Many years later, I started an investigation with a psychic to get to the bottom of this enigma. In reply to questions of who this figure was and what it wanted, one fascinating answer came via two different mediums. It was a quote from Tao Te Ching: *Yet mystery and manifestations arise from the same source. This source is called darkness. Darkness within darkness. The gateway to all understanding.* We were further told that we had not had our last encounter with this powerful and influential spectre!

(Just another note on these hooded shapes: Someone related a story to me in which he observed three hooded figures communicating amongst themselves. One turned and said, "This one has perceived of us," referring to the observer. Yet another hooded apparition similar to the one I saw in the bedroom was observed in the house across the street from us, as you will discover in the following chapter.)

Another incident took place in the backyard, where I would often sit with a coffee and a book on a lounge swing we had set up. The swing was suddenly given a vehement shove from behind, causing my coffee to spill while almost knocking me off the swing. Needless to say I was quite perturbed and made my way to the back of the swing intending to accost the prankster. There I stood ready to rain toads on someone, but there was not a soul in sight, figuratively speaking.

I will never forget the feel of that invisible shove from behind. I can easily relate to a story that a clerk would share years later regarding a haunted courthouse in Toronto. This place had a back staircase often used by the judges and some of the clerks. More than one person recounted tales of being shoved from behind while descending those stairs. The last she heard, no one bothered using the back staircase any longer.

One very disconcerting incident occurred one summer afternoon when I was alone in the house. My parents and sister were at the cottage, and my other sister, Sharlene, was at her boyfriend's.

I was taking a shower when I became aware of another presence in the room with me. I peeked out from behind the shower curtain to check out the room, feeling rather silly for doing so. Silly or not, I was going to conclude this shower quickly. Unfortunately, I was not quick enough. The lights suddenly extinguished. At first, all I could do was stand there, frozen in the dark, listening to the water echoing off the side of the tub. I was too frightened to even scream until the shower curtain was sharply pulled open. That snapped me out of it and I screamed, bolting for the door. I turned the light back on, grabbed a towel, and stood trembling outside the bathroom door. When I had sufficiently composed myself, I called Sharlene and practically begged her to come home, which she agreed to do as soon as she could. Fortunately, Sharlene was very much aware of what was going on in that house, having experienced much of it herself. Meanwhile, I was going to have to make my way back into the bathroom to shut off the water.

Looking back on this now, I recall thinking how everything always happens when you're in the shower: phone calls, doorbells, and ghostly manifestations. One is so ill-prepared to deal with anything while showering. Sleeping with the light on is one thing; showering with your clothes on is a whole other matter.

Jocularity aside, I remain most grateful for two things regarding that incident. First, I was not seriously injured (or worse) dashing out of that slippery tub. And second, at that time I had not yet seen the movie *Psycho*.

The other two most memorable events have one thing in common: the cellar. As an adolescent, I was a real loner and consequently spent much of my time on my own, often reading or painting in the bedroom or the cellar. One evening I was reading in the bedroom when I thought I heard a faint conversation. I strained to discern to whom the voices belonged and from whence they came. The conversing seemed to be carried up through the heating vent. When the furnace came on, I could no longer hear the voices so I just let it go. After all, this was not the first or the last time I would hear strains of music and voices coming up from the cellar.

I did not think about it again until a few days later when I was reading in the cellar. Once again I heard whispering, and it was coming from a part of the cellar opposite me. I got up to investigate but there was no one there, at least no one I could see.

I should explain that houses of this old age did not have the finished basements that newer houses have. This cellar was originally used for winter storage of vegetables, etc. The floor was a type of concrete, and the walls were part of the stone foundation. The cellar was divided in two by the stone wall. There was a small window at the furthest end of the cellar where the furnace and the dryer were located. This was the section that I read in. The other section is where the stairs leading up to the house through a trap door were located. The trap door opened up into a cellar foyer. This in turn led through another door and into the kitchen.

As I mentioned, I was always in the far end of the cellar, mainly because the light fixture in the first section would not operate. The light bulb would always explode. We had a professional in once to remove the remaining bulb filaments, and I asked if perhaps water could be dripping on the bulb from the shower above. He just laughed and dismissed the notion. I suggested this explanation to my mother as well, and we both thought it was a logical explanation. Neither of us really believed it though. I happened to know that the light bulb would go out or blow up when the shower was not even on. I often found the bulb smashed below as though it had been unscrewed.

The last time it happened, I was reading in the aforementioned section of the basement when I heard the whispering again. There was also faint melodic music coming from the blacked out section of the cellar. I gingerly made my way toward the voices and the melody. One of the voices became more distinct. It was female and called my name twice. The second time was the loudest, scaring the daylights out of me. Then the light bulb burst, and I was out of that cellar like a bat out of hell — no pun intended. That was not the last time I would hear my name being called out by a disembodied voice. However, hearing your name called is nothing compared to seeing the apparition to whom the voice belongs.

On a cool, clear fall evening just after nine o'clock, I thought I had fallen asleep while reading in bed. I "dreamed" that I got up and was walking toward the cellar in response to Sharlene calling me. I felt like I was walking through water and had a feeling of unreality, like I was in a mesmerized state. My movements were slow and laborious. I rounded the corner of the bedroom heading into the kitchen and the cellar foyer. I never quite made it, though.

I stopped when the door to the cellar foyer opened, followed by the trap door rising. I saw the back of a girl with long brown hair slowly ascend from the cellar. She stopped and turned to face me. It was my sister Sharlene. Her attire, which was quite dressy, stuck me as very out of place under the circumstances. We just stood there looking at each other, only metres apart but seemingly unable to converse with each other. She was so pale I wanted to ask her if she had seen a ghost or if she was feeling all right. Nothing was uttered though; it seemed like we were both struggling in this bizarre underwater ballet. It even sounded as though I was underwater.

She turned and slowly made her way back into the cellar. For the first time since moving to number thirteen, I seriously questioned my sanity. My brother, who was with us for a few days, snapped me out of this by emerging suddenly from the bathroom. He didn't say anything, just looked at me like I was crazy. That is when it hit me that I had not been dreaming. I also noticed that both the cellar and trap doors were open and quickly went to close them.

The following day I began to discuss this incident with Sharlene, wanting to know what she had been doing all dressed up and hanging around the cellar. Unfortunately, we got sidetracked by one of our numerous arguments.

I never broached the subject with her again, nor with anyone else in the family. I just assumed they would think me crazy and send me off to a shrink. That experience continues to haunt me to this day. What was the purpose or meaning of this phantasmal apparition? Why did it beckon me? Was it a portent of the future? Was I in fact seeing the ghost of my then living sister? As crazy as it sounds, that is exactly what I believe.

Awhile after my sister's death, I was looking at some pictures taken of her on the last night of her life. She was all dressed up in the clothes that I had seen her in over a decade earlier. I will never forget those clothes or the way my sister looked as she faced me from the cellar. Her face was pale and luminescent, and she didn't look distressed. She seemed content, like she was where she belonged, but a bit confused as well. When she turned away from me, it was as though she was saying farewell.

The images of that event would revisit me with a vengeance.

Strangely enough, both Sharlene and I believed we would die young. For her, it was a gut feeling. For me it was due in large part to recurring nightmares I experienced. I would occasionally visit an historic graveyard near our house; it was lovely and peaceful, so I would sit there and read for hours. My nightmare took place in this cemetery. It was during the fall and was very dark, rainy, and windy. I was running through the cemetery because I was lost and wanted to find my way home. Running about was so hard because, once again, I felt like I was moving underwater. I made it out of one side of the cemetery, which led onto a busy road. Out of the darkness came two incredibly bright headlights. I heard the screech of car wheels, then an agonized human wail, and at that point I would always wake up, breathless and shaken. I assumed that the nightmare was a premonition of my own death or some warped Freudian imagery about being lost to myself.

The only specific date I recall having that nightmare was on the evening of Sharlene's birthday because I was anxious that the party go well. It was to take place at my apartment (I had long since been living on my own), and I had been painstakingly planning for three weeks. I must have driven her crazy with the numerous phone calls checking on all her likes and dislikes, but I wanted it to be perfect. All that work was well worth it, because it was indeed the perfect party with all her favourite things. Her last words to me as she and her husband Ron were leaving were, "It's nice to be remembered."

A week later, I felt compelled to call my sister Chris. While I waited for her to pick up the phone, I tried to think of what to say, as I had no idea why I was calling. When she answered, it was in a shaky voice, and I got chills down my spine. She didn't need to say anything. The images of that vision from number thirteen came flooding back to me. On April 27, 1980, Sharlene and Ron were hit head on by a drunk driver. There was another young couple in the car who were parents of an infant. There were no survivors. (Ron and Shar had a beagle they named Blue. He was placed with friends until my brother Bob could return home with him. On the day of the burial, as the funeral procession passed by the house where the dog was staying, he suddenly went right off the wall. He was barking and whining and trying to get out of the house. He was completely inconsolable nor could he be distracted. Ironically and sadly enough, a few years later, Blue would meet a similar end to that of Ron and Shar, having his life cut short by a car.)

All poor Chris could do was to keep repeating that Shar was dead. I called my boyfriend at work, extremely agitated, babbling about not being able to escape the long shadow of that house and how my family was cursed. At times like these, families should be drawn closer together, but I ran like hell, partly out of fear.

My persistent fear that no one would believe me or that they would write me off as loopy cost me the priceless and forever lost opportunity to explore these shared experiences during and after our time together at number thirteen.

At least twice, Sharlene made statements that clearly indicated that we were sharing similar experiences and that the house was having a profound effect on us psychically, spiritually, and psychologically. But we never did discuss it. Opportunity lost with people is often the greatest haunt of our lives.

My family moved out of number thirteen in the late seventies. I left there a bit before that. However, with that house, you move away from it but you can never leave it. Or rather, it never leaves you. Even though it had been many years since I lived at number thirteen, instigated by the trauma of my sister's death was the recurrence of the PMIR (spontaneous telekinesis). In my irrational grief and outrage, the object of my misdirected rage was alcohol, as it had been a drunk driver that claimed their lives. Consequently, even though I was having people drop in and wanted to be able to offer them a drink, I could not keep alcohol in the house. The contents of an unopened bottle would simply dematerialize!

We returned a couple of bottles to the store where we had purchased them. The first couple of times, the clerk interpreted it to be a mistake by the distillers and replaced the bottles. However, although he could offer no explanation, knowing very well that the bottles were full upon replacing them, he could not replace any more, so I made the obvious decision to not purchase any more bottles. Interestingly, the only alcohol that remained intact was the beer and gin I had left over from my sister's birthday party.

This situation was resolved when I redirected my anger in the appropriate place. This is a good example of how a poltergeist can manifest itself physically when there is overwhelming emotion and the reaction is initially immature (especially when a shock has occurred).

Ours was not the only family to have such experiences related to this house. Besides the psychical phenomena, denizens of the dwelling shared a wide range of physical and psychological problems. For some, it ended when they left the residence; others were not so lucky. It is true that we all suffer some misfortune in life, but what befell some of the residents of number thirteen was more like a plague, ranging from the minor to the catastrophic and including death. The psychic manifestations continued for some as well. The numbers and consistencies of those so afflicted rendered this beyond coincidence.

Fortunately, the psychic influence of the house appears to diminish with time. Unfortunately, that influence reasserts itself when contact is made with the house again as I discovered during the writing of this. I am scheduling a number of seances to hopefully get some answers, starting with who or what is haunting that house and the lives of so many who lived or even visited there. Is it a discarnate entity that used to dwell there or a combination of accumulated energy?

There is a lot of evidence to support the theory that material structures like houses absorb the psychic and emotional energy of the people and the events that happen within them. The house, therefore, takes on an atmosphere and a personality of its own. It could well be that many powerful events and tragedies have taken place within the walls of number thirteen over its long history that have resulted in a strong psychic aura about it. People exposed to such an environment, especially over a period of time, tend to absorb the energy and influence of that environment.

On the other hand, it may be disembodied entities haunting the house. Either way, I know far too many people who, having entered the house for the first time, exclaim that there is "something" about the place that just is not right and feel the need to leave as soon as possible.

Those experiencing the poltergeist phenomena probably had natural latent psychic abilities and the house was like a catalyst or conduit for them.

I know the influence of the house affects those who have lived there as well as some who are just visiting. Even the writing of this chapter was interfered with to such a degree that I never thought it could be finished. The chapter is finished, but the story is just beginning. That house casts a long dark shadow. For all I know, it even touches people who merely read about it.

The investigation into the phenomena of number thirteen is ongoing. On a coincidental note, one of the psychic investigators on this book pointed out that my apartment number had been changed to 013 after the new security system had been installed for our building. Good old thirteen again! A fine example of Jung's synchronicity; i.e., meaningful coincidence.

In addition to the message regarding the hooded spectre, one other message was received: *Death does not possess her, she possesses death and acquires its magic.* It is directed at myself, but the source or origin is unknown as of the writing of this.

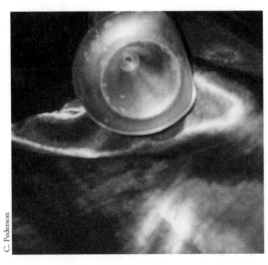

C. Pederson

Warped Brass Candle Holder: poltergeist artifact from 13 Highgate St.

Addendum: I have recently been in touch with the former boyfriend of my deceased sister. He was going to send me an account of his experiences with a Ouija board on Highgate Street while he was dating Sharlene. Shortly after I made the request, an event occurred, on the evening of October 11, 2000. At 7:48 p.m. my living room suddenly became very chilly. Previously, it had actually been quite warm as we were experiencing unseasonably mild temperatures that fall. I retrieved a blanket and bundled up and resumed reading a book.

My reading was interrupted by the sound of a painting rattling against the wall as though it were being shaken. To the left from were I was seated hangs an oil painting of my sister Sharlene. I immediately assumed my cat Dusty was scratching at the painting again, as she is prone to do. I exclaimed, "Dusty!" in a stern voice to warn her away from the painting and proceeded to make my way over to that corner of the room.

Just as I got to my feet, the bell on my grandfather's Christmas stocking began ringing from the bedroom. I felt like I had just been hit with a pail of ice cold water. Since his death, whenever the bell on that stocking rings, someone dies or is in a life-threatening situation. I quickly made my way into the bedroom, almost tripping over the cat, who was dashing out of that same room. Something had frightened her. I entered the bedroom; it was also chilly, but the little bell had ceased ringing and nothing seemed amiss.

And then I saw it. Neatly placed on the foot of my bed were the two black sideguards from Ron's motorcycle. He had asked me to paint something on them for him, but before I had the chance to do so, he died that night with my sister. I picked up the sideguards and made my way back into the living room.

I felt strangely sad and simultaneously lonely yet crowded by some overwhelming presence in the room with me. I closed my eyes for a second and immediately felt I was at the gravesite that Shar and Ron share. I could smell the air and feel the cold ground beneath me. Just as it had been during that vision on Highgate Street, I again felt currents washing about me, as though I were underwater. The message that had been directed at me via the Ouija board was clearly imparted here again with one notable change: *Death does not possess you, you possess death and acquire its magic.* The "her" in the previous message had now been changed to "you."

I opened my eyes and it was all over. The room was no longer cold. Everything was as it had been before and only three minutes had passed. As I coaxed Dusty from where she was cowering beneath the sofa, it dawned on me that it had not been the cat shaking the painting at all. Dusty had been in the bedroom the entire time until she had been frightened out the room. The purpose of the event is not known to me, though I suspect it will become known soon. However, the message about death remains an enigma. At least I managed to get the cat out from under the couch. Dusty gives credence to the phrase fraidy cat!

Addendum two: Whenever I wanted to get away from all the weird-.ness of that house, I used to go to a nearby cemetery; I know that may sound strange, especially considering the circumstance at home. Nevertheless, there was naturally much less commotion there than in a park. I would sit on a bench under this lovely old maple tree and read for hours.

On the evening of the second time I did this, I had a lucid dream that a young man with short, nearly black and sort of curly hair came to join me on the bench. He asked me what I was reading, to which I replied *Man's Search For Meaning*. He stated that he used to love to read, and we began to talk about books and the general philosophies of life. When I awoke, I actually felt lonely for the young man; even though it was just a dream, I quite liked his mannerism.

I returned to the cemetery the following day and took my place on the bench under the maple tree. That night, I was visited once again by the young man from the previous night's dream. We chatted as we did before. He said that his name was John, which I had not even asked nor had he offered in the previous dream. I asked him where he lived, to which he replied, "Over there," gesturing to the far right-hand corner of the graveyard. I was very confused and for the first time wondered if I had run into some kind of nut. He looked very earnestly at me, shaking his head, and assured me that it was okay. He took me to far end of the graveyard and pointed to a simple black headstone. I read the name on the stone: John P. It further read that he had died at age nineteen. I was more confused than ever and turned to ask him if this was a relative, but he had vanished.

I never woke up with such a start. I felt oddly sad, but chilled, too.

I want back to the cemetery the following day, and even though I felt a little foolish, I headed for the far right side of the graveyard. I caught sight of a medium-sized tombstone, the one I had seen in my dream. I stood in front of it and read the name on the stone: John P. Died nineteen years of age. I smiled and cried at the same time. I sat down by my "dream" friend's grave and read my book.

I carried on like this for a few years. It had become a bit of a haven, almost. (I know you may be thinking that I must have been a lonely child, and in some ways, I guess I was. But I have come to learn that we are all a lot lonelier than we care to admit.) I noticed no one else ever seemed to come and take care of his grave or leave flowers, so I adopted the duty.

Many years later, after I had begun doing informal field investigations, I brought Paul, a boyfriend and colleague, with me to John's gravesite. I told him the entire story and pointed out where I used to sit. He said it was a beautiful cemetery in that it was simple but historical. A rather unique combination. He then proceeded to take a few random photos. He was using a Polaroid Instamatic, the kind that develops the picture on the spot. To our astonishment, contained within the photo of John's gravestone was a white orb. The flash was not on; there was no

Photographer, Paul Taylor Papandreou, 1976

Not Even Does Death Do Us Part: tombstone with ghostly orb.

light bouncing off the gravestone. We simply could not explain it. In my mind, this was John's way of saying hello to an old friend. I never had the dream about John again, not after finding the gravesite. I think the whole thing happened because he was a bit lonely too.

I don't know why it never occurred to me before, but I have since initiated a records search to determine what caused this young man to die at such a young age. As for the connection between the two of us, I don't think that can ever be discovered, at least not through any official documents.

Chapter Two
Rubicon Revisited

As I was driving down Highgate Street to give Madeline, the psychic consultant for this book, a glimpse of The House, she commented that a few houses on this street had interesting auras and energy about them. As we neared number thirteen, the tiny hairs on her arm stood up and her scalp began to tingle. A quotation from Shakespeare jumped to mind: "By the prickling of my thumbs, something wicked this way comes…"

She told me to stop the car and there we were, in front of number thirteen, even though she had never seen the house before. We sat there for what seemed like a long time, though it was merely seconds. She appeared to be catching her breath and orienting herself. She took her eyes off number thirteen only twice in order to glance sideways across the street at the home of my former neighbours. "Let's go." As we drove off she commented that there was a cross-current between the two houses that directly faced each other. There was a psychic umbilical cord between these two houses, which is very rare.

Although I suspected it was not the end of the Highgate Street saga, I thought I had at least completed that particular chapter so I could proceed with the rest of this manuscript. Fate often has other plans for us, though…

One day my sister Chris called to say that she had received a phone call from our former neighbour from Highgate Street, Layla, whom Chris had not heard from in over a decade. Layla had been rummaging through some old things and happened across my sister's phone number. It had been so long since she and Chris had spoken that she thought the number was probably obsolete by now but felt compelled to give it a try anyway. She was pleased that it was indeed the correct number. After catching up on old news, my sister mentioned that I was working on a book about ghosts. Layla was intrigued and began to share some of the experiences she and her family had had.

My sister called me and gave me Layla's phone number, and I called her that same day. I was surprised to learn that our neighbours had also been experiencing paranormal activity, but none of us had felt it prudent to share this information with each other back then. We spoke on the phone for a bit and made arrangements to meet in person along with her brother Tony. What is about to unfold is the strange, chilling, and sometimes meaningful account of what happened to our neighbours directly across the street from us. Funny how both houses seemed so quiet back then, with neither family ever suspecting the strange happenings occurring within the other's residence.

Layla is the youngest of four children. She lived in this house until she was eighteen years old, so in all, close to ten years. One of her most vivid memories occurred after she had gone to bed one evening. She shared a bed with her older sister, and while she was adjusting the sheets to get comfortable, she became aware of an object under the blanket. She began to explore it. First she felt a finger, then another one. It slowly became clear to her that the object she was feeling was a hard, disembodied hand. Needless to say, this startled her somewhat. She immediately tried to wake her sleeping sister, who just brushed her off in an annoyed manner. Layla didn't sleep well that night!

Her pet dog, Muffy, would often share the room as well. Like other family pets, Muffy was sensitive to any odd goings-on, including the supernatural. Both Layla and Muffy responded to the sound of someone walking down the hall at five o'clock one morning. The person, whom Layla assumed to be her mother, proceeded down the hall, opened the door to the linen closet, retrieved what sounded like the ironing board, continued to the kitchen, and, once there, commenced ironing.

Layla got out of bed to see why her mother was ironing at such an odd hour. As she came through her bedroom door and headed for the kitchen, she started to say, "Ma, what are you doing?" but there was no one up and about. The place was dark and eerily quiet. Both Layla and

Muffy ran back to bed. This incident is but one of many classic manifestations of poltergeist activity this family would live with for years.

Most poltergeist activity is harmless and playful, more of a nuisance or a curiosity than anything else. Sometimes they can actually be helpful, as the time Layla became aware that her brother Tony was approaching the outer back door and she thought she would get up and open the door for him. Much to both their surprise, the door opened but not by their volition. There they were, staring at each other through the opened door, Tony still with key in hand.

Other times poltergeists are mischievous, possibly getting some innocent, unsuspecting kid in trouble. Such was the case for Layla and Tony upon arriving home for lunch one afternoon. They were still in grade school at the time; they remember it being All Souls' Day. Their mother had recently purchased a new coffee pot, and when they arrived home they were greeted by a somewhat perturbed mother who queried them about the new pot. It seems the entire contraption had been carefully taken apart and strewn about the counter and stove. Both Tony and Layla swore they knew nothing about it, which in fact was the truth. Later, the other two siblings, Gianni and Ann, were questioned, but they too knew nothing about it. Fortunately, the pot was in good working order in spite of the psychic dissection.

This sort of thing came as no surprise to Ann. Before the family moved to Highgate Street, Ann had a ring with a blue stone in it that had belonged to her grandmother. It just disappeared one day. After they had been settled in the new house for awhile, she was going through a cupboard in the kitchen where her dad kept all kinds of odds and ends and there was the ring!

Many of the experiences shared by the siblings were related to the death of their mother, Maria, on July 31, 1989. Ann was of course quite depressed following this loss. The day following Maria's death was Ann's birthday. She was hardly in the mood to celebrate, and the birthday probably would have gone by unnoticed were it not for two peculiar events. On the day of her birthday the light of a nearby lamp turned on and off four times. There was nothing wrong with either the lamp or the bulb. The next thing she noticed was that even though neither she nor her husband had thought to turn the calendar page over to August, it had been turned over for her. Although these events were a bit eerie, they were also comforting in that it was as though the spirit of her mother was acknowledging Ann's birthday: the calendar now read August first, her birthday.

The eldest of the brothers, Gianni, would be the least likely person to have or want to have experiences of the supernatural kind, but we do not decide these things as individuals. It was suggested by the siblings that Gianni may not want to talk about his experiences, but, as I wanted to ask him about one event in particular, I would phone him anyway and let him decide if he wanted to be interviewed for this book. The experience to which I refer involved my deceased sister, Sharlene (mentioned in the previous chapter). Gianni had been staying with his sister Layla and had a candle lit in honour of John Lennon, who had just been shot. He happened upon a picture with Sharlene in it and was thinking about her when the flame of the candle flared up like a blowtorch. This greatly startled Gianni and he had an overwhelming impression of Shar. She and Gianni were close in age, and the news of her death had touched him, but the meaning of this experience is a mystery.

As with his siblings, Gianni was devastated by the death of his mother. So much so that when he returned to the home of his parents after the funeral, having decided to spend the night there, his sisters and brother were concerned he might harm himself. Apparently, someone or something shared that concern because Gianni was literally chased out of the house.

It began upon arriving at the Highgate Street home with the garage door opening and closing in some kind of frenzied greeting or warding off. It didn't get any better inside the house, either. He had had previous paranormal experiences while growing up in the house but nothing like this night! The fact that he had just come from a funeral seemed appropriate because he felt as though he had just entered a mausoleum. The house was cold and foreboding. It was not familiar or welcoming. When he turned on the lights, they would grow bright, then dim with the occasional flicker, or they would simply extinguish themselves. Now surely all the light bulbs on the main floor were not about to blow at the same time! He went from room to room, performing a cautious inspection. Upon entering his parents' bedroom, he was shocked to see the indentation of what he appeared to be his mother lying on her side of the bed. That was enough.

He called his brother Tony, who was more experienced and knowledgeable in these matters. Tony told Gianni to remain calm and suggested that is was probably their mother so there was nothing to fear. He then suggested that Gianni leave the house. If Gianni had any notions about harming himself, it was not going to happen then or in that house; he had been effectively chased out. While waiting for his girlfriend to come and pick him up, he cautiously went about the house securing doors and windows. Upon returning the following day, all the doors and windows were open, and directly facing him as he entered the house was the chair his mother always sat in as if she had been standing watch like a ghostly sentinel.

His previous experiences were not quite so dramatic as to cause him to flee but they were enough to leave a lifelong impression. When he was young, he shared with his brother a bedroom that faced the front of the house, overlooking a veranda. On more than one occasion, while he was sitting on the front veranda enjoying the cool summer evening, his bedroom light would turn itself on or off. He also had many experiences of hearing footsteps and various other noises like bangs and thumps. All these things occurred when nobody was at home. Otherwise, it wouldn't have even caught his attention. One of the more pleasant experiences was that of smelling perfume or flowers, seemingly emanating from nowhere. The source of that odour is a mystery to this day.

He recalls one not-so-pleasant experience that took place in the middle of the night. He was curled up in bed and was disturbed by the pressure of a cold, clammy hand on his shoulder. He felt the strong presence of someone unfamiliar in the room but he didn't want to turn the lights on. He had no desire to see who or what it was. This experience is quite similar to the one Layla had.

There was also a shared experience between the two houses on this unassuming street. It involved the materialization of a rather ominous black phantom. The incident happened to the younger brother, Tony. He is the middle child and was the last one to leave the house. He not only spent the most time there, but would also be considered a natural psychic. He was not frightened by the phenomena that took place around him. In fact he was quite intrigued by it, so much so that he began an intensive, albeit informal, study of the paranormal and spiritualism. You may recall reading in the previous chapter that I had had encounters with a black-robed hooded figure, whose presence remains with me to this day. Therefore, I was quite intrigued to learn that Tony had a similar encounter with a variation in the figure's appearance.

After a long day, Tony went to bed early one evening. Both the lights and the stereo were turned down low. He was lying back relaxing when his attention was drawn to a figure forming in the corner of the room. It evolved into a tall man wearing a hat and a long black cape. It was a very old style of dress, perhaps sixteenth or seventeenth century. When Tony turned up the lights, the entity vanished. What, if any, is the connection between the two black-robed figures? Logic would suggest that these phantom appearances in both houses are beyond coincidence.

On another occasion, Tony set his alarm clock for work the following day for 5:00 a.m. He woke up during the night and glanced over at the luminous numeric display, noted the time, and went back to sleep. He woke again later, but when he turned over to check the time, there was no clock! He leapt out of bed, not knowing if he was late for work. He switched on the light and, to his astonishment, discovered that the clock was turned around backwards, facing the wall. The clock's electrical cord was neatly wrapped around the body of the clock. Tony, quite annoyed by this and not having even considered the poltergeist, went to his parents' room and asked his mother if she knew who the prankster was. She assured him she did not and admonished him not to wake up his father, who didn't like to hear about these sorts of things.

Tony was not late for work, and the only significance of this event, if any, would be that the time of his mother's death later in her life would be five o'clock.

When Tony was a teenager, he used to cut grass around the neighbourhood to make a bit of money. As he was nearing the end of work one day and on his way home, he came upon an elderly gentleman who lived in a house on the end of Highgate Street. Tony asked him if he would like his grass cut, to which the elderly man replied, "Sure, but I don't have any money. I could offer you a cold beer as payment." Tony, who was hot and thirsty, agreed. As they were sipping on their drinks, somehow the topic came around to life after death. Perhaps jokingly, the gentleman said that when he passed on, if he were able, he would come back and give Tony a sign.

Months later, Tony was preparing for work on one of the coldest, stormiest January mornings anyone could remember, with high winds and snow with ice pellets, none of which made for great driving conditions. After accepting a thermos of coffee his mother had prepared for him, he was out the door and slowly guiding his car down the treacherous road. Something unusual caught his eye. He couldn't believe what he was seeing. Standing off to the side of the road in nothing but a pair of boxer shorts was what appeared to be an old man. It couldn't be, though. No human being could survive outside in this weather wearing next to nothing. And than a thought struck Tony: no *living* human being could survive exposure to these elements, and he remembered the words of the elderly man. Even though he was a true believer in ghosts, this was the last thing he needed this morning. Between the blowing sleet and snow and not wanting to take his eyes off the road ahead of him, it was hard to get a good look at whatever it was. As he passed by the apparition, all he could make out in the car's side then rear-view mirrors was a shadow, but a substantive one at that. Ironically, as soon as he arrived at work, the first thing a colleague said to him was, "Hey Tony, you look like you've seen a ghost." Tony would later hear from neighbours that the old man had passed on. It would appear that the old gentleman had kept his word to Tony.

On one occasion, Tony organized a seance that included his future wife, Layla, and Layla's then boyfriend, Kevin. They gathered in the family room downstairs and Tony instructed them to join hands and not to break the circle. They then proceeded in their attempt to contact the usual spirits in amateur seances, such as Elvis and JFK. Tony received a psychic nudge to look up the stairs toward the door and as he did so, he saw it slowly closing. Kevin began to laugh, perhaps out of nervousness or a sense that the entire thing was an exercise in fakery. He decided to check it out and made his way up the stairs to the door, only to have it slammed in his face with an unnatural force. Upon trying to open it, he felt a pressure behind the door as though someone had the weight of his or her body up against it. This frightened him so much that he immediately descended the stairs in a backward motion. He asked if there were any windows open that could account for this phenomenon, to which Tony replied no. Kevin had had enough of this seance and exclaimed, "I'm out of here!" and made his way out the back door. Impeding his passage on the walk was a small footstool that their mother had often made use of when hanging the laundry. In his haste to escape the house, Kevin nearly broke his neck tripping over the little stool. Tony believes these phenomena were targeted at Kevin because he almost seemed to be taunting and ridiculing the spirits.

The day following the burial of their mother, Tony was saying a silent prayer to his mother at her gravesite when he felt pressure on his arm. It was the same familiar pressure of his mother holding his arm whenever he would take her somewhere. He received a powerful impression that he was to gather the siblings together at the house. He was able to reach Ann and Layla but not Gianni. When they arrived at the house they realized that Gianni had the key. Responding to a gut feeling, Tony urged them to just wait, so they went to sit on the front porch for awhile. Shortly thereafter, who should arrive but Gianni.

Once inside, the sisters remained upstairs while Gianni and Tony went downstairs to work on a wooden cross they were going to place on their mother's gravesite until a permanent stone was in place. As Gianni was completing the engraving, Tony's attention was drawn to the lights, which suddenly began to glow with a luminescence beyond their natural capacity. They would alternately dim and glow. Tony, who figured that there must be a reason they had all been called here today, took this to be a sign from his mother. For conformation he asked his mother to give them all another sign and with that, the central air suddenly came on full blast and the windows all flew open. He had his conformation. Upstairs, the girls were excitedly jumping and hugging each other. There was no doubt in their minds that their mother was assuring her children that she was all right and was still with them. These would not be the only "signs" they would receive from her.

Toward her final days, their mother had experienced great difficulty breathing. She would often request someone to open a window. After she passed on, the windows, which were always secured before leaving the house, were often found to be open upon returning.

The last time Tony was in the house was approximately June of 1999 to visit his father, who still resides in this house. As far as Tony or any of the other siblings know, the house is quiet now. The paranormal activity has ceased, but their mother still watches over them, forever the ghostly sentinel.

Postscript: Although she died before they had ever met, Layla's son had seen been introduced to his "Nona" via photographs. One afternoon while sitting in his high chair, the little boy became excited and while pointing called out "Nona! Nona!" Layla looked in the direction her son was pointing but saw nothing herself. The baby obviously recognized his grandmother, who was just keeping an eye on things. As previously stated, the patriarch of the family still resides in the house and all four siblings remain in the city. Although all the siblings have had at least one brush with the paranormal since leaving their home on Highgate Street, Tony is the most psychically active and often receives spontaneous premonitions about future events in the lives of those he encounters.

Chapter Three
The Girl in the White Dress:
A True Tale of Reincarnation

> In the middle of the journey of my life
> I found myself in a dark wood
> For I had lost the right path...
> And so I came forth, and once again
> beheld the stars.
>
> — Dante, *Inferno*

For the protection of those involved, especially in the light of their having re-established new lives for themselves, the names and places in this story have been altered. Also of concern was the psychological state of the protagonist, as her former psychiatrist is concerned with retraumatizing her.

As odd as the following may sound, on September 13, 1931, a girl named Sophie Elizabeth Zandona was born in a small rural county in the state of Georgia. She was killed at age nineteen on October 26, 1950. She was born again, literally, on October 26, 1956. Her name this time was Sarah. Do not stand by my grave and weep; I am not there, I did not die...

Growing up, Sarah had had a quite average life save for the bizarre dreams she experienced at the onset of each of her birthdays. The dreams were very lucid, vivid, and extremely detailed. She had been having these dreams since childhood, but it didn't seem to be anything to be alarmed about. For the most part, they were just average dreams in that we all tend to dream about the people, places, and events in our lives.

And so it was with Sarah's dreams, except that nothing in the dreams was familiar to her own experiences. She seemed to be dreaming about someone else's life. Even the style of dress was alien to her. The clothes were so old-fashioned, like something they wore back in the thirties.

The dreams left her feeling depressed, confused, and empty, but those feelings, along with the dreams, always went away once her birthday was done with. During the rest of the year, Sarah did not have good dream recall, just fragments here and there and certainly not in the vivid colour and detail of the birthday dreams.

Sarah left school at the age of seventeen and went to work in a local restaurant/bar. It was around this time that her dreams took on new and even frightening characteristics. They were tragic and so real! Most disturbing was that the protagonist of her dreams (who turned out to be named Sophie) was being physically and mentally abused by both her father and a much older male "companion." Meanwhile, Sarah was becoming more deeply immersed in Sophie's life, including the experiences of degradation, isolation, and crushed hope.

By Sarah's eighteenth birthday, she had come to know the girl in the dreams intimately and felt empathy and sorrow for her. Sarah was having difficulty extracting herself from the dreams, and when she woke up from them her face would often be wet from tears. She began to feel trapped and desperate like the dream girl. During her waking hours, she was always preoccupied with the dream life. She found she was becoming distrustful of men, as well as experiencing a deep sense of foreboding unrelated to anything in her waking life.

People in rural counties like hers did not run off to see therapists; she could not have afforded one anyway. Nevertheless, she was getting therapy of a sort from her close friends. Dale Stevenson was the lead guitarist/vocalist of the house band at the bar where she worked. His sister, Karen, the local hairdresser, befriended Sarah and was intrigued by her. Karen's hobby just happened to be exploring all things pertaining to the supernatural. She was especially interested in the notion of reincarnation and near-death experiences. She was taking courses related to the subject from a friend at a nearby university, Dr. Andrew Smith, who would prove to be of inestimable aid to Sarah's case.

After Sarah's eighteenth birthday, the dreams did not recede as they had in the past. The sense of foreboding did not recede either. It was an inexplicable feeling in the pit of her stomach that something was going to happen. Her personality was changing as well. She was always on edge and had become shy and suspicious of people. An old drunk who was a regular in the bar particularly frightened her. He was always watching her intensely, like he was trying to remember where he knew her from.

In spite of it all, things had been running rather smoothly until three months prior to her nineteenth birthday. She now had only one recurring nightmare. Due to its intensity and her inability to wake up from it, it was in fact what is clinically referred to as a night terror: A lovely girl in an elegant but simple white dress was hanging a painting in a bar sparsely occupied by patrons. It was a cool, damp, miserable October evening, but this was one of the rare occasions when she herself did not feel miserable. She even smiled as she stood back to admire the work of art. It was good of Pete, the owner of the bar, to allow her to hang one of her own creations in the bar. He said it might give the place a bit of class. Pete smiled at her from behind the bar while Rick, the off-duty bartender, joined the girl in the white dress at the painting. He asked her to dance. She shot a nervous glance at the young drunken man sitting off in a corner table. She really liked Rick and felt like celebrating, so she tossed caution to the wind and accepted his offer of a dance. She appeared so ethereal gliding over the dance floor in that pure white dress that she had made herself.

Everyone was watching them, especially the drunk. Time seemed suspended for her, probably because she was not used to feeling so happy, and also because she was dancing with Rick. Her reverie was violently shattered when the drunk broke onto the dance floor, dragging her away from Rick toward the exit. It was a heart-wrenching scene with the girl in white crying and struggling to break free while being dragged from the bar. Rick, Pete, and some other patrons came after them, but the drunk brandished a gun. He tossed the poor girl into his battered old pickup trick, climbing in after her. She was crying pleadingly while banging on the truck window to no avail. He hit her and shouted something as they sped off into the dark, dismal night to meet their fates. Rick and Pete, shotguns in hand, stood by helplessly as they sped off. Rick mournfully cried out her name, "Sophie..." It echoed through the night and across time.

Meanwhile, Sarah, still trapped in the night terror, was gasping for air and thrashing about. She felt like she was drowning in a dream. She finally broke free and carefully made her way to the bathroom on shaky legs. She held onto the sides of the sink while she tried to calm herself. Leaning over the sink, she splashed cold water on her face. She slowly rose to face the visage in the mirror. Staring back at her was the shattered, bloodied face of the girl from the nightmares, Sophie.

Sarah must have fainted, for the next she knew, she was prostrate on the bathroom floor. She seriously considered the possibility that she was losing her mind as she made her way to the kitchenette. She made a strong pot of coffee and phoned Karen. Her thoughts were racing as she waited for Karen or Dale to answer the phone. She knew in her gut that watching Sophie being driven off like that was not the end of the nightmare but she didn't think she could survive seeing any more. She also knew she was wide awake when she saw Sophie's bloody face in the mirror. Sarah had been having something like flashbacks of this girl's tragic life. Dr. Smith had called it cryptomnesia; i.e., forgotten memory. He was insistent that she begin hypnotherapy at once, but she still felt uneasy about seeing a therapist.

Sarah's nineteenth birthday was fast approaching. Dale was staying with Sarah so he and Karen could keep a close eye on her. Although Sarah was still working, she could not stand being in the bar when that old drunk who stared at her was there. She agreed to see Dr. Smith, and the hypnotherapy sessions were going well, except that she was recalling somebody else's life!

Karen and Dr. Smith did some research into the places, events, and people that Sarah so vividly recalled. They were stupefied when so many of the things she remembered could be found in county records and microfilm news accounts. This in turn led them to people who were actually present when it all happened.

The seemingly insignificant miscellaneous memories really intrigued Dr. Smith because it is such minor events and details that most people would have no way of knowing about unless they were there. One such event was recalled by an elderly black woman who had been a neighbour of Sophie and her father back in the forties: "Sophie never did have any pets. In these here parts, most folk don't keep animals for pets. That crazy old man [the father] wouldn't let her have one by any count. He was a cruel old... Well, I just figured the devil done got a hold of 'im with the drink and all. After Sophie's mamma done died, the poor girl had to take over for her, doin' everything. She was only a child. Anyway, Sophie befriended a stray mutt, all the time she be sneakin' him food. She just loved that mutt. 'Course, that dog be the only friend she had tin the world. Sure 'nough, that old man found out. Slapped her 'round good, saying they couldn't be wasting good food on some mangy mutt. Next time the mutt came around, he sure 'nough shot it. That poor girl was just heartbroken. Blamed herself, she did. There was no consoling her. Weren't allowed to be crying 'round the old man, no how. He'd slap her 'round for that, too. She used to sit in the woods back here by the crick and just cry all to herself. She wasn't just crying 'bout that poor old mutt, neither. That's why I reckon she died so young. The good lord took pity on her. Sure do hope she be at peace now..."

When the episode with the dog came out in one of the therapy sessions, it hit Sarah really hard. Now he was hearing it first-hand from someone who was there. How could Sarah have known about such an obscure event in the life of someone who had lived and died before Sarah had even been thought of? The only people who knew about the dog were Sophie, her father, and the neighbour, Grace Collins.

It was this kind-hearted woman who had never forgotten Sophie that directed Karen and Dr. Smith to the grave of Sophie Elizabeth Zandona. As they stood at the grave, gazing down at her modest stone marker hand carved by one of the Collins boys, they both became cold and numb. They agreed it would be best not to mention the gravesite to Sarah.

Sarah's nineteenth birthday was only hours away. For no apparent reason, she was a bundle of nerves. Dale and Karen had arranged a small celebration in hopes of cheering her up and taking her mind off things. The evening wrapped up at around ten-thirty. Dale, Sarah, and Karen all retired for what they thought would be a good night's sleep. That was not to be.

The nightmare came with a vengeance. It played itself out in the usual way, only this time the end was coming: Sophie and the drunk were speeding erratically down the road. Sophie was hysterical. The drizzle was battering up against the windshield; the wipers weren't working. Only the right headlight was on. Being in the country, there were no street lamps, so they were completely surrounded by the night. They were speeding down an old back road near Claymount Cemetery. The lone headlight allowed glimpses of disfigured trees and swamp as they sped by. Sophie was pounding on the door, pleading to be let out, pleading for her life. She was still pleading when the truck hit a huge tree head on.

Sophie was thrown from the truck and hit another tree head and back first. The back of her head opened. Bone fragments protruded from a cheek. Her spinal cord snapped. Her left shoulder and arm were shattered, the latter hanging at a grotesque angle. Sophie's pure white dress, so carefully made by her own hands, turned crimson red.

Sarah was jolted out of bed the moment Sophie hit the tree. She let out a blood-curdling scream, hands clasping the back of her head as she fell unconscious to the floor. Dale was at her side within seconds. He noticed the blood seeping from her mouth, nose, and ears. Karen frantically called for an ambulance and then put a call in for Dr. Smith.

Sarah had been unconscious for days in a hospital in Atlanta. She had suffered a cerebral haemorrhage and was in shock, both from unknown origins. A battery of tests offered no clues to the etiology of her trauma. Of equal mystery, she was gradually regaining consciousness. On the nineteenth day of her hospitalization, she opened her eyes. Dale had fallen asleep in a chair next to her bed. She did not know what she was doing in this room; she did not know the young man dozing in the chair beside her bed. The last thing she could remember was hanging a painting in the Longhorn Bar. There was something else that happened, something important. It was just on the edge of her mind but she could not grasp it. Any memory of Sarah and her life was gone. Sophie was back.

Dr. Smith was completely astonished by this entire case. He had never encountered anything like this before in all his years of practice and research. With no apparent cause, he was looking at a case of total amnesia. Sarah had just disappeared and been replaced by Sophie. All her memories were those of the deceased girl. Her psyche and even her physical characteristics had become those of Sophie. Even her accent and dialect were of the type that Sophie would have spoken in her time and place. Dr. Smith knew more details about Sophie than Sarah did and he had never shared this information with her. Yet here she was, twirling her hair with her fingers, as Sophie had. Cracking her toes, as Sophie had. There was nothing left of Sarah at all.

Photographer, Dale Stevenson.

Location of the accident that so tragically ended Sophie's life.

Sophie was not sure who Dale, Karen, or Dr. Smith were but she had an uncanny sense of trust in them, which was a very fortuitous thing considering they were all she had. She even agreed to work with Dr. Smith, though she did not understand his reasons for wanting to "do" therapy to her.

In spite of there being little evidence of physical trauma, the amnesia clearly indicated a severe psychological shock. As Sophie would express months later, "Dyin' can be a really hard thing. It ain't nothin' yah easily forgit."

Besides some headaches, numbness on the left side of her body, and a great deal of confusion and apprehension, she seemed normal enough. Talking with Dr. Smith on a daily basis turned out to be a big help to her. For him, it was coming face to face with the girl who had died decades before. The girl he got to know through old people who never forgot Sophie. The tragic girl in white who haunted Sarah's dreams.

Karen was the one to introduce the idea of reincarnation. She suggested they go see a psychic whom the police had used. Dr. Smith had an open mind but he was cautious out of concern for his patient. He had done a couple of past-life regressions himself, but it was her current life that was lost to her, not her past life. He no longer considered this a rare case of split personality. The Sarah of this time is the continua-

44

tion of the Sophie from a past time. Of that, he was sure. What astonished him was that one life picked up where the other left off prematurely. Or so it seemed. If that was true, this case was unprecedented!

After one session with Sophie, the psychic, Madeline Kinney, would comment, "Sophie's life was so abruptly and tragically ended that she reincarnated sooner than what is usual. The sudden jolt of her soul out of that body and life was like a super psychic shock. What happened to Sophie is not a rare event. There are no accidents. The sudden death of this girl, however... it is not typical. It sent shock waves through the ethereal world that resonate to this day. There are unresolved issues, things that should have been finished before her death. These things will have to be confronted and resolved this time around. This is why she came back. There is an awful lot at stake here."

One of the reasons they had decided to consult the psychic as part of Sophie's therapy was that she was still suffering from frequent headaches. She also had arthritis in her left arm and shoulder. She had not yet recalled the crash, which is what everyone attributed the physical symptoms to. Nevertheless, no one had ever shared the details of Sophie's life with her. They didn't need to. Fate would bring it all back to her.

Sophie returned to waiting tables part time at the bar. It had been called the Longhorn until fire gutted the place in 1952. It was now called Diggers. Dale's band was introducing new material this weekend. Even though the weather was drizzly and gloomy, the bar was packed. All the regulars were there, including a very old drunk who had been coming to this bar since before the fire.

Sophie was not working on this night. She was just there to cheer Dale on; they had become very close. She had dressed carefully for him, choosing a lovely white dress with lace accents, although it was a bit old-fashioned for her. Halfway through the band's second set, Dale went into one of Sophie's favourite songs, "Slide on Over Slinky" by Rick Derringer. Nancy's boyfriend asked Sophie up for a dance. As she was coming out of a full turn, her eyes locked onto the bloodshot eyes of the old drunk who was always watching her — the same drunk who, on a night not unlike this one, had driven Sophie to her death twenty-five years before.

She froze in her tracks, oblivious to everything around her. Her nose began to bleed. He dropped his beer and tipped over his chair while backing away from the spectre of the girl he had killed decades before. His sudden movements roused her from her trance. She noticed the blood trickling down her face and dripping down the front of her white dress. She stared at the patterns of blood on her dress. She remembered that night; she remembered the crash. She remembered who the old drunk was, too. They locked eyes again. Both fear and hatred flooded her. She shook her head as if to say no. She ran out of the bar, into the night and rain. She ran from the parking lot out onto the old country road with only moonlight for illumination. She didn't know where she was going or why; her feet seemed to know where she was running to.

She fled by the old, ominous trees, pausing only once to catch her breath. She leaned against a big, old, half-dead tree. The tree had a dent in it, made by a truck that ran into it twenty-five years ago. She slowly backed away, unable to take her eyes from it, remembering it all. She turned and began running down the road again. She passed through the dilapidated gates of Claymount Cemetery. She kept running through the headstones toward the back left part of the cemetery. The ground was uneven, pitted with gopher holes. Her foot got caught in one of them and she fell forward, hands outstretched to brace her fall. She lay there for a couple of minutes and cried, drenched in rain and dirt. She slowly raised herself off the ground, holding an old plain white grave marker for support. A chill surged through her and she let out a gasp. Though she had only the moon for light, she could make out the name on the grave marker: SOPHIE ELIZABETH ZANDONA. She sat there beside it, resting her head against its cold alabaster shoulder.

Karen and Dale had watched Sophie run from the bar. They hopped in Dale's car and slowly made their way down the road after her. Dale suddenly spotted her, pointing at the white-garbed figure stumbling through the graveyard. Karen asked, "Oh God, what is she doing here?" but they both knew the answer to that. They parked the car and headed after Sophie on foot. They both inhaled deeply when they caught sight of her. With the torn dress and the muddied assemblage, she appeared as though she had just dug herself out of a grave. Dale tore off his jacket, wrapping it around Sophie while gathering her into his arms. Slowly they made their way back, guided by the two shining headlights.

The following day, Dale, Karen, and Sophie returned to the gravesite. Sophie had brought some flowers, which she placed at the head of her grave. As they sat quietly by it, Sophie looked over at Dale and asked if he could imagine what it was like to sit at the foot of one's own grave. Without waiting for a reply she said, "On the morning of the day after my death, I shall sit by my grave and wonder…"

1992: Hitherto, Sophie has been unable to recall any of her life as "Sarah" and has had her name legally changed. When she does recall Sarah, it is like catching glimpses of someone else's life. She and Dale are very happy and discussing marriage, but she wants to finish art and design college first. She still paints and designs clothes. It is a talent she brought back with her from the grave. She loves to travel with Dale's band when they are on the road because she still feels a bit claustrophobic in her home county and not always welcome. There is always talk and suspicion. Although it would have been poetic justice, the old drunk was not killed while driving intoxicated. He blew his head off with a twelve-gauge shotgun. There's really nothing poetic about that at all.

Along with his regular practice, Dr. Smith lectures on the paranormal and, in particular, reincarnation, which, up until this case, he never gave much serious consideration. He is fascinated by the many intriguing cases he has uncovered since the Sophie Zandona case. His curiosity is also piqued by the fact that, although reincarnation is a doctrine in many of the world's holy books, in 325 AD all references to reincarnation were stricken from the Christian Bible. He maintains close contact with Dale and Sophie and is working on a book focused on the Zandona case as well as a few others.

Sophie is almost completely free from physical and mental complaints, including the arthritis. The nightmares have not returned either, but they still become a little anxious as each birthday approaches, because the psychic advised them that meeting up with her killer and recalling the accident were not the reasons she came back. The case of Sophie Elizabeth Zandona is not closed yet.

Chapter Four

Stratosfear

In the real dark night of the soul,
it is always 3 o'clock in the morning.
— F. Scott Fitzgerald, *The Crack-Up*

Gregg and Carla moved into the old north Manchester house in the fall of 1988. It was to be a new start for them, as their infant son had died of SIDS the previous year. Carla had been hospitalized for several weeks and was still receiving treatment as an outpatient. It was Carla who found the cold, cyanotic remains of their infant son.

During her stay in the hospital, Gregg began house hunting for them; their old house had already been sold and the closing date was fast approaching. He had not yet found anything by the time Carla was discharged, but a few days after she came home, while they were out on a day trip, they happened upon an old three-storey Victorian that was for sale. They were both struck by the house but for different reasons. Gregg was a lawyer who had a hobby of architecture; he especially loved old structures like this one. Carla, an artist, was drawn to its unique, intricate beauty. However, she also experienced a sense of foreboding, which she ascribed to her still-fragile emotional state. She said nothing to Gregg about it.

They contacted the real estate agent that day and were given a tour of the house while being informed of many of the recent renovations. The attic in particular had been fully renovated and the house had been rewired and a new roof had been installed. Once again Carla felt that sense of foreboding and a bit claustrophobic in spite of the immense size of the house, which included cathedral ceilings. What she didn't know was that Gregg shared her sense of foreboding. They both wondered at the peculiar cold spots that were localized in a couple of places and the trepidation they evoked. Nevertheless, they were both quite pleased (as well as a tad surprised) when their first offer was promptly accepted. Gregg figured it was probably owing to the fact that in spite of the extensive renovations, it would still require a good deal of work. The current owners were also concerned about squatters moving in while the house stood empty. Still, they couldn't believe their luck. Some things just seemed destined to be… That's what worried Carla.

They, with the help of some close friends, were in the process of unpacking boxes and setting up house on October 31, All Hallows Eve. Tricks or treats had long since made its way to England, and they took turns shelling out goodies as they put their new home in order. They were the enjoying the festive mood and the parade of costumes that accented the cool, clean, crisp fall air. Flames snapped in the old brick fireplace as they sat around the hearth and christened their new place with glasses of wine. When two children arrived at the door dressed as ghosts, Carla jokingly mused with her friends about some oddities in their new domain and wondered if they had any unseen housemates. Little did they know…

After their friends departed and the costumed ghosts and goblins retired for the evening, Gregg and Carla collapsed in front of the fireplace and breathed a sigh of relief. They were both thinking they must be more tired than they had thought because they could have sworn they heard something breathe back, followed by some rapping sounds above them. On their way to bed they decided to rent the ground floor and attic flats of the house as they were quite comfortable here on the second floor. Neither had even considered occupying the attic flat. They couldn't put their finger on it, but it was as though some animal had died, trapped behind the walls, leaving the stench of death in its wake. This was not so much an odour as it was a feeling. They neither felt comfortable nor welcome in the attic. The strange noises they kept hearing did not put them any more at ease!

Fatigue finally overtook them and both fell into a deep slumber quickly. Carla dreamed of her deceased son, trick or treating in a little ghost costume. In the far-off distance of her dreamscape, she heard a baby crying. The little boy in the ghost costume looked up at Carla and said, "You should leave here, Mommy, before she finds you." She started to ask him what he meant, but he merely frowned and turned, heading off into the landscape of the dream. The further away the little boy got, the closer the cries of the baby came. She called out after her son, but he was lost to her.

She awoke with a start. Her cheeks were wet with tears. She looked over to see if Gregg was sleeping. She noticed that the clock beside him read 3:17 a.m. Then she heard it: a baby crying. This was no dream, but how could it be real? Where was it coming from? A cold fear was enveloping her, a fear that she was having another breakdown.

She carefully got out of bed to investigate, following the direction of the crying. She made her way down the dark hall, caught in the trance of the crying. The sounds led her to the door that opened into the interior staircase that joined the four storeys of the house. She cracked open the door and peered into the shadowy darkness. The crying was coming from the attic! She could hear her heart pounding in her head. She wanted, even needed, to ascend the stairs but was frozen at the foot of the staircase. She heard movement from behind her and uttered a silent gasp. She almost fainted with relief at the sight of Gregg. They looked from each other up toward the attic. She was not losing her mind; he heard it too! Carla was both reassured and frightened by this. As they stood locked in the moment, not sure what their next move should be, the crying abruptly ceased. As if released from its grip, Carla collapsed into Gregg's arms, sobbing.

Gregg guided her back into their flat. He sat her down at the kitchen table and poured them both a generous brandy. She cupped the snifter in her hands and finally voiced what they both were thinking. "What's happening around here?" Were there squatters up there with a baby? As improbable as that was, Gregg went up to investigate. As he expected, nothing had changed from the first time they inspected the attic flat. Save for a wheelchair and a kitchen table, there was no sign of life. They would hear the phantom crying on only one more occasion.

The following day, Gregg's best friend and partner in the law firm, Marc, came over to help with some repairs around the house. Marc had been a tremendous support to both Gregg and Carla following the death of their son. He was like family, so Gregg felt no compunction relating the experience of the previous night. As the two were installing smoke detectors, Gregg related the events to Marc. They did-n't know what to make of it and so they decided to write it off as a com-bination of exhaustion and stress.

At 3:17 the next morning, they were once again awoken. This time, however, it was by the piercing wail of the newly installed smoke detector. They both lunged out of bed in a frantic haste to find the sup-posed fire. They could smell but not see any smoke or, for that matter, any fire. They quickly checked the rest of the house even though the alarm was localized to their flat. There was no fire to be found any-where on the premises. They experienced a mixture of relief, puzzle-ment, and annoyance. It was certainly feasible that a smoke detector would malfunction, but what was the origin of the smoky odour and haze? This was indeed a strange house!

In spite of it all, Carla was in the midst of preparations for their first Christmas in their new home. While addressing invitations for their Christmas party, both Gregg and Carla joked about inviting an exorcist. They erected what was a very good imitation of a spruce pine in their living room; they would have preferred the real thing but they weren't taking any chances with fires. As it was, the smoke detector continued to wail its false alarms periodically and always at the same time: 3:17 a.m. Gregg was forced to disconnect the contraption, but that didn't bring an end to the recurrences of a phantom fire. Carla suggested they call in a psychic, but Gregg dismissed the suggestion as an overreaction. That was until the morning of December 7.

Carla was wakened from a sound sleep by something. She glanced over at the digital clock. She once again smelled the faint odour of smoke, but this time it was accompanied by what appeared to be flick-ering lights or flames coming from the direction of the living room, just a short distance from their bedroom. Carla was wondering if they had left the Christmas tree lights on, when something casting a dark shad-ow slowly entered her peripheral vision. The shadowy form slowly made its way down the hall until it, or rather she, came into view. The apparition was that of a young woman with long dark brown hair, garbed in a long white night dress. She was floating past the bedroom door, but just as she was moving out of sight, she came to an abrupt stop. It was as though she suddenly became aware of Carla.

The phantom figure turned her head and she and Carla locked eyes. A chill passed through Carla. She wanted to scream and wake Gregg but she was transfixed in the moment, a moment that seemed timeless. Carla felt a sense of grief and overwhelming sadness wash over her; she noticed the shimmer of tears on the young girl's visage as she reached her arms out. Then, much to her horror, the spectre began to morph into a burnt relic of itself, consumed by an invisible fire. The long hair was smouldering, threatening to ignite in flames. The pouting mouth was replaced by a grimace frozen in a silent scream. The hands that had been reaching out were now burnt, gnarled claws, cracked open by fire to reveal ivory bone. The eyes were no longer sad and shedding tears; in their place were gaping, blackish red sockets that seemed to retain the power of sight. The entire figure had turned shades of black, red, and an ugly hue of bluish grey. The horrific image sent shock waves through Carla. Her screams woke Gregg, and the apparition vanished as he bolted into an upright position. He turned to see the cause of Carla's distress. He thought he caught a glimpse of something, like the remnants of a faded image, but he couldn't make anything out clearly. He turned the bedside lamp on and gathered the shaking Carla into his arms.

Eventually, she calmed down enough to relate the experience to him, stating that either this house was haunted or she was clinically insane. She insisted on calling in a psychic, and this time Gregg put up no resistance to the idea. He could no longer shrug things off; it had evolved into something much more serious — and, he feared, dangerous.

They made immediate arrangements via a friend to have a psychic examine the environment. Their friend assured them of the authenticity of the psychic, sharing her own experiences of him with Gregg and Carla. His name was Ian Ainsworth. He was forty-four and, as he phrased it, he had been an involuntary conduit between the living and the dead since he was a boy. After years of struggling with his so-called gift, he finally made his peace with it by employing it to help the living and the deceased. He prayed he would be able to do so in this case.

The seance was scheduled for the evening of December 12. In attendance were Carla, Gregg, Marc, and Deanna, the friend who had introduced them to the psychic. As the majority of the manifestations seemed focused on the second floor, Ian decided to hold the sitting there, but first he did a walk-through of the house.

He began in the attic. As he would later describe it, he was thunderstruck by the vibrancy up there and couldn't wait to leave, as it felt like the walls were closing in on him. He received the same impression on the second floor, but there it was more about grief and excruciating pain. He was not as claustrophobic outside of the attic flat. In the living room, however, he could barely resist the urge to cry and shout out in agony.

Having thus gotten a sense of the psychic environment in the house, the small group gathered in a circle around a table in the living room. It was illuminated by the warm, dancing flames in the fireplace and the Christmas tree lights.

Ian began by invoking a white light to protect all those within the circle. He requested that no one break the circle, and they joined hands as Ian commenced to lower himself into a trance state. All was quiet save for the faint, rhythmic breathing of the participants and the occasional moan of the wind. Several minutes passed before the silence was broken by the soft voice of the psychic beckoning to the spirits of the house. The now familiar sounds of breathing were replaced by the raspy, laboured breathing of an unseen presence. It would seem that someone else had joined the little group.

A cool draft blew through the circle. A faint odour of smoke permeated the room, but this time it was accompanied by the distinct smell of overcooked meat. The atmosphere felt electrically charged, and everyone in the group noticed that their scalps were tingling and the tiny hairs on their arms were raised. The lights on the tree began to flicker frantically. The flames in the fireplace flared and spat sparks. It took the collective will of the entire group to prevent the breakup of the circle.

Ian again beseeched the spirits of the house to reveal themselves. As far as Carla was concerned, they had already revealed themselves plenty! Again they heard laboured breathing as though someone was struggling to speak. Ian assured the spirit that it was safe here amongst people who only wanted to help. Although it was a cool December evening, in the living room it became exceedingly hot, almost unbearably so, but they dared not break the circle to remove their sweaters.

Ian moved deeper into his trance state, reaching for this poor lost soul. His body shuddered and gave off a small jerk when he finally established contact, and his eyes shot wide open as if responding to the shock of it. His face appeared anguished. He began to speak in a low, agonized manner. It was his voice, but, like the breathing that preceded it, he sounded as if he was having great difficulty vocalizing. He would later explain that he felt he was trying to speak with vocal cords that were raw and ravaged.

"My name is Katherine," finally made it past his lips, followed by several rasping coughs. The group feared he may be choking, but instead, he repeated, "My name is Katherine," drawing in a long, slow, difficult breath followed by a horrific howl. One full of torment, sorrow, and utter despair — a primal scream. It was like the wail of a banshee, penetrating right through those in attendance. This time, they could not help but break the circle.

In an instant, it was as though they were transported back to the land of the living. Ian almost crumpled forward onto the table, and, much to Carla's alarm, coughed a touch of red into his handkerchief. He politely waved off her concerns. He, as well as the others, took several deep breaths to reorient themselves. More than one of them was pale and trembling. Both Marc and Gregg were in a state of disbelief. Their friend, Deanna, made a dash for the light switch. Slowly, they regained their composure enough to start conversing. Gregg went to the kitchen and returned with some brandy and snifters. Ian declined and asked only for a glass of water and an Aspirin. When they were all settled, he began to tell them what he had discerned from his connection with this spirit.

It was that of a seventeen-year-old female named Katherine. She lived on the premises (if you could call it living) with her elderly grandmother, who was wheelchair-bound and suffering from a number of ailments, including dementia. The grandmother was totally dependent on Katherine. She remained on the top floor, but Katherine spent most of her time in the flat Gregg and Carla now inhabited, if for no other reason than to escape the old woman. Nevertheless, the old woman would command Katherine from the attic flat by causing a noisy disturbance or banging on the floor. That explained the noises Gregg and Carla heard emanating from the empty attic. It would also explain the perplexing sounds of a squeaky wheel traversing back and forth throughout the flat.

This poor young woman was a virtual prisoner in death, just as she had been in life (she had no friends and was not even able to attend school) until fire consumed them both. Out of sheer exhaustion, Katherine had fallen asleep while dinner was cooking. The second-floor flat became engulfed in smoke. She struggled to make it up the stairs to retrieve the old woman, who was screeching from the attic, but she collapsed halfway up the stairs. She died there, petrified in a crawling posture by flame and heat.

Ian had connected with many lost souls over the years, but never had he felt such a deep need to help release a soul as he did for this poor wretched girl. A false sense of failure seemed to be keeping her trapped, so he would have to make her see the events of her life and death differently, more realistically. He re-established contact and kept working with her until she not only saw the light but moved into it.

The atmosphere of the house was not as ominous and it felt like clouds were lifting. Even though there was no way to be sure, it was felt by all that Katherine had moved on into the light and was at last resting in peace.

Gregg and Carla lit a special prayer candle in her honour on Christmas Eve. Upon preparing to retire, they went to extinguish the candle, but before doing so they held hands and said, "Be at peace, Katherine, along with our son." With that, the candle flame flared a brilliant white and blue for about thirty seconds before extinguishing itself. Carla prayed that was a good sign.

That night, the little boy who had been wearing the ghost costume once again visited Carla in her dreams. A deep feeling of dread passed through her as he repeated his previous admonition to get out of the house before "she" finds them. Carla was awakened from the nightmare by the cries of a baby. Once again, they were coming from the attic. Carla knew it was not her son. These cries were from a malicious entity that was attempting to torment her. As Ian had suspected and the rest of them feared, Katherine had not been the sole entity in the house. But this spirit was no poor lost soul needing guidance to any light. Carla felt in her gut that it was the demented old woman, and she was truly afraid.

Postscript: Although food had been left cooking in the oven, further forensic study indicates that the most likely cause of the fire was faulty electrical wiring, which had been smouldering behind a wall in the attic for hours before finally igniting in the wee hours of the morning. Maybe 3:17 a.m.?

Gregg and Carla remain in the house in spite of whatever presence remains there with them. They have had other paranormal activity, but certainly nothing as traumatic as when they first took up residence there. However, they continue to have difficulty keeping tenants in the attic flat.

Although the experience was frightening, to say the least, Carla feels a sense of peace for the first time since the loss of their son. She feels that having had the opportunity to help free that trapped soul somehow freed her own in a way. She does believe it coincidental that they were so drawn to the house in the first place. Gregg shares her feelings but believes that we remain in the earthly stratosphere for a short time, then we begin to fade, becoming reabsorbed in the stuff of the universe. He believes that tragic events can chain you to this earthly realm whether you are dead or alive. Although he would not relish having another such experience, he is grateful for having been part of this, for he too feels changed and deeply in awe of what lies beneath the lives we live.

Carla wanted to add that she continues to see the psychotherapist who helped her through the tragic events, but now for the purpose of exploring the meaning of it all. In response to a query of Carla's, the psychotherapist stated that at no time, even when Carla was at the peak of crisis or grief, did she present in a hallucinatory or delusional manner. In fact, he was concerned that, if anything, she was too rational.

Chapter Five
The Far Side of the Sky

Groped up, to see if God was there —
And wandered out of life.
> — Emily Dickinson, poem 1062

The following is an eerie account of brotherly love that offers up evidence that blood is not only thicker than water; it also runs much deeper than the average grave. These events happened to David Brinja, a Norwegian-born artist currently working in Canada. David left Norway about a year after his older brother and sole sibling, Jorjen, hanged himself. It was David who found the limp, lifeless body of his brother. No note offering any insight into this tragic event has ever been uncovered. However, David would not only hear from his brother again, his life would be saved from beyond the grave.

Seven years after my brother, Jorjen, committed suicide, I had this incredible brush with him and fate. I was staying at the home of a close friend in Lambeth, England for the Christmas holidays and had retired to bed early due to a chest cold and a headache. I hadn't bothered seeing a doctor so I wasn't taking any medication.

I fell into a heavy slumber and had a vivid dream about being back in high school in Norway. I was walking through some corridors searching for my locker. When I came to the end of a hallway, instead of turning left or right, I felt an irresistible urge to go through the door straight ahead of me. I thought it opened into the teacher's lounge, but once through it I found myself in the front room of the cottage where Jorjen had hanged himself. This gave me such a start that I believed myself to have been jolted out of my dream and woken up back in the cottage. I was quite apprehensive and was immediately struck by the ferocity of the wind blowing around me.

In retrospective, I think I was more afraid about seeing Jorjen hanging from the rafters again. I was in the very room where it happened. I came into position directly beneath the rafter. I was standing there looking up at it, pondering what all this was about, when I felt the sensation of a noose tightening around my throat. I could not breathe. A panic was overtaking me. I was clutching at my throat, gasping for precious air. I could feel my body growing cold and numb. There was a burning agony as every cell in my body seemed to scream for oxygen. That terrible wind was howling all around me.

Is this what it felt like to die? Is this what Jen had gone through while he slowly asphyxiated? I tried to think of a prayer to offer, but for the life of me, I just couldn't remember any. In my panicked mental outreach, I found something else, or rather someone else found me. In the midst of what I knew in my gut to be the throes of death came the voice and very real, puissant presence of my brother, Jorjen. I felt he was holding me up somehow so I wouldn't be choked by this psychic noose or whatever it was. A warm rush of relief and calm washed over me. All the fear and panic vanished with the appearance of my brother.

Clearer than I've ever heard anything before, Jorjen imparted these words: "David, be calm and still. Everything is going to all right. Help is coming. Just wait for Brett. Trust that I will never leave you again." He then gave me the small gold cross and chain he always used to wear. (It is the one I gave him for Christmas the year of his death, so it was quite familiar to me.)

I knew my friend Brett had been watching the telly in the adjoining sitting room when I had gone to bed. All the Christmas commotion had caught up to him and he had fallen fast asleep during an episode of *Are You Being Served?* He certainly did not hear my gasping and struggling for life in the bedroom. He would later tell me of his being shaken awake while his name was being called. He distinctly recalls the pressure he felt on his shoulders and his resistance to being summoned back into wakefulness. He also recalls that it had been Jen trying to wake him up. He expected to see him when he opened his eyes. However, upon awakening he found himself alone in the sitting room.

He was confused and still half asleep and about to go back to sleep when much to his alarm his attention was drawn to the choking, gasping sounds coming from the bedroom as though someone were in a struggle, as indeed I was in the struggle of my life. Upon entering the bedroom, Brett found me thrashing about the on the bed like a "fish out of water" just before collapsing into unconsciousness. Brett called for a car to be brought around and then began CPR.

The poor chauffeur had not even changed out of his nightclothes when I was ushered into the car, still unconscious, and whisked off to hospital whilst Brett continued CPR. I have no recollection of any of this. As far as I knew, I was off in some otherworldly place with my brother, with whom I was completely at peace and thrilled to be reunited.

Things were not so peaceful with Brett, though. By the time we reached the hospital, I had ceased breathing and had only a faint, erratic pulse. The doctors were able to bring me back, and once stabilized, I was sent to the ICU for observation. As it turns out, I had developed a severe case of pneumonia, and my airway passages were inflamed and blocked. If Brett had not been so mysteriously awakened, I would have died of asphyxiation.

When I regained consciousness at around four o'clock the following afternoon, I was feeling quite confused, which is not surprising given the circumstances. The hospital staff were very pleased with my progress but were puzzled and seemingly quite concerned over a physical manifestation: there was around my neck what appeared to be burn marks such as those made by a rope. After extensive interviewing, they became cautiously satisfied that they did not have a case of assault or attempted suicide on their hands.

They did, however, have the resident shrink come down to see me. I related the entire story from what I had experienced. He concluded that (get ready for this) the rope burn marks were an outward somatic manifestation of the unresolved psychological trauma I suffered as a result of my brother's suicide, and that this suffocation experience was the trigger to bring that trauma to the surface. (Don't you just love the way psychiatrists talk?) I wasn't too impressed by any of that but I was sure of the emotive impression I received as I parted company with my brother — it was simple and precise: "I am sorry. LOVE."

Still, I need to know why he murdered himself. I have since read a book entitled *Darkness Visible,* by William Styron, which offered some unique insights on the matter of suicide notes as a result of [the author] trying to compose one himself. He states, "I couldn't manage the sheer dirge-like solemnity of it; there was something I found almost comically offensive in the pomposity of such a comment as 'For some time now I have sensed in my work a growing psychosis that is doubtless a reflection of the psychotic strain tainting my life,' as well as something degrading in the prospect of a testament, which I wished to infuse with at least some dignity and eloquence, reduced to an exhausted stutter of inadequate apologies and self explanations."[1] His writing offered me some understanding and solace. Perhaps no note could ever explain it. Actions speak louder than words.

Something else that cannot be explained is that when I opened the small brown envelope containing my valuables (the staff had removed them upon my admission), there with my ring and watch was the small gold cross that Jorjen had given me in my dream. The thing about that cross is that my brother had been buried in it. What was it doing here, with me?

I was released from the hospital a little more than a week after my admission, just in time for Christmas. Brett and I had no doubt in our minds that it was Jen who alerted Brett to my desperate situation, and just in the nick of time. It was also Jen who was my comfort and support while I lay suspended between life and death. I am more convinced than ever that the curtain dividing those worlds is a very thin one indeed. The psychiatrist and some other mental health workers would explain all this away in psychobabble terms, but their brand of logic does not translate well in the paradigm of reality just beyond that thin curtain. Those of us who have had such experiences know in our hearts and souls the reality of our experiences and we are never the same again. Jen's cross has not left my neck since that Christmas, nor has the faint rope scar. Science has its explanations, and I have mine.

I received something besides the cross from my brother. Ever since his suicide, I had been severely depressed. I had been to see doctors and was taking medication, but nothing seemed to work. After having this experience of my brother, I was no longer depressed. It wasn't anything I did or took; it just wasn't there anymore! I felt like I had got my life back.

Several months after giving this interview, David went through some boxes containing possessions of his brother. He found notes and passages underlined by his brother that may offer a clue as to Jorjen's state of mind. He had always been a history buff, and if he had lived, he probably would have gone on to become a professor of history. However, he seemed to have developed a fascination or even minor obsession with the tales of the Nordic God, Odin. In the old Nordic myth, only those who died by violence — as in battle or in suicide — could enter paradise, the famed Valhalla. Jorjen had underlined many references to Odin and Valhalla and had even drawn sketches depicting some of the stories and poems. The one that really seemed to have captivated him, though, was the following, in which the references are eerily reminiscent of Jorjen's own demise:

> I know that I hung in the windy tree
> For nine whole nights
> Wounded with the spear, dedicated to Odin,
> Myself to myself.
>
> — from *Havamal*

It is not a suicide note, and in a way it raises more questions than answers for David, but nevertheless he is grateful for any clues or insights into the state of mind of his lost brother.

David is currently working as the lighting and sound engineer for the classical rock band Blind Shadow, of which Brett is also a member. David continues to paint and study art. He remains intensely interested in the study of suicide and how to prevent it. Besides playing keyboards for the band, Brett also performs individually as a concert pianist.

When the band is not touring, they reside together in a turn-of-the-century farmhouse, which, if not haunted, has very spooky and immensely strong mice. Brett related to me one of the unexplained events connected with this farm.

Growing up as he did on an old English estate, ghosts and haunts are second nature to Brett. He is not sure if they are drawn to him or vice versa, because even the boarding school he attended in Switzerland was haunted by a former headmaster. I wasn't sure, either; there is certainly an aura about him. Artistic types are often naturally sensitive to psychic phenomena and alternative realities, and Brett is definitely artistic. Although he does not look like the stereotypical concert pianist (with his long chestnut brown hair, stocky build and squared jaw, he looks more like a model for an outdoors men's magazine), he is, in fact, an internationally renowned musician with two earned and several honorary degrees. He actually took to the piano, or as he puts it, the piano took to him, at the tender age of four and a half years old.

One piano in particular captured him at that tender age. It is an eighteenth-century Steinway that Brett inherited when his grandfather died. Brett has always had a special relationship with his keyboards. He says he is very "Zen" about being one with the tools of your creativity; i.e., you are part of each other. He also believes the keyboards can absorb and emit energy so each one has a feel and a personality of its own. He further believes they can imbue you with life or, conversely, suck the life right out you. He says, "I believe they can be haunted by the combined energy of those who have had an intimate relationship with them through the good and the bad times. This one particular piano [the Steinway] has always been my best friend." As he relates this to me in a soft, cultured British accent, his intense brown eyes have an almost mischievous twinkle. I wondered if he was having me on... until I heard the story.

When the band first moved into the farmhouse, one of the first things moved into the place was the antique Steinway. The band would rehearse in a living room/dining room combination, which was divided in the centre by two French doors. A small foyer with a staircase leading up to the second floor separated the double "music" rooms from the large old-fashioned kitchen that spanned the length and ran parallel to the double room. There were doors on either side of the kitchen, allowing one entrance to either end of the music room.

The piano, as well as the other keyboards, was to be placed in the front room (the parlour); the drum kit and other smaller equipment would be in the back section (the dining room).

As previously stated, the only piece of musical equipment in the farmhouse as they moved in was the Steinway. After bringing in a few mattresses and other bits of furniture, they all decided to crash for the day. Upon awakening the following morning, they were astonished to find that the massive, exceedingly heavy grand piano had been moved into the back section of the music room. Since the legs were not removable and the piano would have to have been manoeuvred through the French doors, this bit of redecorating was no small feat! They joked about having some really big mice and suggested to Brett that it just be left there, but Brett preferred the acoustics and the structure of the front room, especially an odd little alcove in one of the corners. So, five of them manoeuvred the grand back through the French doors and into the front room. The next morning, sure enough, the piano was back in the rear part of the music room. This time, it would remain there.

As the rest of the band went to pick up the remaining two vanloads of furniture and equipment, Brett decided to edit some musical scores at the kitchen table. The only other person at home was David, who was napping upstairs. As Brett was busy at the table, he became distracted by the sound of sighing or laboured breathing emanating from the front part of the music room. He thought perhaps Dale had returned and was moving guitars into the music room. Whoever it was moved from the front room to the back room but stopped at the door that led into the kitchen. To and fro it paced, sighing in distress or frustration as though it was trying to get beyond the music rooms but could not pass through the doors into the kitchen.

This became too much for Brett, who stormed into the music rooms to find out what the heck was going on, but there was no one there. (He was almost expecting to see the piano moved again and was relieved to see it in its self-designated position.) Although he is not the nervous type, especially when it comes to paranormal activity, Brett was nevertheless happy to see the other band members return. He told them he was convinced the place was haunted and described what had just happened.

A few days later when the man from whom they purchased the farm returned to pick up his last remaining boxes, Brett described the event to him. He said he was not surprised. In fact it was one of the reasons he reluctantly sold up. He explained that his family, especially the missus, was not happy there. As for the piano moving about, the gentleman explained that the front room, being the parlour, would have been used in bygone days as the funeral or viewing room for the family. (This was before the days of funeral homes.) The man pointed to the strange little alcove Brett had liked and explained that it was called a coffin corner, the place where the body would be laid out for the wake. So, either the piano didn't like being in the "wake room," or one of the dearly departed didn't like the piano in that room.

Either way, some unseen entity certainly liked the piano, as the playing of haunting melodies would often awaken band members, especially Jesse, Brian, and his son Stevie, (all who had bedrooms above the music rooms). She seemed to have a penchant for Bach and Schubert. I specify the gender because of a truly unique manifestation of psychic phenomena.

One evening after everyone had long since retired to bed, Brett, David, and Dale were all awakened by a very loud clap of thunder. This was quickly succeeded by another, only this time it was accompanied by what sounded like the hood on the grand piano being violently slammed down. The reverberations from the piano strings could be heard throughout the house (it in fact it woke everyone else up). Brett thought the piano must have been hit by lightning and went dashing down the stairs into the music room. Close on his heels were David and Dale. The lights came on but their flickering issued a warning that the power would probably not be with them much longer, so Dale popped into the kitchen to fetch a couple of flashlights. He returned just in time to witness another streak of lightning illuminate the rooms, and this time the power did fail.

Brett and Dale switched on the flashlights and scanned the two music rooms for any possible lightning damage, unplugging electrical cords as they made their way to the piano. Another bolt of lighting flashed, but this one did not so much light up the room as illuminate the piano. The amorphous concentration of light appeared to slowly soak into the hood of the piano. As it slowly re-emerged, the amorphous luminescence began to take the shape of a female form. They could not believe their eyes as the phantasm evolved into the figure of a woman in a long dress looking as startled to see them as they were to see her. Her look quickly changed to defiance, as though she were guarding her territory. She tilted her head, staring straight at them, before being drawn back into the piano.

I was not a witness to this event but it nevertheless gives me chills; when I asked them to describe the woman, David and Brett looked at each other and then replied that she looked just like me. Brett didn't want to say anything because he thinks it may have been my doppelgänger, an apparition that is said to herald death. (In most cases, it means certain death only if you see your own doppelgänger.) I assured them that the apparition may have looked like me, but given the lack of light and the environmental circumstances, it could have looked just as easily looked like Whistler's mother. Nevertheless, to this day Brett refers to me as the living ghost of his piano. I have spent many hours on that piano, since 1974, in fact.[2] It does indeed feel like a part of me when I'm with it, so maybe Brett was correct in his theory about pianos taking on some elements of those close to them as well as imbuing life into one… and vice versa.

A few words about the mysterious phenomena of the doppelgänger, which is sometimes referred to as an autophany in research circles (see Glossary). David mentioned that Norway has a long history of doppelgängers, which in Norway is known as the vardger. Norway's Society for Psychical Research notes that most incidences of encountering one's double in Norway are of an auditory nature, where one may hear a family member enter a room, call out a name, or drop their keys. Norwegians seem to be nonplussed by such experiences.

A couple of well-known persons who met up with themselves, so to speak, include the stoic Elizabeth the First, who saw herself lying on her bed looking deathly ill. A few days later, she expired. One of the most intriguing cases of the doppelgänger happened to the French author Guy de Maupassant. It seems that Maupassant was locked in his room battling writer's block when he received a visitor. He was astonished that anyone had gained entrance into his room. He became even more astonished when the intruder was revealed as being none other than the author's double! The double took a seat and proceeded to dictate a story to Maupassant. It was the chilling tale of a man tormented by an evil spirit who, although invisible to the "host," had a life outside and separate from that of his "host." This menacing spirit eventually drove the wretched victim to despair and finally utter madness. This classic tale of horror will be known to readers as "The Horla." Tragically, the fate that befell the protagonist in "The Horla" also fell upon Maupassant. Not long after the publication of gruesome tale, Maupassant plunged into the same kind of madness and suffered an early death.

Denny Taylor of Toronto, Canada shared a more recent and certainly more inspiring tale of encountering his doppelgänger. He is an artist and freelance writer. These events transpired in the summer of 2001.

"I had become seriously ill and so had been unable to work. My partner was only working part time as a teacher at a local university. Money was tight and things just seemed to be getting worse. I had become really burnt out and felt like I was on the verge of losing it. I was unable to write or paint, which has always been a means by which I can remain grounded and centred.

"As this progressed, I seemed to lose a sense of my own identity. For me, and I think for most people, there is this inner sense of the self; whether you refer to it as your higher self or soul, it's that essential part of us that encompasses all we have been, all we could be, as well as all our hopes and dreams. It's that part of us that people who have endured imprisonment or even torture write about when they describe a core part of themselves that remained intact and allowed them to maintain their sense of dignity in the face of the inhumanity and humiliations being imposed on them. It's that part that cannot be taken from us, only surrendered. It's also a constant companion.

"I have never had the experience of losing that inner sense of self before. It reduces your life to a sentence of living death, where you are physically alive in the sense that your heart is beating and your lungs are breathing, but that which was you is dead. You are a hollow carcass barely able to make it through the motions of daily living.

"One day after getting out of the shower, I was drying my face and stared at the mirror. The face was vacant. I asked almost prayer-like, 'Are you still anywhere in there, Denny? Is there anything of you left alive?'

"I had not been sleeping well, but that night I fell into an almost exhausted sleep. I was woken up in the middle of the night by someone entering the room. I thought it was my partner maybe coming back from the bathroom or something. As the figure grew closer to the bed, I realized I was looking at myself! In spite of seeing what I knew I could not be seeing, I was very calm and accepting. The figure that was me drew closer to the bed. I just lay there, observing. He or I stopped about a foot away from the bed. The figure just stood there watching me with a look of compassion and empathy on his face. It was as if he had come in answer to my earlier question about anything being left alive in me. It stood there watching me, and for the first time in over a year, I felt comforted and not alone. In spite of the bizarre nature of this experience, I did not move, not even to sit upright. In the comfort, I fell back to sleep knowing I was not alone and there was 'someone' still in there, watching over me."

It is possible that under the prolonged stress and ill health, Denny experienced a psychotic break with reality. Or maybe it was his living ghost or soul coming in response to his pleas. Whatever it was, the outcome was immensely positive and therapeutic.

Chapter Six
If I Should Die
Before I Wake

I felt a funeral in my brain
And mourners, to and fro.
> — Emily Dickinson,
> "I felt a funeral in my brain"

Gate, paragate, parasmagate, bodhi svaha!
Gone, gone, gone beyond altogether gone
beyond, Free at last!
> — From *Bhagavad gita*

The ancient Greeks have given mankind some of its most profound insights into the human condition. Their philosophy and applied logic endure today. They held a firm belief that life was purposeful. Eighteen-year-old Andreas Papandreou had always been attracted to the wisdom and philosophy of the ancient Greeks. After March 17, 1997, it took on even greater meaning for him. At 9:55:07 p.m. he was pronounced dead in the emergency room of a hospital in Athens. As he jokingly puts it, death really changes your life. He also came to understand the ancient quip: Where there is death, there is hope.

This was the second fatal asthma attack I had in my life. It is this second one I am recounting here, for though my experiences on the so-called other side were similar, the second one had more meaning and its effects were more enduring. This was not due so much to what transpired on the other side, but rather due to what was taking place in the hospital around the body that used to be me. That was the first thing that died in me — an attachment to a physical form. With that comes an attachment to all the various roles and identities we have. They're understandable attachments because it's all we know and it's required to function in life, at least until you see things from the other side of life. Even simply being is different. You are somehow authentic there; you don't try to be anyone or anything because you simply are. It's so easy, unfettered, and uncomplicated. There are no roles for you to fulfill even if you wanted to.

By the time my father, Darien, and I reached the emergency room, I was well on my way out of this world. I was in absolute torment, slowly suffocating to death. It seemed to be taking forever. Finally, my body and the hectic commotion around me started to fade, becoming distant and unreal. I was dying, which is a lot like waking up from a deep sleep while recalling fragments of a very lucid dream.

I could still make out the frantic voices in the ER, but they were growing fainter while another voice beckoning me by name grew louder. I could not see who was calling me, but I received a clear and loving impression from this strangely familiar voice. It was penetrating while the voices from the ER were more like echoes. Simultaneously, I heard the doctor exclaim, "We've lost him," then calling for a crash cart. I was being drawn upwards, as though caught in the eye of a tornado, surrounded by this fully encompassing swishing sound and motion. It was all happening so fast and I was elated to be free from that torture my body had been going through. (Being dead is easy; dying is the hard part.) Now I could not even relate to that lifeless form lying on the hospital gurney; it was like a familiar stranger to me. I couldn't believe I once thought of that body as being me. It is difficult to find the words that accurately convey what an incredible feeling of freedom it was to be out of that body and even out of that world!

All the while, the voice continued to beckon me. As I was drawn closer, I instinctively knew that the voice belonged to my paternal grandfather. I have no memory of him, as he died when I was still an infant, but I have heard wonderful things about him and I am his namesake.

As happened during my previous experience, I was soaring through this tunnel at an incredible speed towards the voice of my grandfather.

There was a luminous, animated living light at the far end of this tunnel. This chamber was alive with colours I've never seen or imagined before. There was a consciousness about them that touched me as I passed by. (Our language is a hopelessly inadequate tool by which to describe these experiences. I liken it to trying to explain colour to a person born blind or music to a deaf person.) Time, space, even consciousness is not as we know it in our normal, waking life. There was such a feeling of belonging, as though I had been away at school and finally I was home. There was an unconditional love and acceptance that grew stronger the closer I came to the light. I thought I had known such love from my father, but apparently I was wrong. It was so intense and powerful that it engulfed me without obliterating my sense of autonomy. I imagine you simply blend in with the light and continue as one with it or them. Far off, there was a bright light, but it was so bright, it appeared as a cold, blue light. I am cognizant of how esoteric and fanciful that sounds, but I know of no other way to describe it.

Between the light and myself was a great canyon. It reminded me of the great abyss Goya termed Noda. I clearly recall this gulf from my previous encounter with death, a sense of déjà vu. There was something that sounded like rapids gushing from deep within the chasm, though I did not see water. I felt flowing currents, though, like an ionic atmospheric effect (as you sometimes experience around a waterfall). I felt my being caught in the rhythm of gushing, turbulent forces. As with the lights in the tunnel, there was a consciousness associated with this energetic activity. I could easily have spent eternity being by these rapids and this gulf, just absorbing it all.

In my previous visit, I was compelled to peer into the abyss and experienced a brief review of my time on earth. Being so young, the principal theme was the effect my existence had on others, especially my father and, much to my surprise, his best friend, Edgar Lavour. I became aware of the interconnectedness of everything. Things that on the surface appear unrelated in fact have a deep, subterranean correlation. Our thoughts and actions affect events and people in ways we just can't imagine, but in death you see it quite clearly and it all makes perfect sense. You don't understand why you didn't see it before. It is so transparent there that you come to realize how blind we are in life. We're blinded by so many things: our fears, biases, distractions, and ignorance. That is one thing I never fail to recall everyday, though: we are blind in this life.

If I Should Die Before I Wake

There was no compulsion to gaze into the abyss this time. Instead, Papaus [Grandfather] appeared at the other side of the gulf with the most warm, loving smile on his face. It was all so wondrous and overwhelming. I wanted to rush right over to him but was prevented from doing so. I recall thinking how happy Pateras [Dad] would be to know that Grandfather was happy and content. With that thought, Grandfather beamed and nodded knowingly, but he was keeping me at a distance. It was communicated to me that the choice to cross over was mine, but once over, there would be no going back, like crossing the Rubicon. Caesar's words as he crossed the Rubicon flashed before me and not just in my mind: *Alea iacta est*, the die has been cast. I could feel the weight of those words.

It was imperative to Grandfather that I be made aware of some important things and time was of the essence. I immediately found myself back in the ER of that hospital. I was far above it all and ambivalent as they worked over the body that used to be me. I wanted to remain on the other side, which seemed like home, but became thunderstruck by the state my father, Darien, was in. To say that he was devastated would be to make a ludicrous understatement. He knew I had departed this world as soon as he looked into my eyes as I lay on the gurney. They had performed an emergency tracheotomy and my eyes had not been taped shut. Darien saw no light in the lifeless orbs. As far as he knew, I was gone. And technically, he was correct. I had already been pronounced dead.

I was desperate to reach him. Edgar stood by, grim-faced and helpless. The grief and shock I could feel from both of them was unbearable. Edgar's wife, Bonnie, was out in the hallway attempting to drink something, but she was crying and shaking too much to manage the cup. There was so much going on, but I was naturally drawn back to my father. I have obviously never lost a child before, but I certainly know what it feels like. If there is a hell like the church says, my father was in it. His mind was completely blank. He was in a state of shock and disbelief. I was amazed to feel what he was feeling and to hear, through his ears, the screaming flatline tones from the vital sign monitor. It was excruciatingly loud and piercing, reverberating through the depths of all four of us. I saw through his eyes the corpse of his only child as his eyes darted between the vital sign monitor and the body. (There is a song that always gives me chills because of this experience. It's entitled

"Through My Father's Eyes") I felt him suppress the urge to smash the wailing monitor against the wall as if silencing it would bring me back.

I could not bear this any longer. The decision was made, and with that, I was instantaneously drawn away from the gulf in a flash of blue light. It was windy but not from air currents. I believe it was emotion that had electrically charged the atmosphere. Things were swirling around me: people, events, books, places… They were things I had yet to accomplish and affect in my life. Instead of a life review, this seemed to be a life preview in fast-forward mode. I felt compelled to go back, though I would have preferred to stay. I was violently sucked back with such speed and force that I literally crashed back into the lifeless form. (I gave everyone a start with that as the body jerked backed to life on the gurney.) It was such a shock for all of us. It reminded me of jumping into the icy cold sea near home.

The vital signs monitor ceased its monotone wail and began soft, erratic beeps. I was back. My father collapsed against the wall. He told me that sudden change in tones was like music to his soul. As soon as it was established that I would be all right, Edgar and Darien left the hospital and went to get some fresh air and quiet — at my grandfather's grave. Neither of them could explain why they chose to go to a graveyard after what happened except that Darien felt the need to be close to his father.

Though I do not regret my decision to return, I often feel almost homesick and a yearning. I am not certain for what purpose I returned, besides the obvious things like my father, but I know we are all here for a reason. There was a reason for my dying experiences as well. They have changed not just me forever, but Edgar and Bonnie, too. My father, he has always been a spiritual man with Buddhist leanings. These experiences strengthened him and confirmed his spirituality. As for Edgar, he had always been the typical businessman, preoccupied with acquiring things, including ulcers. He also devoted much time and energy keeping depression and a sense of futility at bay. He said that this experience was a real wake-up call for him and he has his priorities in life reorganized.

Although dying can be hard, I in no way fear death itself. Both my father and I volunteer with hospices in hopes of making [the patients'] journey to the other side a bit easier. I hope I can impart on them the knowledge that no one passes through the process of dying alone.

I still feel intimately connected to the other side and I perceive my presence here as being on a sabbatical from real life.

I also came out of this with a deep, psychic connection with my father, my grandfather, and Edgar. This I truly treasure because it is the people and the love in our lives that offer meaning and purpose to our existence. I state that as someone who died and lived to talk about it!

Most people who have had these close encounters with death share strikingly similar experiences regardless of their religion, race, or ethnicity. Especially intriguing is the profound influence these experiences have on the lives of the people who have been beyond and back. Their attitudes and stance on life come from a place of compassion and empathy. They are genuine in their faith in the basic benevolence of the world and all its inhabitants. Not all subscribe to a traditional religious doctrine, but their belief in a loving, sentient energy with a plan is unshakeable. Life often doesn't make sense from our vantage point, but when viewed from the other side, it's quite a different picture. Not one of them fears death.

They become cynical about those things taken so seriously by most. I am referring to the material possessions that we spend so much time and energy acquiring and protecting. That aspect of life is foreign to them, though it was not so before they died. They attribute that to the life review. Hitherto, in all the documented life reviews, none have ever been asked about the make of their car, the size of their house, or how much money they were "worth." Worth is an arbitrary value judgement not applied on the other side. What is measured and valued there are things such as how we treat each other, including strangers. As Immanuel Kant so aptly phrased it back in 1775: "Act in such a way that you always treat humanity, whether in your own person or in the person of any other, never simply as a means, but always as an end."

The most common questions put forth to those who died were: What did you do with your time in life? Is the world a better or worse place for your having passed through it? These questions never stray too far from their consciousness and serve to guide them on their journey through this life. These are questions most of us are not faced with until we are on our deathbeds, and by then it is often too late. In many life reviews, people re-experience the pain and harm they have caused others from the recipient's point of view. Those who have been beyond and back consider such an experience the greatest spiritual gift anyone could receive. I recall seeing a bumper sticker that read, "Whoever dies with the most stuff wins." Anybody who believes in and lives by that credo is in for a shock when they die.

After relating his experiences to me, Andreas stated that it was a shame that most people would not experience the life review until they actually died. It is a most efficacious means of taking stock of one's life and putting things in their proper perspective.

He also pointed out that although his grandfather met him, different people or symbolic representations meet others. However, none of these people are the judges in the life review. They are our guides who are with us always in life. We are our own judges, in life as in death.

It should be stated that the term "near-death experience" is a misnomer. All the people I have interviewed who share this experience were not near death — they had actually died and were literally retrieved from the condition we know to be death, only to discover another state of being. They return with an altered state of consciousness as a result of having transcended this basal reality. As Stephen Levine writes in A Year to Live, "Our centre is vastness, there is nothing to die. There is nothing to die and nothing to hang our hats on."[1]

Additionally, those who come back to life are more keenly aware of the effects their actions have on the lives of those around them, so they tend to live more altruistically. Those changed by this experience have what is termed empathic resonance for others. (A quality we could all use.) They avoid falling into the trap of attachment to and overidentification with things we use to identify our lives and ourselves. This frees up a tremendous amount of time and energy normally dedicated to dressing up our lives and ourselves with props so the world views us in our constructed social persona, no matter that this is a false representation that we can lose ourselves in.

Andreas has just entered university. He is taking courses in philosophy, archaeology, and psychology. He continues his hospice work with his father, Darien, a well-known photographer who is applying his specialized techniques in photography in hopes of giving people a glimpse of the other side. They reside together in Oia on the island of Santorini.

As a result of his experiences, Andreas has been freed from the painful sense of abandonment he suffered as a result of his mother leaving him when he was a baby. A philosophy for living he returned with is to live your dying and make peace with your life. Along with the empathic resonance he also came back with the ability to see auras around people. He has an inexplicable calming effect on those around him, which is of great benefit to him in his volunteer work. He also has the uncanny (and unnerving) ability of knowing when one of the patients at the hospice is going to cross over to the other side. That enables him to make a point of being there with them even if it means doing a double shift. That is the only time this ability is useful to him. He says it's not just the colour and feel of the aura that devolves, but rather the body is like a large office tower that is gradually shutting down floor by floor until the last light is extinguished. Your work here is hopefully complete and the building is shut down.

Since Andreas' close brush with death, Edgar has reprioritized his life while disentangling himself from some of the trappings of an undesired and meaningless lifestyle. He is no longer a slave to his cellphone, pager, or even his watch. Although he still works in corporate law, he does a lot of pro bono work for the underprivileged and not-for-profit groups. Edgar has struggled with bouts of major depression throughout his life evolving from what Darien believes to be an existential angst (a pandemic in our time), but this death experience has added a spiritual dimension to his life that was not there before.

While on the other side, Andreas became aware of an attempt Edgar had made on his life while in university. (Much to everyone's shock, Andreas broached the subject with Edgar. The subject had certainly not been discussed with Andreas, who was still quite young at this time.) It goes to demonstrate how the life (and death) of one individual can touch the lives of so many others.

In April 2001, Andreas was one of the models in fashion show. The fashion and art gala was a fundraiser for AIDS and hospices. Darien, who was also in attendance, had donated a piece of art to be auctioned. Also included for people's entertainment was an informal psychic fair where you could have your palm read, your handwriting analyzed, get tarot and astrological readings, and other various things of that nature. Andreas decided to have a tarot, astrological, and palm reading done. Much to their confusion and amazement, none of the psychics were able to pick up on his individual energy or psychic engram, which we all have. Even his palm seemed to indicate that his life ended many years ago. One of the psychics commented that he has a strong connection with the other side and that he did not have a readable aura. She just looked at him in utter mystification.

Andreas related this to his Darien, who was somewhat disturbed by it. It is as though he came back but not all the way. He has dropped off the psychic radar map. Other researchers and I are looking into this to determine its meaning or significance. We have never encountered anything like this before in all our combined years of investigation. In all cases of near-death experience, the deceased was required to make a conscious and deliberate decision to return to his or her life. I reinterviewed Andreas on the particulars of his returning to this life. He returned because he felt drawn back by the overwhelming anguish of his father. This leaves us with a psychic paradox. Is Andreas supposed to be here? Why can't psychics tune into him? Is it even possible to be here if we are not supposed to be? We are still looking into this fascinating development.

Chapter Seven
The Night Owl

Hark! The death-owl loud doth sing
To the nightmares, as they go.
                    — Thomas Chatterton,
                    "Song from Aella"

In December 1993, Beth Howard was awakened by what she knew must have been a dream — but it was so vivid and lucid that it left her feeling a bit "otherworldly."

It began with a warm hand lovingly and gently stroking her face while calling her name. She awoke (or at least perceived herself to be awake) to see her grandfather at her side repeating in urgent tones, "Not your mother; *mashi-I hal* [things are all right]." Then a *bomi* (Arabic for night owl and a symbolic representation of doom to many Lebanese) flew up from behind, coming straight at her, uttering a horrific, soul-piercing screech. She recalled being captivated by her grandfather's tales of the *bomi*, the equivalent of the Irish banshee. She awoke for real this time with her hands flaying at the fluttering wings of the *bomi* in her face. As she was regaining her composure and orientation, a clear vision of an *ubwa nassifal* (an explosive device) was juxtaposed on the night owl.

She sat up in bed trembling and overwhelmed by dread and panic.

Beth was born in Lebanon to a British father and a Palestinian mother. Her father, whose profession was in international finance, afforded

Beth the opportunity to live in a number of countries, including England, France, and Jordan. After completing high school abroad, Beth returned to Beirut to attend the American university there. Shortly after her arrival, the Israelis invaded Lebanon, laying siege to West Beirut. Beth was seriously injured during one of many air raids and was miraculously evacuated to Jordan for surgery. It was in Jordan, during her rehabilitation, that she met a very handsome and intriguing young man who was injured in the same war. That subject was rarely discussed even though he was greatly disturbed by it; he was also secretive and evasive. They felt an immediate affinity for one another, and the circumstances in which they found themselves (and each other) only served to cement the bond. There was much they had yet to learn about each other, including that he was an Israeli pilot, a fact he withheld for fear of losing her.

At the urging of her family, Beth decided against returning to Lebanon and she and Chad moved in with each other. As his "company" was transferring him overseas, they lived in Israel only long enough to tie up some loose ends before moving to Canada.

The two had been through a lot together over the years (including the trauma of war). Chad had remained a great source of comfort and support for Beth while she watched her homeland be consumed by violence, politics, and hatred. They had such experiences in common. Neither of them, however, had any experiences with the paranormal. Therefore, they were both shaken by what turned out to be an event of the supernatural kind.

Beth was seriously agitated by the night terror and could not get back to sleep. After an hour of this, Chad insisted that Beth call her family in England and Lebanon, but before she had a chance to pick up the receiver, her mother was ringing her from England to say that Beth's grandfather had passed away. Her mother informed her that she was leaving for Lebanon, via Jordan, to attend the funeral. Once in Jordan, she would depart for Lebanon with a group of aid workers from the Red Crescent Society. As she did a lot of work with this group and knew many of them quite well, she was comfortable with the arrangements.

Beth suddenly grew very cold. Alarms bells went off in her head. The meaning of the night terror suddenly became chillingly clear to her. Her grandfather was trying to warn her mother against following through with her travel plans. (Beth hadn't even absorbed yet the fact that her grandfather had died at the very time she "dreamed of him," which was more likely a crisis apparition than a dream.) The problem was convincing her mother of this. If she failed to do so, she just knew there would be a second funeral in the family.

She was feeling desperate. She made some calls to Lebanon and Jordan in an attempt to abort or change her mother's travelling arrangements, but to no avail. She was finally forced into bed by a migraine. All she could see through the blinding white pain was the foreboding image of the night owl. Chad brought Beth her migraine medication and stood watch over her until the pills finally took effect. He then quietly slipped out of the room to make a few calls to Israel. Fortunately, he had more success with his contacts. The travelling agenda of Beth's mother was now radically altered; she would be landing in Israel, bypassing Jordan altogether, and from there she would be ushered across the border.

Although she could not for the life of her fathom why Beth and Chad had changed her hastily made arrangements, Beth's mother was too distraught and anxious to debate it.

Everyone arrived safely for the funeral, and although it was a sad occasion, the impromptu family reunion was quite lovely and badly needed for this weary wartorn family. For the most part, the country was free from strife and relatively peaceful throughout the family gathering. There was one notable exception, however. A bus carrying aid workers and medical supplies into Lebanon from Jordan hit a landmine within the Lebanese border, killing everyone on it. Had Beth's grandfather not come to her bringing with him the night terror in the form of the *bomi*, a symbol he knew would capture his granddaughter's attention, no subsequent interventions would have been made and Beth's mother would have been amongst those killed.

Chad and Beth are still residing in Kitchener, Ontario. They have both been back to the Middle East on numerous occasions and are expecting to be transferred back to Israel soon. Beth now regularly keeps a dream diary. A couple of days after this event, Beth was vacuuming and caught sight of what she first thought to be dust bunnies on the floor. Upon closer examination, she discovered they were not dust bunnies at all but rather large white feathers — three of them — the same kind that the *bomi* was coated with!

Chapter Eight
Chillers

From ghoulies and ghosties and long-legged beast-
ies and things that go bump in the night — good
Lord, deliver us.
                                        — Cornish prayer

In this chapter I have presented a number of short accounts shared
with me by people who, although their encounters with the paranormal were brief, were nonetheless left with lifelong impressions.

Sharon in Ontario, Canada shared the following fascinating and
touching accounts.

Mabel, Are You There?

When I got married, my mother, Mabel, gave us a trendy teak floor
lamp with a tall woven orange shade. I had been married eight years
when she passed away.

A few months after she was buried, strange things began happening with our lamp. As we sat reading in the living room, the light
would begin to flicker. Replacing the bulb did not stop this flickering,
nor did plugging it into another outlet. We had an electrician examine
the lamp and no mechanical malfunctions were discovered. We found
it puzzling that this flickering did not occur every time the light was in

use. We could go months without an incident and then it might act up every night for a week.

Mabel and the lamp are both gone now. I decided to put it in a garage sale and a neighbour was thrilled to carry the lamp down the street to its new home. Every now and then, I get the urge to ring her up and ask her how "Mabel" is doing.

The Boy in the Wall

When Cheryl, our youngest of three children, was learning how to vocalize, bedtime was often a disturbing and frightening time for her. In a state of agitation, she would gesture toward the wall beside her crib, often crying. We just assumed she was objecting to having a nap or going down for the night.

Months passed and Cheryl's vocabulary developed to the point that she could verbally express some things. One day when I went to her room to get her up from her nap, she was particularly upset. As I lifted her from her crib, she pointed and cried, "Boy in the wall!"

There were times I would find her lying in her crib, facing the wall and chatting away as if to someone unseen in the room with her. When I queried her about this, her response was always, "Boy in the wall." It seemed to have become an acceptable form of companionship to her, so she was no longer frightened or agitated. We moved from that house shortly after Cheryl's first birthday. She is twenty now and does not remember anything about her little companion, the boy in the wall. But who or what was this strange companion?

It Must Be Noah

It was going to be a great house! Everything was moving along on schedule and without a hitch. Flooring, tiles, cupboards, and waterbed all went magically into place all with the wave of the Maestro Noah's baton.

Noah was proud of this, his latest construction and masterpiece. Noah and I made a great team, with me choosing the colours and styles and he conducting his well-polished craftspeople toward the grand finale.

My family of five moved into our dream home just before Christmas. A few details were yet to be completed but nothing that could not wait until after the holidays.

On Christmas Eve, before final completion, Noah died. We were very sad, both for his family and for ours. We were also sad that ours would be the last wonderful home ever constructed by his clever hands.

After months of living in the house, accusations, suspicions, and reprimands arose as a result of strange occurrences. Things like late-night stair creepings and door slammings brought our family to the debate table in hopes of flushing out the culprit responsible for sneaking about and scaring the bejeepers out of everyone. Much to the dismay of everyone, the guilty party would not fess up, and the mysterious creaks, thumps, and midnight escapades continued.

We finally deduced that it had to be Noah. Unfinished business must be keeping Noah from moving on.

And so it went on. We would leap out of bed and rush to the great winding staircase that was often the location of footsteps; a door would close while everyone was in the same room and not a breath of air circulating throughout the house.

One very hot, still night, we all went to bed and I left the patio door leading to the family room open; only the screen door was locked. Shortly after midnight, a thundering crash from the family room awakened us. We leapt from our beds, meeting at the top of the stairs behind our nephew who was visiting. The poor chap was frozen on the top step with an expression of terror on his face. We slowly began our descent of the staircase and cautiously entered the family room. I thought that perhaps a wind had come up and disturbed something on the mantle or side table, but no air moved inside or out. To the contrary, there was an eerie stillness to the night.

At the farthest end of the room from the door, an object lay on the carpet. Upon closer inspection, I saw it was Raggedy Ann, a salt dough figurine that had been hanging on the wall. The doll stared up at us, one leg snapped off, its jagged edge laying a few inches away. I just could not figure out how this ornament had crashed. The nail was still securely anchored to the wall; the hanger on Raggedy Ann's back was intact. There was not a wisp of air coming from the screen door, which was a good fifteen feet from where the figure had been hanging. It would have to have quite the gale force to do this.

"It must be Noah," we chimed, as our nephew scratched his head and followed us back upstairs.

The following is a chilling account of what can happen when you use a Ouija board as just another board game as it most assuredly is not.

The Beckoning

A number of years ago, when Norm's family was together for a small gathering, some of the younger ones decided to play with a Ouija board. Norm was not too thrilled with the idea and attempted to discourage them, warning them that it was no game, but his efforts were in vain.

The kids became very excited when the planchette actually began to move, spelling out the message, "Bill, come, Helen." This same message was to be spelled out again, but its intended meaning would not become evident for a week.

Bill and Norm were brothers. They had a sister named Helen who was deceased. A week after receiving this cryptic message from the Ouija board, Bill suddenly died. The message was like a summons or an omen. It struck everyone that the deceased Helen was beckoning to her soon-to-be-dead brother. For what purpose, one can only speculate. It was not a warning; perhaps she was acting as a guide so he would remember at the moment of his death her message and know that he is not alone. Whatever the reason, to this day Norm will not allow a Ouija board in his home. It's not hard to appreciate why.

A young woman from Vancouver who wishes to remain anonymous offers the following sad and truly haunting account.

Haunted Christmas

Christmas of 1999 was evolving into one the most difficult ones ever. Nothing seemed to be going right, and worse, she was getting lost in the dense fog of an eerie depression. This was not just the usual holiday blues and fatigue we can all experience at Christmas, but rather a much more pronounced, "wet, heavy blanket of gloom." Interestingly enough, she was intrigued to later learn that other members of her family were experiencing the same thing. She was particularly feeling the loss of loved ones, especially that of her deceased sister.

A couple of weeks before Christmas, she was given a sound effect machine that also contained a radio. The only time she would have the radio on was when she was on her way out and needed to hear the local weather report. She happened upon a local station that was playing old-fashioned Christmas tunes; one in particular was emotionally evocative. Its title is "Have Yourself a Merry Little Christmas," a sad, forlorn melody, but not completely devoid of some hope. The Christmas music was mixed with oldies music. The station was way too corny for her taste, but it aroused a memory in her. Her mother and her sister both listened to such stations. She recalled teasing her sister about it and that is why the station call letters seemed so familiar to her.

The oldies became too much for her so she kept the radio on the CBC, which also provided local weather forecasts. Nevertheless, whenever she returned home, the dial would inevitably be back on the oldies station and that haunting little tune, "Have Yourself a Merry Little Christmas," would be playing. It was way beyond coincidence that the dial had been changed and that particular song was playing every time she turned the radio on.

At first she took some small comfort in the strange incidents, relating to them as though they were her deceased sister's way of letting her know that she was not alone this Christmas or that the situation was not necessarily hopeless. She listened to the lyrics carefully at one point. The words that really gave her chills were: "Have yourself a merry little Christmas. Make the yuletide glad. From now on our troubles will be far away. Through the years, we all will be together if the fates allow. Until then we'll have to muddle through somehow. So have yourself a merry little Christmas now."

It was anything but a merry Christmas and the Fates were not smiling favourably down on her life. The recurrence of this song was beginning to spook her as well as exacerbate her depression. She finally unplugged the machine and it remained unplugged until well into the New Year. The radio dial has not since moved on its own.

Debbie Allen relates the following account. She and her husband currently reside in Margate, Kent, England, however the events here occurred in their former home in Hillside, England. Debbie has herself been published, having written an article on the murder of her son, Alfred, who I am sorry to say is the little boy in her story. Tragically, Alfie is not the only child Debbie has lost.

Ghostly Playmate

When Alfie was about two or three years old, we lived at the old Hillside house. It was around nine or ten o'clock one evening; Alfie was up in his room asleep, and Steve and I were sitting downstairs in a room directly beneath Alfie's bedroom. We were watching the telly with my mom and dad when we heard Alfie up in his room as though he were moving around, banging toys about and talking to himself. It was abnormally loud, so Steve and I got up to investigate and put the baby back to bed.

We were surprised to find upon reaching the nursery that Alfie was sound asleep, oblivious to all the noise and commotion we heard

Debbie and Steve Allen.

from this very room not two minutes before. However, all his toys were strewn about the room. Curiosity got the best of us and we reluctantly woke him up and asked him if he had gotten up at all to play with his toys. He replied that he had been playing and talking to Rita! He was adamant about the identity of his playmate. Steve and I were quite shocked; the entire situation was so bizarre. He had been cheerfully playing and talking and a minute later was deeply sleeping. Strangest of all is that his playmate, Rita, was our daughter who died of crib death on October 31, 1979. How could he have been playing with his dead sister whom he didn't even know?

In the old Hillside House, you often felt a lot of unusual sensations, like you were being watched. We've all felt someone touching our skin. Things like that.

Dawn

> "Demonic frenzy, moping melancholy,
> and moonstruck madness"
> — Milton, *Paradise Lost*

A basement sitting room/apartment on Cheshire Street in Guelph, Ontario was home to a young woman named Anne, who was completing high school. This particular room would have originally been used for a wine and vegetable storage compartment for the house. It had its own separate entrance on the side of the house.

She shared this small flat with a very unwelcome ghostly tenant who became known as Dawn as a result of an automatic writing session with a psychic researcher. The words that came through did not make any sense at all. However, four years later, Anne would run across those words verbatim in the form of lyrics to a song by a sixties band called The Nice. The message read: Dawn, for she is surely a maiden, is born and raped 365 times a year. The Dawn is born pregnant with anticipation but is murdered by the hand of the inevitable. The innocent Dawn asks forgiveness for the sins man brought on her.[1]

To this day, it is not known who Dawn is or why she was haunting this basement flat. She was an especially malignant entity who seemed trapped in her own dying, unable to transcend the state of death and decay. Her face was only seen once in a mirror as the lights were flickering on and off. In the far corner of the room, there sat a chest of drawers, a dressing table with a mirror, and, directly across from that, a wardrobe with floor-length sliding mirrored doors. There was something about this area of the room or even the wardrobe itself. It was always freezing cold. It wasn't as though it was in a drafty area; this was a very localized freezing spot.

It was there that Anne would catch her first glimpse of the spectre's gruesome visage in the mirror while brushing her hair at the dressing table. It belonged to a female, perhaps in her late teenage years, though she also seemed beyond time. Her visage was cadaverous with a greyish hue and scars suggesting open wounds from a slashing. The eyes were yellowish, fierce, and penetrating. The medium-length hair was matted and dishevelled. The lips were chapped and slowly parted into a grimace as she realized that Anne was seeing her. The nose appeared broken and had a crusted layer around the nostrils like dried blood.

Anne was too shocked to even scream at first. She felt herself caught in the grip of those cruel eyes and was overcome by a sense of unreality. The horrific image facing her in the mirror was being reflected from the mirror directly behind her. Perhaps it was some sort of mirror mirage abetted by the flickering lights. She grasped at any explanation, no matter how implausible, to regain her foothold in reality. The power stabilized and she bolted out of the room. She tried to call a friend but her hands were shaking so badly she couldn't punch in the numbers. She grabbed her coat and made her way up to St. Joe's church, which was just a block up from her flat. There she stayed for awhile, letting the calm of the environment settle into her. Then she called her friend from the pay phone downstairs and pleaded with her to come over. By this time, enough had transpired in the little flat that no one she knew was too enthralled with the idea of spending much time there, but her friend nevertheless agreed to come. Fortunately, the place was quiet as a mausoleum for the remainder of the evening.

Unfortunately, the same could not be said for many other nights. Anne would often be startled out of a sound sleep by the clatter of glass breaking from the wardrobe. On other occasions, a vibrating knocking sound emanating from within the wardrobe as though someone was trapped inside, struggling to get out, awakened her. The majority of the noises ensued from the vicinity of the wardrobe. However, on a couple of occasions, noises like scratching, popping, and rolling could be heard coming from the ceiling. There was no sign of mice so no one knew what to make of it.

If that wasn't strange enough, something happened one evening while Anne and the aforementioned friend were studying. Once again they heard the scratching and rolling noises and wondered if squirrels were storing nuts. Suddenly, they heard a resonant intake of breath issuing from the wardrobe followed by pebbles of various sizes plummeting from the ceiling directly above them. It lasted for only a few seconds, but

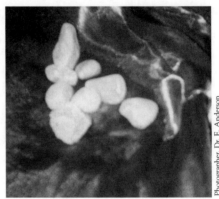

Pebbles Fallen from Ceiling: poltergeist artifacts.

Photographer, Dr. E. Anderson

that was long enough to compel Anne to look for a new flat.

They both fled from this little crypt, as it had been dubbed, and once again made their way up to St. Joe's church, which had become a safe haven. Anne had already had a priest in and a psychic investigator, the latter being a professor from the university who introduced the element of automatic writing into the situation. Although it proved to be a useful tool in other areas of her life, all it provided in this instance was the cryptic message about "Dawn." If the message somehow applied to the current haunting, no one could determine how.

When she heard the message in the form of a song many years later, it sent shivers throughout her entire being. A friend even commented that she appeared ashen. If only you knew, she thought, but she has never uttered a word to anyone about her experience on Cheshire Street — until now.

With no explanations or resolutions forthcoming, there was nothing left to do but vacate the premises. It was not easy, especially with the financial limitations most students live with, but it had come to the point where she had no choice. She felt literally driven out of the place!

Looking back on that time, she recalls one rather amusing event. In the midst of all the frightening phenomena (much of it in the shadowy dark, as it was an arduous task keeping the lights on), she never needed to purchase garbage bags. There seemed to be an endless supply of them in the bottom of the wardrobe. No sooner would the supply be getting low than an entire new batch would materialize. They were not in any store or brand packaging. Just loose, neatly folded garbage bags! Her boyfriend once joked that the "man from GLAD," in reference to an old garbage bag commercial, was haunting her. She also had a bowl that continuously replenished itself with almonds.

Anne had a memory triggered once while listening to that song "Dawn." Because it was so difficult to keep lights on, she tried a candle once. It remained lit, but unfortunately she fell asleep while it was still burning. She recalls hearing her named being bellowed as well as experiencing a physical shove. She sprang bolt upright on the couch just in time to see the candle flame slowly licking its way up a speaker cord, heading directly for some curtains! Did this "Dawn" entity save her life? And if so, why? It seemed uncharacteristic. Like everything else that took place there, that too remains a mystery.

Who or what was this energy or entity in the vicinity if the wardrobe? Was she as malevolent as she appeared? Or was she just a wayward soul unable to get beyond her own death? What were the origin and meaning of the cascading pebbles? (She still has them in a plastic baggie.) After all these years, she remains haunted by the place and suspects she always will. Whenever she passes by her former residence, she still questions the meaning of the strange events and can sometimes hear the name Dawn being faintly called.

A Fatal Fortune

Dr. Deni Diejen is a Swedish-born doctor specializing in neurology and neuroscience. He is a very intelligent, soft-spoken man with a supremely logical mind. Deni was a mentor and long-time friend of mine so I had no compunction in asking him questions about the paranormal, questions some may view as a bit off-the-wall.

He began his career as a family doctor and then specialized in neurosurgery. He is now in research while still seeing patients. With his wide range of experiences, I thought he might be able to offer a unique perspective on some of the phenomena I have been writing about.

Like any open-minded and honest scientist, he will tell you that he is not convinced that people's experiences are of a supernatural etiology. He spoke of the fact that people have had experiences similar to near-death experiences without actually having died or suffering a medical trauma. There is also the dying brain theory. Simply stated, the theory is that as the brain dies it undergoes a condition called anoxia, or oxygen deprivation, during which it releases high quantities of endorphins, causing hallucinations. But as there are people who have had near-death experiences with normal blood gases, anoxia is not a feasible explanation. Dr. Diejen has been able to induce near-death experiences in people by stimulating particular areas of the brain, especially the right temporal lobe, which seems to be the region of the brain that is wired for paranormal activity like telekinesis and telepathy. Canadian neurosurgeon Dr. Wilder Penfield believed that if there was an actual physical location of the soul, it was there in the right temporal lobe.

Biology and neurology aside, Dr. Diejen does not discount the purely psychic reasons, either. There are many things he has seen and heard from patients that science hitherto has no adequate explanation for. He recalls one surgery in which, when a patient's brain was being electronically probed in specific regions, she began to re-experience the past, complete with the accompanying emotional elements, a reaction that is quite common with this type of surgery with one exception: it wasn't her past!

The woman couldn't get that experience out of her mind, so, with a bit of detective work, she was able to verify the existence of this man whose life she recalled in such vivid detail even though he lived more than a hundred years before she was born! She has since become an ardent student of Carl Jung's theories of the "collective unconscious" and on life after death and reincarnation. Dr. Diejen was quite intrigued with the information she was able to uncover.

Many patients have over the years shared with him their experiences of having died only to be revived. He has also witnessed the life and personality changes that accompany such an experience, and he is not sure if it is all down to brain chemistry and doesn't think it really matters. That is, at least, to those who have been beyond and back.

He did have one personal experience that still disturbs him to this day. Dr. Diejen undertook his residency in a mid-sized city in Ontario. He was the youngest resident the hospital had ever had and there was some suspicion about him and even jealousy amongst the other physicians. Due to his unique circumstances, the CEO of medicine, Tony Devonetti, made a point of "running into" the young doctor frequently, and they fast became good friends. A couple of years after they met, at the urging of Tony's wife, a small group of them would go and see a psychic Mrs. Devonetti had heard so much about. Tony and Deni were skeptical, but Tony's sister, Angela, Deni's girlfriend, Michelle, and Mrs. Devonetti were quite enthused.

As the psychic progressed with individual readings through the little group, Tony and Deni were growing less skeptical. The psychic reassured everyone that she doesn't reveal "deep, dark secrets" or disclose an impending death. Everyone had a little chuckle, and she began. She was frighteningly accurate, pointing out little obscure things that only the individual or someone very close might know. The women were getting gooseflesh. When it came time to do Angela's reading, the atmosphere took a decidedly ominous revolution. Up until then, it had been intriguing and exciting with everyone in the group, including the psychic, enjoying the lighthearted exchange. But when the psychic tuned into to Angela's aura, it was as though a light switch was flicked off. The colour drained out of her face as she slowly withdrew from the young woman and tried to regain her professional composure. She didn't want to upset anyone.

In spite of himself, Tony was upset. The psychic apologized, explaining that she was unable to read anything on Angela due to an oncoming migraine. Deni explained that he was a physician and offered her assistance, but she brusquely declined and made a hasty departure, looking back once at Angela to say she was sorry. She was lying about the migraine and about not being able to see into Angela's future. They didn't know that for sure, but every one of them suspected something was wrong. Nevertheless, they covered up by making jokes and commenting on how that last trick really added to the performance. Beneath the surface, they were all uneasy. Tony was annoyed with his wife for having dragged them into these silly parlour games, and they didn't utter a word about it again until they received a phone call a week later.

There had been a car accident. A young woman was brought into the emerg whom Deni immediately recognized. Angela was DOA, but it was his duty to pronounce her dead and fill out the death certificate.

Time of death: 2:45 a.m. He went off to call Tony about his sister, trying not to think about the session with the psychic. He couldn't get it out of his mind, though, and he still can't!

This next incident chronicles a record-setting long-distance call. The daughter of the woman to whom it happened related it to me.

A *Final Goodbye*

It was the spring of 1987. Angelica and her mother, Sofia, were doing a major spring cleaning. She helped her mother with this every year, but this year was especially significant. The previous summer, Sofia's husband and Angelica's father, Joseph, had died after a mercifully short illness. Needless to say, Sofia took the death of her husband badly and was just now starting to come around. The spring cleaning was therapeutic and symbolic of starting out new. Much of her husband's belongings would be donated to a local charity. She carefully packed his things away while reminiscing about him. She brushed away the odd tear, but she wasn't crying out of anguish anymore.

The ringing phone interrupted the work and reverie. Angelica carried a box downstairs while Sofia answered the phone. When Angelica joined her mother in the kitchen, she was startled to observe that her mother was pale and trembling. She heard her mother exclaim, "Joseph? It can't be!" She began crying and then fell into a dead faint. Angelica grabbed the phone and reached for her mother at the same time. She called into the phone but there was only static on the line.

When her mother regained her composure, she explained to Angelica exactly what had happened. When she answered the phone, she was greeted by the unmistakable voice of her deceased husband. He repeated her name several times — "Sofia? Is that you? Can you hear me?" It sounded like long distance but a bad connection. Her daughter had not heard the voice of her father, but her mother was unequivocally convinced that it was her beloved Joseph. She reasoned that as she was reminiscing and offering up a final goodbye to her husband, he had wanted to say one last goodbye to her. Whatever truly happened, her mother felt blessed by the event and achieved long-awaited closure and peace of mind.

In 1979, D. Scott Rogo and Raymond Bayless co-authored a book entitled *Phone Calls from the Dead* in which they documented such phenomena. They state that "despite the purely anecdotal nature of so many of these phone call cases, there are nonetheless on record many well-authenticated cases of this phenomena."[2]

They go on to say that there are a wide variety of these calls and that the ghostly callers usually seem surprised or stunned that they are able to get through to the living! No wonder.

The following recounts the experiences of Bill Ryder of Guelph, Ontario, although the events occurred whilst in his homeland of Ireland.

An Irish Tale

Bill was born in the lovely coastal town of Dun Laoghaire. He and his family are quite engaging, especially as he can trace his maternal ancestors (the Lawless Clan) back to thirteenth-century Ireland. The ancestral home was a fifteenth-century castle called Shankill (which means old church). As a boy Bill used to spend his summers at an eighteenth-century house that sits right next to the castle. Bill's uncle owned the place at the time and it was a dream come true for an inquisitive young lad, what with the winding metal staircase and all the secret rooms.

As Bill was sharing his family history with me, I enquired hopefully if there were any ghosts or a familiar banshee. He did recount the legend of the banshee, which was not only employed as a semi-efficacious means of intimidating young children into behaving, but, especially during war times, was a common siren of despair for those families left at home. The unearthly wail of the banshee served the dual role as harbinger of impending death and announcing that a death had already occurred.

Of course Ireland has many ghosts, known as thevshi or tash. The Irish believed that if one died suddenly, especially leaving unfulfilled duties, passionate attachments, or unfinished business with the living, he or she would remain trapped between this world and the next. They also cautioned against excessive sorrow or grief-letting over the deceased, advising to "Be quiet now; you are keeping him from his rest." On the Western Isles you would be told that, "You are waking the dog that watches to devour the souls of the dead." The Irish also have their unique variant on the doppelgänger, which they call the fetch. Legend has it that if you see the double of someone in the morning, no ill harm will come to him or her, but if you see the double in the evening, death is certain to follow.

Bill's first ghostly encounter was during his college days. He attended Blackrock on the East Coast of Ireland. It was operated by a group of priests called the Holy Ghosts, ironically enough, though the locals simply referred to them as the French fathers. Bill heard many a ghost story during his stay at Blackrock, but it was not until his second-last year that he experienced anything of a personal nature.

The students shared a common lavatory up in the dorm, and one evening, after everyone had turned out the lights and retired for the evening, one of the students who had gone to use the facilities came running frantically back into the dorm room, dived for his bed, and literally hid under the sheets. He was quite obviously terrified of something. He explained to his roommates what had transpired to give him such a fright. He had met up with the ghost of a priest. The incredible detail he provided while relating the experience gave them all pause for concern. Perhaps it was more than just this poor lad's imagination.

As ghostly stories continued to make their rounds of the college, the dean called together the seniors at the school — which included Bill — and ordered a stop to such stories. He made Bill a prefect, which meant he was to watch out for the new, younger students. Furthermore, if all this ghost nonsense frightened the new students, poor Bill would be expelled. A tad extreme considering there was very little anyone could do to halt the spread of the haunting tales. To exacerbate matters, Bill himself experienced a ghostly manifestation of a classical form. He observed a man making his way briskly down the hall, and as Bill watched his progression, the spectre simply vanished into the wall. He was witness to this spectacle on more than one occasion.

There are two other incidents that have left a lasting impression on Bill. The first involved the death of his mother, Jane. She had been ill and lived alone in Dun Laughaire, Ireland. Bill was visiting from England when she shared the oddest dream with him. She dreamt that she had died and was laid out in her coffin in St. Joseph's church in the nearby town of Glasthule. She found this to be puzzling, as her parish and church had always been St. Michael's. The other church was about five miles from where she lived. A week after this, while undergoing some electrical work, St. Mike's burnt to the ground. Within days of the fire, Jane passed away at age seventy and had to be laid out in St. Joseph's, just as she had envisioned in her dream. Many people who are nearing the end of their lives have a gut feeling about it. She may have sensed that her days were numbered, but she certainly had no way to predict that the church she belonged to would go up in flames, necessitating the change in funerary venue.

The second incident involved the sudden death of Bill's older brother, Dick. Dick had just returned home after attending a dinner in his honour. He went to bed straight away, as he was tired but otherwise in good spirits. He died suddenly of a massive heart attack. Meanwhile, back in Canada, Bill got one of the frights of his life when the family crest he had hanging on the wall suddenly came crashing down to the floor. The metal remained in one piece but the wood backing the coat of arms was mounted on cleanly snapped in two. Soon after this, Bill would learn of the death of his brother. Uncannily, the time of death coincided with the time the family crest came crashing down!

Of Jung and Freud

For anyone who is familiar with the work and writings of psychologist Carl Gustav Jung, it will come as no surprise that he not only had personal experiences with the paranormal, but also came from a family that shared such experiences. Jung used to attend seances conducted by his fourteen-year-old cousin, Helene. She claimed to have established contact with their grandfather, who was purported to have visions. Even though she was caught out in trickery, she nevertheless made quite an impression on Jung. So much so that he gave his doctoral dissertation on the various stages and transformation young Helene would undergo during her self-induced "trance" states. Jung's attitude could best be expressed in his own words when he asked, "Why, after all, should there not be ghosts?"

Before their infamous break, Jung would recount many tales of supernatural experiences to Sigmund Freud, his then mentor. For professional reasons, Freud could never let his genuine interest in the topic become publicly known. It wasn't until many years later, when death, loss, and illness began to take their toll that Freud spoke more openly about the validity and meaning of such experiences and further expressed his regret that he had not examined it more closely. At the time of his chats with Jung, however, he didn't know what to make of such phenomena. Indeed, during the course of one such meeting, while Jung was feeling frustrated by Freud, a loud bang issued from a nearby bookcase, causing both men to jump from their respective chairs.

Jung writes in his autobiography:

"It interested me to hear Freud's views on precognition and on parapsychology in general. When I visited him in Vienna in 1909 I asked him what he thought of such matters. Because of his materialistic prejudice, he rejected this entire complex of questions as nonsensical, and did so in terms of shallow positivism that I had difficulty in checking the sharp retort on the tip of my tongue. It was some years before he recognized the seriousness of parapsychology and acknowledged the factuality of 'occult' phenomena.

"While Freud was going on his way, I had a curious sensation. It was as if my diaphragm were made of iron and becoming red-hot, a glowing vault. And at that moment, there was such a loud report in the bookcase, which stood right next to us, that we both started up in alarm, fearing the thing was going to topple over on us. I said to Freud: 'There, that is an example of a so-called catalytic exteriorization phenomenon.'

"'Oh come,' he exclaimed. 'That is sheer bosh.'

"'It is not,' I replied. 'You are mistaken, Herr Professor. And to prove my point I now predict that in a moment there will be another loud report!' Sure enough, no sooner had I said the words than the same detonation went off in the bookcase.

"To this day I do not know what gave me this certainty. But I knew beyond all doubt that the report would come again."[3]

Interestingly, it seemed important to Freud to deny such phenomena altogether as suggested in a later interpretation of the event:

"I don't deny that your stories and your experiment made a deep impression on me. At first I was inclined to accept as proof if the sound that was so frequent while you were here were not heard again after your departure, but since then I have heard it repeatedly; not, however, in connection with my thoughts and never when I am thinking about you or this particular problem of yours. My credulity, or at least my willingness to believe, vanished with the magic of your personal presence; once again, for some inward reasons I can't put my finger on, it strikes me as quite unlikely that such phenomena should exist. Accordingly, I put my fatherly horn-rimmed spectacles on again and warn my dear son to keep a cool head, for it is better not to understand something than to make such great sacrifices to understanding.

"*Consequently, I shall receive further news of your investigations of the spook complex* [italics mine] with the interest one accords to a charming delusion in which one does not oneself participate. Yours, Freud."[4]

Jung attributed this discharge as his own psychic energy. Two other experiences had particular significance to Jung. One summer afternoon, Jung was in his room studying (he was attending college at the time) when a resounding crash caused him to rush into the room next door. There he found his mother staring at the family dining room table. It was made of solid walnut and had inexplicably cracked from the edge clear through to the centre! Jung was stupefied by it. His mother stated that "it meant something" but Jung needed to understand how such a thing could happen.

A few days later, upon returning home from class one evening, Jung found his mother and sister visibly shaken. They told him they had heard what sounded like the report of a gun coming from the sideboard in the dining room. Jung was expecting to see more wood cracked, but much to his amazement, he instead found that the metal of a bread carving knife had been shattered. Jung promptly took the knife to a repair shop for examination and was told that somebody must have applied tremendous force in order to smash it, as steel does not simply shatter of its own accord. Jung, of course, knew better!

Interestingly enough, with all his considerable personal experiences, Jung considered ghosts to be human projections from our psyche, a belief he stated in his paper "The Psychological Foundations of Belief in Spirits." True, this stance of his caused some cognitive dissonance in him, especially having spent some time in a haunted house where he experienced loud rappings and foul odours. In fact all those who stayed in this place left in fear; how could so many different people be engaged in duplicating the same projections? He finally came to the conclusion that, "After collecting psychological experiences from many people from many countries for fifty years, I know longer feel as certain as I did — to put it bluntly, I doubt whether an exclusively psychological approach can do justice to the phenomena in question."[5]

Like many others, Jung was a devoted believer in spirit guides. Whether it is the inner wisdom of the unconscious, collective or otherwise, he utilized this practice frequently and even assigned his guide a name: Philemon. He first made his acquaintance in a dream but he evolved beyond a mere dream symbol, taking on characteristics of his own, independent of anything in Jung's life. He would often share long talks with him in moments of solitude.

The following is an exquisite example of an apparition of the living with a very happy ending.

Home Sweet Home

Steve and Rene where residing in a rather small but quaint apartment in Montreal, Quebec, not far from where the Forum was located when it was still home to the Montreal Canadians. After tripping over each other for years in the cramped quarters, Steve finally persuaded Rene that it was time to buy a house. She readily agreed provided it was in a more rural setting. She had dreamed of living in a country cottage since she was young.

Now that they were in the market for a place, her childhood dreams returned more vivid than ever. She could actually feel herself moving through the house, checking out even little things like closets and pantries. She would float about the rooms mentally decorating everything, thoroughly enjoying the experience. When she woke up, she would often make detailed drawings of her dream house.

They contacted a real estate agent and spent the summer and a good part of the fall looking at dozens of places, but nothing said "home" to Rene. Poor Steve was beginning to regret the entire venture. Then finally, one day they came upon a place they had almost driven past because it was so far back from the road. When the owner of the house opened the door to greet them and saw Rene, her jaw dropped and she had a shocked expression on her face. She quickly regained her composure.

They hardly required a tour of the bungalow, as Rene recognized the place as the one from her dreams. It even conformed to the sketches Rene had made upon awakening from her nocturnal excursions through the place. She practically gave the tour of the house herself! In response to this oddity, the lady of the house said that they should be aware that the house has "a bit of a ghost. Nothing to worry about — never bothers the family. She just busies herself about the place." Steve and Rene were not at all put off by this and in fact found it to be a bit charming. They knew right away that they were going to purchase the house. They felt right at home here. The lady of the house said that they should feel at home because the spectre the family saw roaming about the place in every nook and cranny was none other than Rene! She was home at last. Steve and Rene purchased the house in 1993 and remain happily there.

Till Death Us Do Part

This very sad tale happened to Lianne Osbourne of Birmingham, England in the spring of 1984. Lianne was happily preparing for her nuptials, as she had just become engaged to her boyfriend, Keith. They had known each other since Grade 7 and now that they were both out of college and working, they decided it was time to settle down and start a family.

Lianne harboured some misgivings as she suspected Keith was not ready to settle down and maybe never would be. They had many heated arguments in what could be a tumultuous relationship. She felt him to be too "untamed." He engaged in reckless and dangerous risk-taking behaviour. According to Lianne, he drove too fast and drank too much with his buddies. As Keith would say, the list of concerns was endless. His biggest complaint was that she was trying to mould him, and she admits that he wasn't too far off in that notion.

Nevertheless, they were the very best of friends and never failed to be there for one another in times of need. Like many other close couples, they had an almost psychic bond and could sense when the other was troubled. Lianne remains in that bond to this day, in spite of the events that took place on the evening of April 2, 1984.

One week before their wedding, Keith and Lianne had a major blowout. It was a combination of wedding preparations, pressures from both of their families (especially regarding which church to marry in as religion can be a hot topic), and a sense Keith had that he was being railroaded into this. That caused Lianne to go ballistic, as she put it. In the heat of the moment, she made a grave, rash error as many of us can do under such circumstances: she called off the wedding. She took off her little gold engagement ring and flung it across the room. Keith angrily agreed and went storming out of the house.

She watched him tear out of the driveway and kept watching until the rear lights of his Camero faded from sight. She suddenly grew very cold and grief stricken. She searched for her engagement ring and upon finding it, placed it carefully back in its box. She then burst into an uncontrollable fit of weeping and remained in that state for many hours until she finally fell into an exhausted sleep. She had a horrific nightmare in which Keith was trying desperately to reach her. She knew he was in trouble and the frustration of not being able to help him was unbearable.

She was awakened by the proddings of her sister, who was also to be her matron of honour, and upon seeing the expression on her sister's face, Lianne immediately went into a panic. She just knew something had happened to Keith; in fact, she knew he was dead! She shouted, "No!" and, pushing her sister aside, made for the dresser where she had left her engagement ring. In her grief and anguish, she figured if she just put the ring back on her finger none of this would be real and they could proceed with the wedding plans.

Meanwhile, Lianne's sister was attempting to get a physical grip on her so she could tell her what she wished with all her heart she did not have to tell her. Last night, Keith lost control of his Camero and it spun out of control, slamming into a phone post, exploding into a fiery pyre. Lianne knew it was true but refused to believe it anyway. If she could just get the ring back on her finger — but upon opening the ring box, much to both sisters' horror, the engagement ring was warped, the stone had been dislodged, and the box had been singed. On the cushion that cradled the ring, an image of a cross had burnt into the fabric and was also reflected onto the lid. It was as though the box and its contents had been exposed to an intense heat. As for the image of a cross being impressed into the box, Lianne can only hope it symbolizes Keith being at some sort of peace. She remains bonded to him and often senses his presence.

In this account, a middle-aged detective who had previous experience saving the lives of strangers had his own life saved by a mysterious stranger. Due to the ignorant and stubborn stigma attached to illnesses such as depression, the name of this individual has been altered. These events took place in late April 2001.

Look Before You Leap

Dominic has been with the police department in this large metropolitan centre for eleven years. When he made detective he thought the gloom that had been hanging over him for months now would finally dissolve. It did not. In fact it intensified. A good friend who was also a doctor told him in no uncertain terms that he was suffering from clinical major depression. He was completely burnt out by his work, which included bearing witness to all the deplorable things humans are capable of doing to each other. She urged him to seek professional help, preferably counselling along with antidepressants, but at the very least some medication until he came to a decision about seeing a therapist.

He eventually agreed to consult with his family doctor about a course of antidepressants. His friend cautioned him against becoming discouraged with the drugs, as they generally require a few weeks to have an effect. In the meantime, she continued encouraging him to see a psychotherapist. She was concerned that his repeated exposure to what at times can be the worst elements of humanity was causing him to want out of this world and, consequently, his life. He was not sleeping well, and when he did fall asleep, he was haunted by nightmares. He had developed a genuine disdain for the human race and he summed up his general attitude toward life once as, "What the hell's the point in it all anyway?" Although he remained adamant in his refusal to see the police staff psychiatrist, he did relent and take sick leave and he had his GP put him on a waiting list to see a psychiatrist in private practice.

Things went from bad to worse rather quickly. He stated that the depression was like quicksand that wouldn't let him go, drawing him deeper into a bottomless pit of despair. He came to believe that death was the only way out of this quagmire.

For several months now he had been going for extended walks along the banks of a river that ran through the city. He would always pause by a small waterfall, the only source of tranquility in his life at the time. He felt strangely drawn to this location, almost compelled by it. He would sit listening to the water and gazing at the rocks. It was almost hypnotic. On one occasion something deep inside him clicked and he knew what action he must take. Even though he had ready access to a gun and was an excellent shot, there was no question in his mind as to how he would quit this life. He would descend from the bridge above the little waterfall to the rocks below. He would execute his plan early the following Monday morning, when there were not so many people about as there were on the weekend.

That weekend, he sat by the waterfall, once again staring at the rocks and contemplating what it could all mean; what was the point to all the suffering? So much of it seemed senseless and random with no rhyme or reason.

"I looked at the rocks I would be crashing into and I remembered a couple of the suicide calls I had responded to. One chose to live but the other one... As I was recalling that incident it suddenly grew quite chilly, so I turned to the left to get my jacket and was startled to see a woman sitting quite close to me on the ground. This struck me has highly unusual, as I hadn't heard anyone approach me, and also because, with so many other places to sit, why would she pick a place so close to a stranger? I was also struck by an odd sense of familiarity about her and by the way in which I took in every detail about her in a brief two seconds.

"She said good morning and I replied the same and as I was turning my attention back toward the rocks, she added, 'The water is so cold and murky.'

"I thought that a strange comment to make and turned back to ask her what she meant, but she was gone! Once again there was no sound of her leaving. She left as quietly and mysteriously as she had come. I wondered if I had finally snapped and was hallucinating.

"Then it came rushing back to me and I realized why she was so familiar to me. The short red her, the round innocent face with the wide doe eyes, even the sporty jogging outfit. This was the female suicide from eight years back when I was still on the beat. I rode with her in the ambulance, holding her hand the entire way. She had taken an overdose. I kept telling her to hold on but I could see in her eyes that she was fading fast. She was at the critical point of no return. They pronounced her dead at the hospital. The emergency room physician said it was too bad she overdosed on these particular antidepressants, as they were especially hard on the heart. She expired of cardiac arrest as a result of the overdose. I had felt a connection to her in the ambulance. I'll never forget those eyes. She kept them locked on me as if she was trying to communicate something and I was her last chance because she knew she was dying. And now, here she was, or had been. There was absolutely no mistaking her.

"The hair on the back of my neck and arms stood up and I got chills. Those chills stayed with me throughout the day. I just couldn't seem to get warm. I developed something else, too: second thoughts about my plans for Monday morning. I still cannot comprehend the nature of the experience. Was it a ghost or did my mind conjure up this image or hallucination out of desperation? Whatever the explanation, it was a life-altering experience that had taken place for a reason. It certainly did give me second thoughts about my decision and I obviously reconsidered."

Dominic was able to get into the care of a private psychiatrist a week following this event. He never mentioned the experience to the psychiatrist and states he has no intention of doing so. He is only sharing it here in hopes that it may cause some other vulnerable person thinking of taking a similar plunge to have second thoughts too. Shortly after coming under the care of the therapist, Dominic saw that same woman. Once again he was on one of his regular walks around the bank of the river. He had paused in a wooded area to absorb the sound and smell of the water, when he happened to glance over at the other side of the riverbank. There she was, sitting with her knees pulled up around her chest watching him. He couldn't believe his eyes, but there she was, clear as crystal. Same outfit, same hair, same eyes! He didn't get chills this time. He felt she just wanted to say a final goodbye and let him know he made the right decision. And then she was gone.

Tend to My Grave

The last place in the world you would venture to in the hopes of spotting a spook is a cemetery. Spirits tend to remain connected to the people or places in death that they were attached to in life — if they remain attached at all. That, however, is not the case in this extraordinary graveyard encounter.

Melina Selvestri of Reggio Calabria, Italy relates the following unearthly tale: "I had been visiting my husband Gino's grave twice weekly ever since his death, three years back. It was springtime and I couldn't help but notice the large number of open, waiting graves. I made mention of this to a friend of mine, and she too had noticed the high number of death notices there had been in the papers. Maybe the long dark, wet winter we just came through had taken its toll on some of the more vulnerable souls; *non so perche.*

"One Tuesday afternoon I noticed a freshly dug grave just three spaces down from where my Gino was. They already had the concrete block in place waiting for the casket. It is often referred to as our final resting place, and this slab of concrete with its alabaster cover reminded me of a macabre bed. I crossed myself and wondered about the newcomer. How did they pass? How is the family coping? Those sorts of questions. I said a short prayer for them then resumed my work on Gino's grave.

"When I came back the following week, I was greeted by the melodious humming of a young woman, maybe in her twenties or so. She was tending to this new grave, which was still covered with flowers from the service, though they were dying now. She seemed quite content, or at least she wasn't crying or anything. I mean *irr conoscure?* [Who knows what she was thinking or feeling?]

"I was thinking how young and fragile she appeared. She had long blond hair that was blowing slightly in the breeze. She was very pale with fine features like a figurine. She must have been from the north looking as she did, or may be from della Sicilia. I wondered what her relationship to the person interred in the grave was. Was she the young wife, a daughter or sister? I also thought (silly me) that she was wearing nothing but a plain white dress. Sitting on the ground as she was, her dress would become soiled. And no shoes, either. [At this point Signora Selvestri paused to hum the tune she had heard.] It's sort of sad. A feel to it that is a lamenting. My grandmother used to hum it all the time, but I just can't recall the name of it. It's very old, though, and I think it's actually from della Sicilia.

"Anyway, I decided I had better get back to my own work and stop being so nosy. I returned the following Friday and noticed the grass was starting to come in already over the freshly dug grave. But there was no sign of the young woman this time. Again, being nosy I guess, I strolled over to read the name on the stone. Maybe I would recognize the family name. As I came closer it became apparent to me that this was one of those tombstones where the family encased a picture of the departed loved one in the monument. Well, I could not believe my eyes. The picture on the tombstone was that of the young woman I had seen just a week before at this very grave. Her grave! *Santo Cielo!* Perhaps that's why she had no shoes. They don't bury you with your shoes on."

I asked Singora Selvestri why she had not been scared off by such an encounter, as surly many others would have been. She waved me away, explaining that in her family, they were use to this sort of thing; besides, the living are more of a threat than the dead could ever be and certainly this poor young soul was no threat to anyone. She was saddened by the lack of visitors to the young woman's grave but thought that the family might still be too distraught by their loss to face the actual gravesite.

Still she could not stand the thought of this woman's final resting place going unattended as though she didn't matter to anyone. She just knew this was not the case or they would not have bothered to include a photo of her. So along with the accoutrements she brought for her Gino's grave, she included extra flowers for the young woman's grave. Toward the end of summer, members of the family did visit the grave and they were so moved by the actions and concern shown by Singora

Selvestri that they became friends, often going for a cold drink at the end of their mutual visits. They remain friends to this day. I should add that a couple of Signora Selvestri's questions were answered. The young woman died suddenly of a blood clot. She was the youngest of eight children. Her name was Anna Marie, and may she rest in peace and know that her grave was being lovingly tended to.

Brandon and Craig are yet another couple of people who swear they are the last "type" of people to whom you would expect this sort of thing to happen. As has been illustrated throughout this book, there is no type, and living in a new home instead of a turn-of-the-century one "built on an ancient burial ground" is no guarantee that your home will be haunt-free. Brandon is a nurse and Craig a bartender. They reside in Toronto, Ontario, Canada. Both are in their late 30s and have never had an experience with the paranormal before or since this incident.

A Conundrum from the Attic

We were so excited about finally getting into our new home. It was one of those "fixer-uppers" and it seemed like the renovations had taken forever. Finally it was all done — or so we thought. Everything seemed to be according to specifications and was in good working order except for the ceiling; more specifically, the part of the ceiling where the attic door lowers down from.

We first noticed what we thought was an oil stain from paint forming around the outer parameter of the trap door. We touched it up, but it came back. We could not determine the origin of this stain but as we couldn't do anything about it, we just ignored it until the morning our attention was drawn sharply back to it.

It was a typical Monday morning with the alarm going off and Craig muddling down to the kitchen to make the coffee. The attic stairs, which had been pulled down, stopped him. He called up to me before remembering that he had left me in the bedroom. He shouted for me to come and then asked if I had forgotten to retract the attic stairs. I had no idea what he was talking about and told him I had not even been up there. Then we both noticed two peculiar things. First, there was a cold draft blowing down from the attic and this was the middle of heat wave in July. Second, there seemed to be a sickly sweet odour like decaying flowers.

We were both perplexed, and when Craig replaced the stairs back up into the attic we noticed the stain had grown considerably bigger. "Oh great, we need to call the contractor back," was the only thing Craig could mutter as he continued on his way to the kitchen in a huff. Personally, I was more curious than miffed. How did the stairs come to be lowered in the first place, and why is it we never noticed a draft before this, and a cold one at that? I've always been interested in the paranormal and sort of thought, though not seriously, that maybe we had a spook or something.

Craig called the contractor and we forgot about it for a few days until we found the attic open again with the stairs lowered. The cold draft was present as well, but this time I noticed that it really wasn't so much of a draft as a cold spot. You would have to go three-quarters of the way up the stairs so that you were almost in the attic but not all the way. I thought to myself, "Wow! A genuine cold spot." And when I say cold, I mean it was freezing. You could literally see a bit of your breath when you exhaled. The cold spot wasn't very large, either; it was more like something you might get when you open a freezer door on a really hot day, only colder. I had heard about these things, but this was my first personal encounter.

Craig didn't know what to make of any of this and he went from being worried about how much more money we were going to have to sink into this place to being pretty freaked out by this weird stuff.

The contractor came in a couple of days later and had a look around. He pronounced the place structurally sound with no need of repairs. It didn't even need more insulation. He didn't know what to say about the cold spot and he checked the hinges on the stairs and door and said there was no mechanical reason why they were not remaining in the retracted position. Finally, all he could say about the brown stain was that it could not be due to sweating oil paint as we had figured because the paint around the ceiling was not oil based. Nor was it any kind of mould or mildew. All he could say was that we had a bit of a mystery on our hands. Not what Craig wanted to hear.

This "mystery" with the attic continued, only with an added touch. We began to hear scratching noises and thought squirrels had made a nest up there because it was too loud to be mice. Upon investigation we found no trace of any kind of animal up there. We had a real mystery on our hands, as there was no physical cause for the disturbance nor did it seem to fit the profile of a haunting — unless it was a really stupid boring one.

There were a few things that really stood out in my mind suggesting it might be a ghostly manifestation. Early one Saturday morning, at around five o'clock, someone quietly calling my name and gently stroking my arm was waking me up. The touch was very cold, and I thought what a strange dream before realizing I wasn't dreaming at all. With that my eyes shot open and simultaneously the attic stairs came crashing down. Both Craig and I leapt out of bed. Craig asked, "What the hell was that? What was this place before we moved in, an insane asylum?" I noticed that my arm was still cool as though it had had ice on it. I've also had the covers pulled off of me more than once.

Another really odd thing happened one morning when I was running late for work. I had a quick shower and was trying to brush my teeth and blow-dry my hair while getting dressed. The bathroom mirror was all fogged up from the shower so I couldn't really see what I was doing. I turned to the towel rack on the left [to get a towel] to wipe the mirror and when I turned back, the condensation on the mirror had been wiped away. Judging from the pattern, it was done with a hand. I just said thanks, shrugged, and spit the toothpaste. I didn't mention it to Craig, as he had no patience for this sort of thing, especially if it costs us money, which it had in the beginning.

Other than those two things, the manifestations remained localized at the attic. The cold spot remained, and we would occasionally hear noises coming from above, but mostly if you banged on the ceiling it would stop. The stain didn't get any bigger but we had to remove the rug because we found that it occasionally dripped; not a lot but enough that the dark spots where noticeable on the rug. After the rug was gone, we would occasionally find a small puddle of water, but as the contractor had already given the place the once over and there were no pipes where the drip was, we decided against calling a plumber in.

There were some other odd things, but how do you determine if it is supernatural or not? For instance, one morning the coils in our toaster started glowing an incandescent bright red and were literally frying the toast. We pulled the plug on it and the next time we used it was perfectly fine. The real disturbing thing about that incident was that a couple of days later I switched on the coffee maker and when I came back all four of the burners on the stove were glowing red. I turned them off immediately and even unplugged the stove. You don't want that sort of thing happening when there is no one home because of the fire hazard. Actually you never want that sort of thing happening, but nothing like that ever occurred again.

One really funny thing I remember is one morning just as dawn was breaking we were lying in bed enjoying the sound of the rain on the roof and splattering against the windows. Imagine my surprise when I got up and discovered it wasn't raining! In fact it looked like it was going to be a really clear and beautiful day. I was about to say something to Craig, but he just waved me away and put the pillow over his head. He didn't want to hear about it. So long as it didn't wind up costing us anything he basically made light of it like with the rain. He said how nice it was that the house came with sound effects. He is eminently practical.

Some of this stuff still goes on, like trying to keep the attic door closed is impossible. We even tried a padlock once and we found it sitting nicely, still locked, on the floor beneath the attic steps, which of course were down again. So we just gave up on it. The cold spot remains but Craig just looks at it like a bit of free air-conditioning in the house. It's a real mystery because we've never had any indication that this stuff is being done by a ghost like learning that someone died here and this is his spirit. A friend of my sister's is psychic and she said it was a male who died in his 40s. Apparently he had become intoxicated and fell down the attic stairs, which are steep. He broke his neck. His name was Raymond. He is mostly playful and makes for good party conversation, so we don't really mind. As Craig is fond of saying ad nauseam, so long as he doesn't cost us anything more.

Throughout our recorded history there has always been mention of dreams and the special part they play in our lives. Great significance has been projected on them by us for ages. They were a way for the gods to communicate with us, a vehicle for uncommon wisdom, a portal for diabolical inhabitants of the underworld to attack or influence us, and they have been used as a royal road to the unconscious by which we can gain a deeper insight into ourselves.

One enduring quality about them, however, is their role as a portent of the future and a looking-glass into things happening in real time that we could not otherwise have conscious knowledge of. Such is the case in the following dreams.

It Was a Dream Come True

Ulanda Lang emigrated from Germany when she was just fifteen years old. She is now in her 60s and lives in a mid-sized city in Ontario, Canada. One of her most significant dreams involved the foretelling of the death of her beloved brother, Fred. One night she dreamed that she was out walking her baby in a pram. Although at the time of this dream she was too old to have a baby of her own, she did not consider her maternal role odd. She came to a sidewalk that was on an upward incline and had a railing. She noticed many people were standing around as if waiting for something. She asked someone what they were waiting for. The individual replied that someone very popular and famous was going to be coming by and they wanted to catch a glimpse of him. It began to rain a bit and, wanting to get the baby out of the rain, she left.

Two weeks later, she received the heartbreaking news that her baby brother Fred had been killed in a single-engine plane crash in which he had been the pilot. He had been flying since he was very young and was an excellent pilot, but accidents do happen. It was during the funeral procession that Mrs. Lang noticed a sidewalk on an upward incline with a railing. The place in her dream. She felt a chill pass through her and got goosebumps.

I asked her if being one of the older children she had ever had the responsibility of looking after her brother when he was a baby. She replied that she had never thought of that before, but yes indeed, she had helped to care for him as an infant. Although he was not famous, he was very well liked and respected and was indeed very popular, just as the figure in the dream had been.

In another dream, she found herself in a long building with many private entrances. Her vision was such that she felt as though she were viewing the surroundings through a sheer veil. She saw sparks and then

110

a fire erupt in the back of the building. Frantically, she began pounding on doors to get people out of the building. No one answered the doors or seemed to even take notice of her. She came outside to the front of the building and was alarmed by how large the fire had become. By now there were fire trucks all over the place. She accosted one elderly lady who was in some type of enclosure. The lady said she simply wasn't capable of leaving.

The very next day she and her husband were watching the news and a story came on about a tragic fire in a nursing home in the United States. Many elderly persons had perished in the fire, as they were physically infirm and the rescue personnel were unable to reach everyone on time. The nursing home on the television was the one she saw in her dream — or in this case, nightmare.

Mrs. Lang related to me a fascinating dreamlike experience. It may not be an actual dream so much as a vision. Dawn was approaching and she was in that twilight state between wake and sleep known as a hypnogogic trance. She was aware of the sun slowly rising and could hear the birds singing, when quite suddenly all became silent and dark as though her senses of sight and sound had been turned off. It was replaced by a click, click sound — the kind of sound a slide projector machine makes when you advance the frame. At the sound of the click a picture of a man not known to her came up. It was a head and torso shot, the type taken by the police of convicts. This was followed by another click, and the picture was replaced by the sounds of agonizing screams and crying. Another click and the image of the man reappeared. Finally this ceased and her normal vision and hearing resumed.

Once again she and her husband were watching the news and a disturbing report came on from out of Quebec. A man had locked some people in a house and burned them to death. The police photo was that of the man in her hypnogogic "slide show."

Fortunately not all her visions from the night were so dramatic or disturbing. For a considerable length of time, she had been waiting for the delivery of a table and chair set from a large department store. One night she dreamed that the table and chairs had finally arrived but upon opening the boxes she discovered that all the chairs were different and that something was wrong with the table.

It was a vivid dream, and she shared it with her husband the following morning. Sure enough, that very day the table and chairs were delivered. When they finally got around to unpacking them, they discovered that the legs on the chairs were different from each other — all in all, rather mismatched. Considering how long she had waited for her new dining suite, this was not exactly a dream come true. Mrs. Lang remains quite interested in dreams and has read many books on the subject. At the time of these experiences she was practising yoga and meditation, which she feels helped her open her mind and be more relaxed psychically.

Mrs. Lang has a daughter we will call Katrina. She was very close to her uncle and was devastated by his sudden death. There is a particular event that took place immediately following the plane crash involving Katrina and her grandmother. This is how she recalls it: "At approximately noon on Sunday June 8, 1997, I got a call from my Uncle Bob, who was desperately in search of his sister, my mother. He told me that my uncle's plane had crashed in the field shortly after takeoff and that it sounded really bad. Horrified but never assuming that my uncle was actually dead at that time, I told him that I would track down my mother.

"For some reason the first person I called was my Grandma Lily on my father's side. Although she is not Uncle Ian's mother, when he was a little boy he used to visit Grandma and Grandpa's cottage. He was well bonded to them.

"When I called my Grandma Lily, I immediately asked if my parents were there. She replied that they were not there and then tried to keep me engaged on the phone, chatting. I didn't want to worry or upset her so I certainly didn't mention the plane crash but I needed to get off the phone and find my mother. This was no easy task and I'm afraid I had to be rather abrupt, cutting her off saying that I really needed to go and find my mother. Weeks later I discovered why she so desperately wanted me to stay on the phone.

"At the time of my call, she was sitting alone in her condominium paralyzed with fear. She had just seen a man in her kitchen. She later related the entire episode to me. She explained that while she was sitting quietly in her living room sewing buttons, a movement caught her attention. It was coming from the kitchen so she turned to see what it was. When she looked up from her sewing, she saw a man walking from the kitchen on through the length of her dining room toward the window. He could not have been more than ten or twelve feet from where she was seated. His head was turned away from her so she was unable to see his face. She said he had dirty blond hair that was nicely cropped and curling about halfway up his head. Overall, he was large across the back and thick across the middle of the chest. He was wearing a short-sleeved shirt, reddish in colour but faded as though it had been through many washings.

"Her first thought was that someone had broken into her home and she was terrified. She turned her head toward the dining room, fully expecting to see him enter it from the kitchen, but he never appeared. She was very puzzled, not understanding where he had disappeared to or, for that matter, how this man had entered her premises without her hearing the door.

"She was cold with fear and glued to her chair not knowing what to do when the phone rang. She later shared with me that she had never been so happy to hear someone's voice. She was so frightened and confused that she tried to keep me on the phone for as long as possible. She had not even hinted to me as to the events that had just transpired, so I had no way of knowing she was in distress, and I needed to get off the phone quickly. In fact, by the time of my call she already knew what she had seen was a ghost. After discussing all of this, she understood why I had to get off the phone so quickly just as I had learned the reason behind her trying to keep me engaged in conversation.

"Later our family was to learn that Uncle Ian was killed on impact as the plane exploded in flames. The time was around noon — approximately one hour prior to the time of Grandma Lily's ghostly visitor. We also discovered what Uncle Ian had been wearing at the time of death from his wife: a faded red shirt! His widow told us that Ian just loved that shirt. No sooner would it come out of the laundry than it would be back on him because it was so comfortable. My uncle's overall physical appearance matched that of the visitor as well: a heavyset man with light hair. Grandma Lily told me that before this experience, she was never sure about such things as ghosts, but if someone were to ask her now, her reply would be that she does not simply believe they exist, she knows they do.

"I never could figure out why Uncle Ian had appeared to Grandma Lily. My mom thinks it may be due to the fact that Grandma's mind was more receptive, as she was unaware of the crash and was in a relaxed state sewing. Meanwhile, the rest of the family was in a mad panic rushing to the crash site or trying to reach relatives on the phone. I asked Grandma why she thought Uncle Ian had come to her place. She replied that the only reason she could figure was the last time she spoke to him, she told him that she needed the condo painted. Being a professional painter by trade, he offered to come by and evaluate the place. She thought that perhaps this was some unfinished business and he was looking at her walls!

"To this day I feel it was more than mere coincidence that I called Grandma Lily just at the time she had this experience."

Mathew Connor of New York City shared a hotel room with a poor lost soul on a visit to Pennsylvania.

Spirited Holiday

While staying at an inn in Lancaster, PA, I woke to see a girl at the bottom of the bed and I asked her who she was and what she wanted. She replied, "Please help me. Please help me." I knew she wasn't from this world so all I could say was, "I can't help you because you're not of my world so please go away." This happened four times throughout the night, and each time she repeated her sorrowful request for help.

I was some bothered by this and in the morning went straight to the front desk and asked to be moved to another room. The desk clerk said that they frequently have guests make the same request so I told her what had transpired during the night. The clerk, who was an older lady, explained that many years ago this inn had been an Amish farm. A young girl became pregnant out of wedlock and was murdered by her own father. This experience has left one very lasting impression on me!

Bob was born and raised in the town of St. Catharines, Ontario. He has had psychic experiences on and off for most of his life beginning when he was only eight years old and had an extraordinary "dream" experience involving his grandfather, to whom he was very close.

Second Nature

"I dreamed that my grandfather came to me and told me to take his hand and come with him. He said to hold tight and don't be afraid. We went flying through the house down through the basement and straight through a spiderweb and a tiny hole. We came through the hole and began flying higher and higher right up to the stars. I could see planets around us. It was so incredible. We arrived at this entrance; I even recall seeing something like street signs pointing to various destinations. We were greeted by a disembodied voice. You could feel the power radiating from it. The voice said that I was not to go beyond this point as I did not belong here. My grandfather had to go on, though. He bent down, hugged and kissed me goodbye, and after saying he loved me he told me that I had to go back and that I was to return by the exact route by which we came to this place. I agreed to this and began my flight back home. I even went through the little hole and past the spiderweb. When I woke that morning I was told the sad news that my grandfather had died in the night."

Bob has also had experiences with precognition, such as the time his wife was beginning a new job at a local bank. He described to her in precise detail the surroundings in which she would be working. He went on to describe her boss to her and warned her that he was a "pervert" and not to be surprised when he made a pass at her. When she arrived home that evening she told Bob, not without some astonishment, that he was correct in all he had foreseen, including the pass. He had no reply when she asked how he knew. He simply shrugged it off, not wanting to make a big deal out of it in case it worried her. He had more or less become accustomed to such things.

Other instances of precognition may have actually served to save lives. Such was the case at work one day when Bob saw the image of a large piece of machinery hanging over a coworker's head fall on him. Bob, in a very casual manner, asked his co-worker if he would mind just moving down the line by a couple of places. Of course the co-worker laughed, and Bob, chuckling back, said, "Yeah, yeah, I know, but just humour me on this, okay?" The co-worker obliged Bob's odd request, and a few minutes later, the piece of machinery fell on the location where the co-worker had been standing.

On another occasion, Bob saw a horrifying image of a friend of his. It was in 1975 and both Bob and his friend were still residing in St. Catharines. His friend worked for a division of Health and Safety. Part of his duties included painting danger, warning, and caution signs where needed on buildings. Bob received the image of his friend engulfed in flames from the shoulders up, his face dark red like a Halloween devil mask. Two days later the combustible chemicals Bob's friend was working with ignited, engulfing this poor man in flames. He was at Bob's place of work, and upon seeing what was happening, Bob responded immediately in an attempt to put out the fire. The ambulance arrived quickly, but one of the things that stand out in Bob's mind was that the image he had seen in his vision matched that of his friend surrounded by flames in real time. One of the reasons he was able to respond so calmly and quickly (not that he wasn't frightened and alarmed) was that the vision had almost prepared him for the true-life event.

Bob has also seen a couple of ghosts in his time. In one unique encounter, he and a friend were out walking their dog late one night and decided to take a shortcut through a graveyard. They were coming to an above-ground concrete encasement. As they came closer, the dog began to growl and strain against the leash. At the same time they noticed a woman in a long white dress lying on top of the long flat memorial. She was almost glowing in the dark. Bob wanted to say something to her, but his friend — and for that matter the dog — was too terrified, so they just inconspicuously made their way past this ethereal spectre. She seemed not to take any notice of them. She lay there prostrate on the monument, apparently oblivious to the world around her, just taking in the moonlight.

His second ghostly encounter took place in a house he and his wife had just moved into. One night a few days after they moved in, Bob woke up to see a man coming toward the bed. He was in old-fashioned attire, wearing a bowler hat and a three-piece suit. The man came to the foot of the bed and stopped briefly. He looked directly at Bob, smiled, and then headed off into the closet. Bob naturally got up to investigate but found no one in the closet or any sign of an intruder. This scenario was to be repeated a couple of more times. Bob's wife was easily frightened by such things, so after the man made an appearance to her, Bob decided it was time to have their pastor come in. They held a prayer vigil and for two weeks all was quiet, which led them to believe that the spirit had been set free.

Shortly thereafter, a new neighbour took up residence. The man introduced himself and then cautiously broached the subject of a possible intruder. He said he didn't want to sound crazy or alarm Bob, but was he aware that a man was hanging around the outside of their house peering in the windows? Bob asked if the man in question was by any chance wearing a three-piece suit and a bowler hat. The neighbour looked wide-eyed at Bob and replied in the affirmative. Bob said not too be concerned about it and made light of it as being just a familial ghost. So the prayer vigil had indeed set their ghost free, but he hadn't gone far and either wanted back in or had evolved into a ghostly peeping Tom!

No Newfoundland Joke

Newfoundland, on the east coast of Canada, has a reputation for its hospitality and familial atmosphere. It is one of the most friendly and picturesque places in the country. It is this part of Canada many of the victims of the SS *Titanic* were brought to after she failed the sea. Newfoundlanders are also well known for their history, which is rich in folklore and superstitions.

Penny is from Gander, Newfoundland but now works in a city in the province of Ontario as a property manager. When I asked her if, being from Newfoundland, she had ever heard any tales of the supernatural, she chuckled, saying that she never discusses such things even though one experience had made her a believer. She shyly shared a childhood memory with me.

Penny was five years old when her family left her place of birth of Gander, Newfoundland. They moved to the city of Grand Falls within the same province. The patriarch of the family had secured an apartment in a very old green house. What he withheld from his wife and children was that the occupant of the house had died just two weeks prior to the family's occupancy. She was an elderly lady who, presumably, died of natural causes. He withheld this information in justified concern that it would be a worry to his wife and children.

Until their upper-level compartments were ready, the children all slept in the same room with their parents. Penny was sharing a bed with her sister Annie. Long after they had both fallen into a restful sleep, both sisters were awakened at dawn by an elderly woman in the kitchen, not far from where they were sleeping. The woman was wearing a long black dress and carrying a pot to the stove. The younger sister was so frightened that she ran to her parents' bed, leaving poor Penny alone and frozen in her bed. She managed to put a pillow up over her head to hide, but when she removed it, much to her dismay, the apparition remained.

This sounds like a typical childhood dream except for the fact that children were unaware of the demise of the elderly lady, that they both saw the same figure simultaneously, and finally, that there was a strange event the following morning.

The bathroom in this house was located in the basement, a place the children were not particularly fond of as many children are not particular to attics or cellars. On this particular morning, they had good reason to be a tad unsettled. Upon their entry into the cellar, they discovered a bag of knitting that belonged to the deceased former occupant. It had not been there prior to her dawn visit to the kitchen.

Although Penny remains aloof about the subject, this shared experience with her sister has left her convinced that there is more to this life than meets the eye. Perhaps superstitions, myths, and legends enter our culture as a result of experiences that, although we cannot readily explain, nevertheless have profound impact on our collective psyche.

Chapter Nine
Breathless

The lights burn blue. It is now dead of midnight,
Cold fearful drops stand on my trembling flesh
Methought the souls of all that I had murdered
Came to my tent.
— Shakespeare, *Richard III*, Act v, sc. 3

This chapter begins as the classic cliché ghost story, as the evening we first arrived was indeed a dark and stormy night. But then again, almost every night in the summer of 2000 was dark and stormy. There were four of us preparing to investigate a house that I had been procrastinating on for quite awhile, as it was the site of a gruesome murder/suicide. Truth be told, I was beginning to wonder if this chapter would ever be written. It was continuously delayed, and when it finally was nearing completion, we were wondering if it should even be included within this volume because it was too fantastic for even us, who are not new to such phenomena, to fully comprehend. The psychic of our group didn't find it "all that fantastic" and the psychologist believed it contained educational components involving trauma and even death. After all the work, which was at times painful, that has been put into this chapter, I certainly wanted to see it included. The psychic also felt it would give witness or lend a voice to the victims. The technician was uncomfortable, feeling that recounting aspects of this tale would be an invasion of privacy to the deceased, who cannot say whether they wish to be included in the book or not.

The psychic disagreed, countering that being deceased does not nec-essarily preclude you from having your intentions known. As a scien-tist, my primary concern centred around our preconceived notions of the house due to the prior events that occurred in it and the degree to which that would contaminate the field. For integrity's sake alone, the ability for a field investigation to stand up under scrutiny is of great import. I cannot in all honesty say that either of those concerns have been fully satisfied (I doubt they ever could be), but I am comfortable in asserting that to the best of our abilities, we handled this case in a professional manner, and, being fully cognizant of the complex issues involved, we were highly conscientious and perhaps even overly ana-lytical of ourselves and the manifestations. And so went our debate until we finally agreed to share this story. The names and locations have been altered under legal constraints and to protect the identity of the living and at the request of the owner of the property.

Our group was composed of Madeline Kinney, the primary psychic consultant for this book; Ian Howe, the technician who would set up and operate the modest amount of equipment we were able to beg; Dr. Michelle Douglas, a psychologist well trained in trauma related mat-ters; and me.

If there was ever a place that could serve as evidence that physical structures could retain the energy of events that occurred within their periphery, this place was it! Approaching the three-story Germanic building, nobody was feeling "clichéd" in spite of it being a dark and stormy night. In fact, if it were not for the intense curiosity evoked in us by the stories this house had generated, none of us would relish the idea of visiting a place so rife with violence and tragedy.

Upon entering, I was reminded of the quote from Dante's *Inferno*: "Abandon all hope, all ye who enters here." Superlatively malignant, the walls seemed to vibrate in a negative harmonic. (This particular affect on its own could induce vexation, and we couldn't allow our-selves to be drawn into the negativity of the house if we were to main-tain objectivity. We could not indulge in negative emotions and felt we had to remain hyper vigilant against such effects. Still, there was no denying that we felt gloomy and irritable here.) The ionosphere was simply menacing but there was an underlying sadness to the place as well, an unspoken tragedy of lives violently extinguished before their time, not to mention a number of "freak" accidents.

The air also seemed to be thin, so much so that we were actually conscious of taking deeper breaths. Ian, who was a climber, said it was like the air you encounter in higher altitudes.

Because the sources of the accounts were so reliable, we had taken special care in putting together this little team. Anyone with active, pre-existing health problems like asthma was excluded from the investigation because breathing difficulties were a major paranormal manifestation in this environment. What rendered asthma and chronic bronchitis especially problematic is that inhalers often became inoperative in this house and were later found to be void of their contents, including in those cases where the script had been recently filled.

Due to what was later determined to be wildly variable electrostatic fields, hearing aids and, more worrisome, pacemakers have been known to malfunction. There has been one death associated with the failure of a pacemaker on these premises, but the device itself may have been defective. By necessity, the death was investigated by the authorities but no recall or warning about the device was issued, as there were no structural faults found with it.

Hearing aids not only malfunctioned, but those wearing them also claimed to be hearing voices as though their devices had tuned into a short-wave radio frequency. Only bits and pieces of conversation would be picked up. As one man described it, it was as though you were picking up bits of a telephone conversation. It is impossible to ascertain from where these frequencies were originating, but judging from the contextual nature of the conversations, it would appear to be otherworldly — just random parts of people casually talking to each other in person. Most disconcerting, though, was when muffled screams and mournful sobbing was overheard. These were all faint, but there was no mistaking the nature of the sounds. (There are some structures where mechanical devices often fail for no discernable reason. These include everything from microwaves to watches. This is not to suggest the structure is haunted. Indeed, the theory runs more along the lines of electro/geometric fields interacting with some inhabitants and even the electromagnetic environment of the property the structure stands on. This is true of granite structures or houses on or near mineralized sands.)[1]

Former residents of the house claimed to hear a child calling out as if awakened from a nightmare in the night. One former resident, Mrs. Illeen Hill, said that she was awoken one night by the sound of a woman sobbing. She sat up in bed and was shocked to see the image of a distraught woman looking for something in a very confused fashion. She woke her husband, believing it to be an intruder, but the image had vanished by the time he responded to her.

In another account, it was asserted that neither pets nor plants fared well in this place. The pets became skittish or ill tempered and the foliage of plants simply turned yellow, dropped their leaves, and then either died or went into a "vegetative coma" as one very annoyed and frustrated plant lover put it. There were also accounts of small play items appearing out of nowhere, mostly those old bouncing balls with the stripes. The residents who had children just assumed the kids had found the items and brought them home. In one case, however, a couple who had taken early retirement and had no children living with them had a very different encounter with the bouncing ball.

Like others who have lived there, this lady (who does not want to be identified) would often hear the monotonous tone of a ball being bounced off the floor. On one occasion, while she was upstairs making the beds, she heard the bouncing ball again, coming from downstairs. This time it sounded as though it were being bounced from the wall to the floor. She went to the top of the staircase, and as she was peering down into the foyer, she lost her balance, falling nearly to the bottom of the stairs. She lay there for what she estimates was nearly an hour before her daughter arrived to take her shopping. She suffered a broken hip and leg, two fractured ribs, and a concussion. Still, she is very lucky to be alive. The odd thing about the fall is that she swears to her daughter that as she was looking downstairs, she felt a cold, sharp breeze behind her and before she had a chance to turn around, she felt a shove and went on her descent. The daughter said her mother is not prone to flights of fancy and is in good health so would not be susceptible to sudden dizzy spells or falls. The husband feared his wife had "knocked a screw loose" when she fell, to which she sharply replied, "I did not fall; I was pushed!"

Even though they had just recently moved in, she insisted that they find a new place to live. Until they did, she would be staying with her daughter. I had the opportunity to meet this lady and would agree with her daughter that she is not inclined to even consider such things as the supernatural. Prior to this event, she always considered people who made such fantastic claims to be suffering from either an overactive imagination or an overactive drinking habit. She added, "Now I'm

Ghost Sliding Down Staircase: artistic rendition by the author.

one of them! I still don't believe in that sort of stuff but I certainly believe what happened to me had nothing to do with natural forces and no one will ever convince me otherwise. And I'll tell you something else; I lived through the London blitz, with air raid sirens going off in the dark of night and all, but I have never known terror until that time, lying there, trapped in that house with whatever pushed me, waiting for my husband or daughter to show up."

We began to set up the equipment in the front living room. We were interrupted by what sounded to all of us like a protracted yawn. We all shared in a little nervous laughter. Madeline added to it by saying, "Oh dear, I believe we have bored the place already." Ian agreed and added that I could entitle this chapter "Ghosts I Have Bored to Death."

The only accoutrements we would be using for this investigation would be a audio tape recorder and a video tape recorder (VTR) with infrared film on standby mode. Ian had also managed to borrow an electromagnetic field monitor as well as a radiation monitor, both to measure any anomalous fluctuations within the normal electric, magnetic, and radiation fields. What we didn't have was an electronic ultrasensitive thermonitor. We could really have used that as it was not merely cold and damp in this place, but unnaturally so, and the temperature varied within parts of each room.[2]

Michelle said what we were all feeling: "It's like a bloody crypt in here. All that's missing is Vincent Price." This time there wasn't even a nervous chuckle. It suddenly felt deadly serious, and some of us were wondering what we had gotten ourselves into. We took a moment to ground ourselves. In a house with a history like this one, it was not hard to become unduly influenced and melodramatic, so all further jokes pertaining to crypts or Vincent Price were suspended.

Before settling down for the first seance, we made our way around the house in an attempt to get a feel for the place. We gingerly made our way through the various rooms. A deep sense of sadness overtook us as we entered the bedrooms where the wife and the children had died, or, more accurately, had their lives taken from them. The two children — Robbie, seven, and Mary, five — were suffocated with a pillow. The wife, Elizabeth, had been strangled. It was in her bedroom that the first unsettling encounter would befall us.

All that remained in the master bedroom was a double bed, a chair, and a large mirror that would have sat on a dressing table. It was now upright against a wall on the floor near the entrance of a deep-set clos-et whose door had been removed. We immediately became aware that the temperature was considerably colder near this closet than in the rest of the room. As we wondered out loud if there was a draft, we were answered by an icy breeze fanning out from the closet.

Madeline made her way to the entrance of the closet and reached out to make contact with whatever may be manifesting from within it. She took a strong, sharp breath in — in fact, we were alarmed because she seemed to be struggling to catch her breath. She certainly appeared to have made contact with something. Meanwhile, our flashlights were struggling to maintain their luminance. She gasped out, "Oh my God, I can see her! Elizabeth!" and had to break away with some difficulty. Before she did, we all got a glimpse of what Madeline had connected with. At first, we couldn't believe our eyes and thought it was a trick of the failing torches, not to mention the overall atmosphere. But the lights grew more stable and the image in the mirror became distinct and undeniable. Staring out from the mirror were two stark bloodshot eyes, wide with terror and panic. Beneath the eyes was a black and blue hue, the sign of broken blood vessels caused by the force she endured. She must have put up quite a struggle. These eyes cast a piercing light brighter than that of our feeble torches. To this day, none of us can get the image of those eyes out of minds. I doubt we ever will.

Madeline hurried out of the bedroom and collapsed against the wall, trying to steady herself. She repeated one expression: that poor woman. She was shaking her head as though attempting to dislodge the image from her head. We told her of the image we had seen in the mirror, and she simply nodded, still trying to regain her breath. She later said the victim, in having been face to face with her killer, was staring straight into the eyes of insanity and malevolence. This "man" was devoid of any conscience; he was a true psychopath. It took Elizabeth less than two minutes to expire, but it felt like an eternity. So tightly tuned in to the victim was Madeline that she was able to put the time it took Elizabeth to die at one minute and thirty-seven seconds. Not only did her life pass before her eyes, but also her final thoughts were that of her helpless children. In her shock and disbelief she mentally reached out to both of them. As she was nearing the end, she became resigned to her fate at the hands of this murderer and was finally able to force her eyes closed in a feeble attempt to shut it out.

It is difficult to convey in words the experience of being connected to someone as her life was being extinguished, especially under such horrific conditions. Most deaths are peaceful and flow easily, psychically speaking. Her last thoughts revolved around her children and the returning disbelief that this was actually happening to her. Mentally, it was an icy cold consciousness that closed in on her. It was overwhelming to Madeline that so many thoughts and so much consciousness could be concentrated into such a short time and space, a space that was collapsing in on her.

We moved downstairs, and after discussing what we had just experienced, set up around the circular wooden table. We were all wishing we had brought some gloves. Our fingers and even the tips of our noses were freezing. We were also trembling, but we doubted that was solely due to the cold. We gingerly set things up. There was no electricity hooked up to the house so we were relying on battery packs for the VTR and, more importantly, the audio recorder. The other two monitors were not showing anything significant.[3]

We linked hands and waited for Madeline to run through the purification ritual, which included the lighting of the ceremonial candle to purify and sanctify the immediate environment. (We were also hoping it would give off a bit of heat to warm our poor digits.) Madeline advised us to get comfortable as the spirit of the house was a trickster — and a mean one at that — so we could be in for a long night. In fact we did not have long to wait at all. Madeline was able to re-establish a connection quickly as it had only been a few minutes ago that she had made first contact.

She was staring intently as though she was trying to make something out off in the horizon. Her face became strained and she whispered the name Elizabeth. Then she uttered these chilling words, "He holds me still." It was Madeline's voice but it was strained and breathless as though she were really struggling. The grip of her hands tightened. I was becoming concerned for her. She seemed to be trying to keep herself anchored. Finally, after a minute of her deep, regular breathing exercises, all seemed more relaxed and her grip loosened a bit. It was in the calm and quiet that we first heard the noise. Scratches, slow and methodical, so they certainly couldn't be attributed to any animal. They were emanating from deep within the wooden table. Slowly and gradually they grew louder and more frantic. This frenzied scratching climaxed with a terse, stifled scream from Madeline, who quickly withdrew her hands from ours.

I quickly made for the battery-run lantern that was just by my feet. There was a collective gasp as we looked at Madeline. An angry welt was forming on her left cheek and, much to our astonishment, four scratch marks were materializing on her right hand (the very hand she had extended into the closet). The scratches were superficial but enough to draw blood to the surface. We decided then and there to call this seance to a halt. Besides, we were already feeling overwhelmed and confused by all that had happened in the short time we had been there. Before we broke for the evening, Madeline informed us that the reason for the energy being centred in the closet was that Elizabeth was hiding in there, hoping to escape that lunatic who was pursuing her. She was also under the mistaken belief that he was preventing her from crossing over into the light, getting on with her death as it were.

We just stared wide-eyed at her, feeling more confused than ever. What did she mean, it wasn't him? Our psychological and moral bias was showing. She assured us that it was not this madman's psychic ability that was keeping her trapped here, but her own terror, disbelief, and guilt. She had become a prisoner of the traumatic event and was, in effect, trapped in her own psyche. She was still engaged in a futile search for her children; although they were long dead, she maintained feelings of guilt for what in her mind had been her failure to protect them from that awful fate. Both Michelle and Madeline agreed that it was at least a good sign in that she knew her children were dead. It would be easier to help her to move on.

"We must help her to move out of this place," Madeline stated with determination. We all agreed and the sooner we got her out — if we could do so — the sooner we could get out too!

After we left for the evening I hit the books, looking for clues or suggestions on how to "unstuck" a trapped soul. Why is it that some spirits become trapped by a shocking or violent end but not others? There is no easy answer to that question because even in life, some get through devastating experiences intact while others are left in ruins. With guidance they can move on and reclaim their lives. In this case, we would have to help her reclaim her afterlife. What was I considering here, anyway? Brief, goal-orientated psychotherapy to help this woman get over her murder? Then again, why not? If you can't find peace in death, where can you find it?

This poor soul had endured enough torment. The trick would be in making her aware that she was delegating her power over herself to her killer. He was not anywhere present in this environment. Michelle and I discussed this topic on the way home. She specialized in trauma treatment and said the only way you can ever heal from past trauma and move on is through forgiveness. We have many misconceptions about forgiveness in the West. We think of it as condoning past actions or weakness on our part. We don't mind doing all kinds of psychotherapy to gain understanding of the ways in which the trauma has shaped our psyche and lives, but what do you do with that understanding once you've attained it? Without forgiveness, you remain trapped in the events and your perpetrator remains with you. Most importantly, forgiveness allows personal healing to take place, and although there may be scars, it is that forgiveness and the healing that it brings that allows you to finally move on.

This case was further complicated by the mother's sense of guilt that she had failed her children. Guilt or regret over our seeming failures can also trap us in life. It became clear that the things that can trap us in life are the same things that can keep us earthbound in death. Madeline interjected that what would be required in this case was a "soul rescue."

None of us slept much that night, so when we arrived at the house in the morning, again with our large coffees, we were bleary-eyed but not one of us felt tired. In fact, we felt charged up, whether from caffeine or adrenaline. We were not without a sense of apprehension, either, and we did not want to have to come back to this location.

We entered the foyer and were again greeted by a sigh-like sound. This house had three fireplaces, and we wondered if these sounds of groaning, sighing, and breathing could be attributed to that. We doubted that was the case, as fireplaces don't generally give off exhalation noises. We were also once again aware of the unnatural silence within these walls. We quickly made our way into the front room and resumed our positions around the oak table. As Madeline engaged in her rhythmic exercises, we looked around, noting that the house seemed to be breathing right along with her. Being as this was ten o'clock in the morning, light was not a problem this time and we barely noticed the cold, as we were too absorbed in the proceedings.

Madeline abruptly discontinued the breathing exercises and quietly called out Elizabeth's name. A few seconds passed before Madeline's eyes shot open and focused up toward the ceiling. Our gazes all fell in line. There was a light fixture directly above us. The bulb appeared to wax and wane with a dull blue glow. (It wasn't until several hours later that we realized that it shouldn't have any glow to it as the power was off throughout the house.) Once again, Madeline called out woman's name. We watched her as she went into "the zone" or what used to be referred to as a trance. A few minutes passed, then she began to speak in a whisper.

"Elizabeth is terrified. She is hiding in the closet of the master bedroom. She feels like a coward. Where are the children? She can't think straight. She had entered their son's room and he was standing over the boy, holding a pillow and laughing! She screams at him, 'What are doing?' He turns to face her with an insane grin on his face. Oh God, what's happening? She runs. She is in the closet. She doesn't believe he will hurt Mary. Where was Mary? She waited second after agonizing second, all the while straining to make out any sounds. She hears him whistling. Whistling! She can't believe it. He is coming this way. She grabs for the door handle and grips it tight. She is not strong enough to resist the force he exerts on the door. It flies open. She is face to face with him. He is still grinning. In less than two minutes, it will all be over. Don't fight it anymore. Let go. You did all you could do."

We all looked at Madeline. She must be talking to the woman. She was staring intently, straight ahead and right through the surroundings.

"You loved your children and took many beatings yourself so he would leave them alone. You know that's the truth. You've got to let go. He can't hurt them or you anymore. Go on and be with them."

Madeline had tears running down her cheeks. This was all very intense. I could feel something churning in the air around us. Madeline was choking back tears and pleading with the unseen presence to let go and go on.

"You've earned your peace; now go on and join your children." And then Madeline smiled, and her face was so peaceful and relieved. We knew she had gotten through. You could feel it in the air like a tension had broken. We could smell ozone. Ian strained to see the monitors. We all jumped at once because we heard simultaneous bangs and cracks. We just looked at each other, not knowing what we should do. Madeline assured us that it was all right. We discovered that the source of the bangs were some doors and windows that had "blown" open — specifically, the bedroom window, the front door, and the closet door, which had been dislodged with the loudest thud. It had fallen flat onto the floor from its resting position against the wall. The cracking was the sound of the mirror, the one in which we had been witness to those horrified eyes staring out at us. Madeline looked at it and said that this was one time when a cracked mirror was actually good luck.

We were almost feeling giddy as we made the rounds of the house. Madeline could not detect any presence. The house was clean. As we came to the bottom of the staircase, Ian told us to stand still and listen for a minute. We did. He pointed out that this was the first time we had heard the sound from the outside world within these walls. He was right! We could hear the commotion of life penetrating what had been this lifeless tomb encasing an innocent victim whose soul was now set free.

Chapter Ten
Mysterioso Visita

The following account is a classic poltergeist case. It contains certain elements that make it quite exceptional, even for a poltergeist. First, the suspected source of the poltergeist was a woman in her 30s with no history of psychic phenomena. It is rare that an individual that old would become the centre of poltergeist activity, especially in the absence of a psychic history. In fact, there is no such history in the entire family. As they themselves put it, they are the last family on earth who would ever have such bizarre experiences (a common refrain from many throughout this book.) The second exceptional point is the high volume of spontaneous materializations or aports. Such phenomena are customary with poltergeist activity, but rarely to this degree. Finally, the accounts of the astral projection are inexplicable in that they are actually cases of biolocation, of which there are very few recorded cases.

The family wishes to remain anonymous and was very reluctant to even grant this interview. I am grateful to the family member who did agree to share these experiences because they add to the scientific body of literature that guides us in the comprehension of the science of parapsychology. That in turns helps all of us expand our understanding of life and our purpose for being here.

Elsbeth, the woman relating this story, is originally from Spain. She now resides in Canada with her husband and children. Her husband, Gary, was present during the interview and is no stranger to this topic, having experienced such things personally. She returns to Spain to visit her family almost every year. One year, the visit had many unplanned activities and was a vacation she will never forget.

Author: Your family had some experiences that may have been a poltergeist?

Elsbeth: It looks like it, yes. It started in the summer 1983 and it went on for about four or five years. Understand we've never had experiences like this ever, ever in our lives.

We wanted to have a summer by the beach so we rented an apartment in Palamos, outside of the city, Barcelona. It was a big apartment with three or four bedrooms. We packed up everything we would need for the summer: dishes, bedding — everything. When we arrived there very few of the apartments had been rented because it was a new building, just barely finished. After supper that first night, we were so tired that I, my mother, I think one of my sisters, and all of the children went to bed. Everyone else, three sisters and a brother-in-law, stayed up enjoying the night air and conversation. It was a beautiful summer night so they had all the windows wide open.

It was around one o'clock or so when I was woken up by the sound of something being thrown against my bedroom door. There was an unnatural force and loudness to it. I thought to myself, "Are they throwing something against the door?" But why? That made no sense. It happened again and then again. Just as I got up to call down to those in the living room, they were about to call up to me to see what was going on and where all the noises were coming from. So nobody had been throwing anything. We turned on the light to have a look around in the corridor and could not believe our eyes. All over the place were tops! Tops from the toothpaste. Tops from the oil and vinegar, shampoo, bubble bath — tops from things all over the villa. We first went into the bathroom and the top of the toothpaste was missing. It was the same all over the place.

Author: So they had indeed been coming from objects throughout the villa?

Elsbeth: Yes, but all landing in the same place, just outside my bedroom door. We found so many of these things we were asking each other, "What is this? How can this be?" We thought that somebody was playing a joke and didn't want to admit it. As these things continued, we came to believe that the youngest, Marguerite, was the source. Not on purpose or consciously.

Author: What was her age at that time?

Elsbeth: She would have been thirty-five. That was the start of it. We didn't go to bed that night at all. We were too scared. We continued hearing the noises throughout the night. We wondered if maybe it was a spirit. Perhaps one of the workmen died while they were constructing the building and it was his spirit trapped here. Everyone said, "Oh, come on!" We had never before been inclined to think in such terms, I mean spirits and such, but this was all so unreal! We then wondered if maybe God was warning us to get out of the building because something was going to happen to it. It was so recently built, maybe it's going to come crashing down or something. So we spent the night trying to figure things out.

Then came the buttons. Dozens of buttons, some we recognized from our clothes, which, when we checked, were missing buttons. Also some of the buttons were from clothes that we did not even have here with us like winter coats. And from clothes that belonged to my sister who lived on the Island of Palma de Mollorca. She wasn't even here with us on holiday. But you tell me how, from another place, these buttons came to be here?

Then and there we decided to pack up and go home. Even though we had fully paid and would lose all our money, we were so scared we just took off. Just as we were getting ready to go, my brother-in-law could not find the keys to his car. We looked everywhere, turning the place in side out. We needed the car to leave! We finally checked the balcony (not expecting to find them in such an unlikely place) and there sitting on the ledge were the keys. We left. My mother said, "But you paid all that money," and so on, but we thought, you know, maybe something bad was going to happen.

Author: That was a short vacation, but you're not alone. There are many others who have fled places out of fear, leaving belongings and taking a financial loss.

Elsbeth: That wasn't the end of it, though. Our first night back in Barcelona I was the first one to go to bed while the family stayed up talking (they can talk endlessly). So I am in bed and around one or one-thirty, and suddenly BANG! against the closet. The same thing as before in the villa. Tops from all of the bottles — from everything in the house. So I ran from the bedroom into the living room where the rest of the family was. We thought it was finished and done but it was happening here also! It went on the next day and the next day. You would be in the kitchen and something would come flying at you from the living room. It would happen mostly at night but sometimes during the day also. Time and time again, the big things usually happened after 2:00 a.m. The objects that would come flying at us would come from another room. The door would be closed to the living room, yet things would come in from the bathroom. And when we picked them up, they would be warm or hot.

Other times things would change location. We had this older television that was [contained] within a cabinet. We moved it to one of the bedrooms after buying a new television. We wanted to keep the old one because it was a nice piece of furniture. Well, one night when we went to bed we discovered that the old television was not in the bedroom. We couldn't find it anywhere in the house! We finally found it — outside in front of the house! How? You would need at least two very strong people to move it. We also used to find suitcases outside too, time and time again. I was so afraid that my passport would disappear and I might not be able to get back into Canada. You never knew what was going to go next.

We had a telephone gone for days. And then one day it was back again just like that. It was so frightening. You would feel like you were losing your mind, asking, "Is this real? What is all of this?" And always the anxiety of what would come next. So far, it had been mostly little things that would fly and hit you smack in the back of the head or something, but never strong enough to hurt you. But then you think, what if a big picture or a whole cabinet comes crashing on you?

Author: So prior to this visit you had heard over the phone and the mail that strange things had been going on for some time.

Elsbeth: Oh, yes. My sister told me that once when they had all been over to our mother's for Sunday dinner, objects from her house appeared. My sister owned these African figurines, beautiful carvings. When they finished dinner and got up to clear the table, right beside her chair were four of the big carvings. How did they come to be in our mother's house, practically at her feet?

Author: Spontaneous teleportation.

Elsbeth: I remember on my next visit [to Spain] I was in the taxi with my sister, Marguerite. We were heading for home from the airport. All of my suitcases were in the boot of the taxi. I put the keys to my house in Canada inside my suitcase. While in the taxi, I said to my sister that I had brought the keys to the house with me in case my husband would be unable to meet me at the airport in Canada. I was concerned that I would lose them. No sooner had I said that to her than the keys I had been talking about came flying forward from the back of the cab, crashing into the front windshield in front of the driver. He was so startled, he shouted, "What is this?" He thought we had thrown the keys. We just sat there like mutes. He picked up the keys and demanded to know why we had thrown them and we denied having done so. I could see that they were the keys to my house that had been in the suitcase in the trunk of the taxi.

Author: You are very lucky. That could have caused an accident.

Elsbeth: It just went on and on. One time my sister from Palma de
            Mallorca came to see us at my mother's house. My mother,
            she was thrilled to have the family all together for dinner. So
            we were sitting around the dinner table just chatting about
            all kinds of things. My sister from Mallorca — she collected
            stamps — mentioned that she would like to go to downtown
            Barcelona to see if she could find three or four stamps she
            had been looking for. These were rare stamps so Barcelona
            was the perfect opportunity because it was such a large city
            with a wide variety of places in which to look for them. We
            all agreed that it was a good idea and we would go shopping
            with her. As we got up to collect the dinner plates and get
            the coffee, there were the exact stamps she wanted! Brand
            new! Well my sister thought she was going to have a heart
            attack. This was her first big exposure to this [poltergeist]
            stuff. She was shocked. She picked them up, examining
            them. She checked the dates and sure enough, they were the
            exact stamps she wanted.

Gary: I wonder if they disappeared from some place, as they were
            rare stamps.

Elsbeth: I know! But next came the money appearing out of nowhere.
            Not big quantities to make you a millionaire or anything
            [laughing] but enough to give you a fright. There were rolls of
            money appearing. We have this long corridor and would hear
            this noise and rolls of coins would be coming down the corri-
            dor. All brand new like they had just come from the bank. So
            we knew it wasn't a matter of used coins, trying to figure are
            these yours or mine? They were all freshly minted.

Author: Did something happen to precipitate the materialization of
            the coins?

Elsbeth: It may have been that Marguerite had been thinking about it
            but we never discussed these things. (Better to ignore it.) But

that wasn't the last time for the money. Late one night, maybe around one or two, we were playing poker. The hand was dealt and we picked up our cards. Well, we fanned them open to look at our hands and there, in between the cards, were neatly folded bills. Like a twenty-dollar bill and again, all brand new. Another thing about the money was that the numbers on the bills were in perfect sequential order. Unbelievable!

This other time we were playing poker, we said, just as a game or test, let's wish for a full house or one of the top winning hands. Sure enough when the cards were dealt it was the hand the person had wished for. The next time, someone would wish for something else and they would get that, too. For the longest time everybody would get the hand they wished for. It was unbelievable. My daughters had seen money behind the curtains, too. How the bills were being held there, we don't know.

Author: I know I'm never playing poker with you.

Elsbeth: Well, there were scary things, but there were playful things, too. Like another year I was visiting, my sister, her children, and myself, my other sister Marguerite, and her boyfriend decided to take this trip together [within Spain]. And when we got to the hotel my sister said it would be nice to play poker that evening. Everyone agreed, so we went to have dinner first and would play afterwards. Following dinner, we went to our separate rooms, and as soon as we got in we found a pack of new playing cards on the top of each bed. My sister and I both said, "Oh great. Cards," as we realized we had forgotten to bring some along with us on this trip. We would ask the hotel manager about the cards later but first we wanted to tell our other sisters about it. First we went to Marguerite's room, which was right next door. She said that she and her boyfriend had also found two packs of cards on their beds. We also discovered two more decks in the bathroom. These cards were new and unopened. They were fancy and ornate with gold embossing — all golden in colour. They must have been expensive as they were of such high quality. The manager knew nothing about the cards. They did not have a casino in this hotel, but these cards must have come from some place.

Author: Your poltergeist can be very helpful. Many poltergeists can be destructive and costly.

Elsbeth: That reminds me of this other incident. You know there was so much going on for so long, we never took the time to write these things down. Besides, we preferred not to think or talk about any of it. So, when I was over visiting one year, there were so many of us in the house that I had to share a bedroom with two of my sisters. We were in a large room with two beds. I shared a bed with my sister Marguerite and my older sister had the other bed all to herself. One night after we had gone to bed we had just begun to fall asleep when I noticed this strange sensation coming from under the mattress. My sister was lying close beside me and I thought maybe it was her, but she couldn't be moving under the mattress. I whispered to her, "What are you doing?" And she whispered back, "Nothing. Don't move!" Her voice was shaky and tense. She was dead scared.

Author: So it felt like movement underneath the mattress?

Elsbeth: Exactly. We were both holding our breath, lying very still, and in one moment, VROOM, the whole mattress was on the floor, with the two of us under it. That was the most scary, threatening thing that ever happened to me. It only happened that once. But if it can do that with that strength or force, what else [can it do]? Another time when I was sharing this bedroom, I had the bed to myself, and when I moved my hand touched something solid under the sheet. It was very cold and soft. I thought maybe an animal had gotten into the bed, so I jumped out of the bed and told my sister what was going on. I threw back the covers and there was a large black garbage bag full of [what turned out to be] water. Water! Who would think of doing such a thing? And there was no spillage, no drop of water anywhere on or around the bed. It was very heavy, so the two of us had to drag it to the bathtub and flop it in the tub and the water came gushing out.

Author: As you didn't notice it when you got into bed it must have materialized afterwards.

Elsbeth: Yes. There was just so much happening and this was the only time I had been there for a whole three weeks, but for my family, it continued all year long. It was overwhelming and exhausting. Things would happen while we were in church. Once while we were sitting at the back of a bus — whoosh — a shoe came flying at us from out of nowhere. These shoes would either hit you or stop dead and drop.

Author: What happened in the church?

Elsbeth: Once we could see the collection plate was coming our way and while we were deciding what to give, out from under the kneeling pads comes a few rolls of money [coins]. I think some people noticed but you don't believe your own eyes when these things happen.

Author: Does it continue through to this day?

Elsbeth: No. My mother died in 1989 and I was over in 1988. By that time it was happening less. The odd thing would happen. For example, one day Marguerite and my two daughters were at the table playing some game and I was over on the couch knitting. I stopped for just a minute and when I went back to my knitting the needles were gone. I looked everywhere, underneath and behind the cushions. One of my daughters looked over and shouted "Mom," and the knitting needles were in my hair [laughing]. Things still disappeared, too, like all these empty bottles we had stored away were just gone one day. My sister Marguerite thought maybe I took them. Of course I hadn't; what I am going to do with a bunch of bottles? But a few days later when someone opened up the bar, they were there again.

I think Marguerite realized she was the source of this thing. How could she not when she could see some of her thoughts become realized in material form? So she was pretty defensive. For her all this was especially disturbing. She also didn't want to give the impression that she was going nuts. I mean she was perfectly okay mentally. In fact, for three years after my mother's death, she just couldn't seem to get over it. She took it especially hard but none of these things happened at all during those three years.

Author: This defensiveness and becoming suspicious of each other is a common characteristic in families where such phenomena are occurring for understandable reasons. There is also a lot of confusion and apprehension, as you never know what's going to happen next. What do you think may have precipitated all of this? Is anyone in your family psychic? Do they use cards to tell fortunes or anything like that?

Elsbeth: No, we don't believe in that sort of thing. We're Catholics. They don't go in for any of that spiritualism or any stuff like that. We never had anything to do with it.

Author: Was there any one location where it happened the most, such as the house in Barcelona?

Elsbeth: No, it was wherever Marguerite was. It even happened at her place of work. Her boyfriend worked at the same place and he was very nervous that something big would happen there and they might both lose their jobs; you just never knew. But things did happen. One thing was very funny. My sister's boyfriend was also her boss at work. He had had a previous relationship with another woman who also still worked there. Marguerite believed that this other woman wanted to resume the relationship. One day they both met up in the bathroom, and my sister, who didn't like this woman, thought some negative things about her. Shortly after they had both returned to their work, the boss opened up his desk drawer only to find a pair of panties. He thought they belonged to my sister [and this was some kind of a joke] but when the other woman suddenly cried out that her panties were missing, they learned who actually owned them. She just suddenly realized that she wasn't wearing them [laughing] but how they got to the boss' drawer — it must have had something to do with Marguerite. That shows you how all these mental things like thoughts can be realized; the interaction between the mind and the physical world. Since that event, the boyfriend has been especially nervous about things happening at work that might get them fired. He is open to these things, but at work — no! A few other small things have happened, but not anything big that the bosses would notice. She is too scared for things to happen there.

Author: Has anything ever happened to you while you were home in Canada?

Elsbeth: No, never. I was so afraid of it starting up here. Even the flights home made me anxious because after you've been through all of that, you just never know what can happen next. I mean supposing the door flies open or something — you just never know.

Gary: We've been back twice since all of that. I was there in 1992 for the Olympics but nothing of this nature happened.

Elsbeth: It slowly stopped and just as well. The family couldn't take much more. There was so much of it, especially the first two to three years. For me, I was only around it a few weeks of the year, but for the family it was all year round. And these things happened a bit in the day but mostly at night, so they were afraid to go to bed because you never knew what was going to happen.

Author: Sure, like being tossed out of bed, mattress and all.

Elsbeth: At first, I didn't want to bring my girls with me. I didn't know how they would react. I didn't know if they would be shocked or frightened. So for the first two or three years, I went on my own. Then I brought them over with me. In a way, I needed someone apart from the family in Spain to see what was going on. My husband believed me, but still, it was so unbelievable.

Gary: So the girls saw the shoes — always the one shoe. It was almost as though the shoes were following them around. [Everyone laughs] They also found money when they were playing cards.

Elsbeth: Yes, and things appearing and disappearing. [Laughing] I'm glad they were there because it backs me up that these things were happening.

Author: Did anything ever happen involving sentimental pieces of jewelry?

Elsbeth: Jewelry, no. We had things like colognes and perfumes appear in the church. We were standing in the pew and when we went to sit down, there were four or five bottles of perfume on the bench. We recognized them from home. What were the people behind us thinking? We never talk about these things in the family. The subject just isn't brought up. But it makes you realize that there is more than just this material world. We have to be more opened minded and not just rely on our senses and mental reasoning.

Gary: [Addressing the author] Have you come across many poltergeist cases while doing this book?

Author: Oh yes, quite a few, but none of them as helpful as the one in this case can be. I've encountered cases where people have been slapped, bitten, and scratched, so not quite as innocuous as the one Elsbeth is referring to.

Elsbeth: We never had anything like that. We would often hear scratching noises. Even though we never saw any sign of mice, that was what we thought the noises were. It was just part of everything else that was going on, like lights and televisions turning themselves on and off. We considered stuff like that minor, not like things flying around hitting you. It's all so unreal, and yet it was happening, so you can't just dismiss it even though the rational part of your mind says no way.

Author: There are plenty of things we cannot explain away. The reply to the statement that there must be a rational explanation for this is, not always, and anyway, why must there be? Science doesn't have an understanding of everything, but it really bothers us when science can't provide us with a neat little explanation. I think it makes us feel less in control. We feel so powerful scientifically, on the brink of conquering death and controlling life, and then this thing happens and it's almost mocking us.

Elsbeth: It makes you wonder why these things are not happening more and spread out to more people.

Author: Well, we don't really know how often it does happen or to how many because people are afraid to talk about it, just like your family is.

Elsbeth: I wonder if the person who is the centre, they must know they are the source because if you're thinking something and shortly after it materializes, you have to think it had something to do with you.

Author: In most poltergeist cases the sources of the manifestations know it emanates from them but that is a hard realization to come to terms with. What does it mean? And, why me? In the seventies Mathew Manning was the source of a poltergeist and it was very difficult for both him and his family, but he went on to channel that energy into helping others, so it can help you evolve.

Elsbeth: But if Marguerite was the source of all that energy or what-ever it was, what was it all for? She hasn't become a healer and it hasn't radically changed her life.

Author: But did she allow it to change her life or did she focus her energy on denying it? You really have to examine it and look into yourself for the underlying meaning and purpose in it all. Explore the possible symbolic messages in the various manifestations. Why always the one shoe and why a bag of water in the bed?

Elsbeth: That's right. She was very frightened. I think she was also afraid that we thought she was doing it on purpose and in a fraudulent way. She was really touchy about it and defen-sive. She was also concerned that she was going mad or that we thought she was crazy. She didn't want anything to do with it so she blocked it all out.

Author: That's understandable, but in doing so, you also block out any chance to learn or evolve from it. Even her own broth-er, who is a psychologist, didn't want to talk about it.

Elsbeth: Yes, he would have considered this to be like magic even though he witnessed so much of it, but for me, it offered so many possibilities. It shows that there is so much out there, so much beyond our [limited] senses and reason.

Author: Did you have an open mind like this before you experienced all of this?

Elsbeth: No, no. I was very skeptical. Even now when I hear such things I think that there must be some [rational] explana-tion for it. But then I go back to what we experienced. We even went to see our parish priest about it once. We thought that maybe he could come and bless the house or something. He just sort of shrugged it off, telling us not to worry and that it wasn't the devil or anything like that. [Laughing] I don't know if he even believed us. Here is this

143

group of sisters coming to him [with this fantastic story]; he might have thought we were crazy. So we didn't get any help from the church.

(At this point, Elsbeth's husband relates a charming story about a former student who had an experience that could be considered one of Carl Yung's "meaningful coincidences.")

Gary: I remember this boy who had a teacher who had to be taken to hospital because of his appendix. The day following that this boy was in my class and he seemed very upset so I asked him what was wrong. He explained that the day before his teacher had to go to hospital, the two of them had had a very bad disagreement and the teacher was quite mean to him. So the boy went home and after making a voodoo-like doll of the teacher proceeded to stick pins in the stomach area. It was the very next day that this teacher had to be taken off to hospital, and the boy asked me if I thought he could have been responsible for it. I was trying not to laugh and said I didn't think so, but just to be safe, he had better not do anything like that again.

Author: Poor kid. At least it taught him a lesson I bet he never forgot even if it wasn't part of the curriculum. You mentioned something that happened to Marguerite in the nature of physical projection or biolocation?

Elsbeth: Yes, it was very strange. It happened in August and that month is very hot in Spain so everyone has a siesta. It was around three o'clock and we made the house dark. We also locked everything up tight. We have double locks on the doors and windows. My family didn't lock things up at night but during the day, yes. So, Marguerite went to bed, and because it was so hot, she just lay on top of the bed wearing just her bra and panties. My mother, a sister, and myself stayed in the living room talking. At around six-thirty the sun began to let up and my mother said we had better wake up Marguerite. She had been sleeping since three o'clock.

When my mother went to wake Marguerite, she was not in the bedroom. We checked all the other bedrooms but she was not to be found in any of those either. Then we began to search the rest of the house, including the balcony, but she had just vanished. Just as we asked, "Where could she be? She didn't say she was going out and we didn't hear her leave," the front door bell rang. My sister went off to answer the door. I could hear the double locks being unlatched and as she opened the door, there was Marguerite, wearing nothing but the underclothes she had gone to bed in. She looked ghastly. The expression on her face was like she had just come from some place where she saw something horrific. And her face was also distorted. My mother cried out, "Where have you been?" but Marguerite could barely talk. She came into the house and went directly to the bedroom. We were afraid she was having a heart attack or something because she looked so bad. She had rapid shallow breathing and kept repeating, "My legs, my legs." All she could tell us was that she had gone to bed and when she woke up was shocked to find herself on the street in her bra and panties.

Author: Very different from merely finding a television outside of the house. Was she cold?

Elsbeth: She was very pale and all the strength was drained from her. I don't know, maybe she had been dreaming she was outside, and then like the other things she relocated. How, though? We didn't hear her leave. All the doors where double locked. Her sandals remained in the hall where she had left them.

Author: And she never discussed it?

Elsbeth: No, she wouldn't. She was the closed type who always bottled things up and kept it all to herself. And as I said, the family never pursued these things either. All this stuff that I saw, though, it made me realize how marvellous the universe really is. It's like getting a glimpse beyond the everyday barriers we know. Even if we want to be open minded, we're so reluctant to take it all in. It doesn't frighten me, but I want to understand it. Like something that happened to my oldest sister, Cassandra. She is very religious — orthodox — and not open to any of this stuff at all. A traditionalist in that she believes in the devil and so, but not in the sense that she thinks the devil drops by to toss about bottle caps and shoes [laughing]. One Sunday during mass she looked up at the columns and pillars and and thought how dangerous it would be if one of them were to break off and come crashing down. A second later a piece of a pillar did break off, missing the priest by only a few inches. It was like a premonition or something. She had been going to this church for years and nothing like this ever happened before. That is the only personal experience she had but it was enough. So those are some of the things that happened to my family when I was there.

Author: I would like to thank you and your husband for granting this interview. I know you were reluctant to do so, but hopefully it will open others people's minds just like it did yours.

Postscript: The family that resides in Spain is no longer experiencing any poltergeist phenomena — at least that Elsbeth knows of.

Chapter Eleven
Dispatches From the Medical Front

In this chapter I have combined three separate but related stories in that all three persons work in some capacity of the medical field. I have also included several other related stories.

The first woman, who will be identified herewith as Jessica, has been registered nurse for twelve years. She had spent a good part of her career facing the unique challenges posed by the limited resources that accompany small community hospitals. When we speak of small here, we are referring to hospitals that are no larger than your average modest home. She is currently on a temporary leave of absence for personal reasons.

Author: I understand that you have possessed psychic abilities for your entire life. Do you recall the experiences you had?

Jessica: Yes. I was born in 1965. My grandfather passed away on Christmas Eve of 1963, so I obviously never had the opportunity to meet him. I am, however, his namesake and had always felt like I had missed out on something not having known him. Maybe even a bit cheated, I guess, but certainly that there was "something" missing in my life. I had of course seen pictures of him but not more than that in the way of getting to know who he was.

When I was twelve, every summer day when school was out I had this routine where I would ride my bike all the way down to this little beach, and then on the way home, I would stop at this confectionery stand and buy something cold to eat or drink. One day I stopped in a nearby park to have my snack. Like most kids, I had been taught never to talk to strangers, but on this day I met an elderly man who just seemed to come out of nowhere, you know? He was just suddenly there. I immediately got a sense of safety, nurturing, and caring from him. When we finished chatting, I felt oddly at peace with my grandfather and his passing. I also came away feeling as though we knew each other. Although we had obviously never met (being that he died before I was born), there was now a sense of love and peace between us.

Years later I related this experience to my mother, who is a very logical, rational person. At first she was frightened to hear that her young daughter had been talking to some strange man in the park. But after I gave her a physical description of the man, she recognized him and realized that the man I was describing to her was my grandfather. What really got her, though, was when I said that this man had an almost overwhelming odour of Wrigley's Spearmint chewing gum about him. That clinched it for my mother because I had no way of knowing that in order to quit smoking, my grandfather had taken to chewing this gum ceaselessly. Even his house smelled of it. I had of course seen pictures of my grandfather but I had never heard a thing about the gum.

Author: You were carrying on a conversation with him so you obviously didn't think something was amiss. Did he appear solid in form?

Jessica: In hindsight, I honestly couldn't say. I remember having no fear or hesitation. I was disappointed when the conversation ended… would have like to spend more time.

Author: You have had psi experiences throughout your life?

Jessica: Yes, but that is the one I consider most spectacular. There was another incident that stands out in my mind. I was working the night shift at a hospital along with a colleague and two RNs. This wing was L-shaped and there was no way you could get on or off the unit without passing the nurses' station. All of the patients on this unit were chronic care and none were ambulatory.

There was one patient in particular that all the staff were fond of. Her name was Bunny. She was completely paralyzed on one side. The upcoming weekend was to be her sixty-fifth wedding anniversary, so her son was going to take her and her husband out for a celebration. My partner and I told her that we would come in early tomorrow so we could do her hair, makeup, and whatever else she needed to be ready for the party. With that agreed, we resumed our work.

Later that night, the two RNs went on their coffee break, which left my partner and I alone on the unit. We had to get all the patients ready for bed, which involved positioning them in their beds so they would not develop bed sores. We had already finished getting Bunny down for the night, and I went off to use the washroom. On my way back I noticed that the light in Bunny's room was on. This was an over-the-bed hospital light with the attached pull chain, so there was no way she could have reached back and turned it on. I turned it off and returned to the nurses' station.

A short time later my partner got up to do rounds and discovered that the overhead light was once again turned on in Bunny's room. She asked me if I had turned it on, and I had of course had just recently turned it off and said no. We didn't really think much of it at the time and made our way down to Bunny's room together. This time, along with the light on we found a chair beside the bed! We just looked at each other, not knowing what to make of any of this. I noticed that Bunny was awake and asked her if she was okay, and she said, "Oh, I see the light. My husband's here! Everything is all right, dear." We thought she was just confused because she did suffer from episodes of disorientation. I explained to her that her husband was not here but that she would see him tomorrow when her son arrived to take her to the celebration. She just looked at me, almost chuckling, and said, "Okay, dear."

Author: As if she were humouring you?

Jessica: Exactly. I bent down so I could see the view from her vantage point. In that position, I noticed a streetlight in her field of vision, which I thought explained her comment about "seeing the light." I closed the blinds, moved the chair, and turned off the light again.

We returned to the nurses' station just as the two RNs were coming back from break. The phone rang and one of the nurses answered it. It was emerg. Little did we know that while this odd stuff was going in Bunny's room, her husband had been brought in by ambulance. He had been pronounced dead about fifteen minutes prior. Emerg wanted us to alert the day staff so they could prepare Bunny for when her son arrived. As I said, we were all very fond of Bunny so we decided to go down and break the news to her ourselves so we could be there for her if she needed us. When we got to her room, we discovered she had passed away.

Author: So she saw her husband at the same time that they were working on him in emerg even though she had know way of knowing that he had been brought in?

Jessica: Yes. We worked out the timeline and then just looked at each other in astonishment. We figured he had come to get her.

Author: If that's true, they were together on their anniversary after all. What about psychic impressions? Do you receive clear images about people, places, or events?

Jessica: Absolutely. One time my husband and I were on holiday in Savannah [Georgia] and we couldn't find a hotel room anywhere. We finally settled on this room and breakfast inn. We checked in and as soon as I stepped into the room, I turned to my husband and said that I could not stay in this place. He looked at me as if to say, "Oh, this [psychic] stuff again." He has gotten to accept it, though, so we left. The following day we found out that there had been murders in that house decades past.

Author: You indicated that you have psychometric abilities? [Psychometry is the ability to glean information about a person or event by touching a related object.]

Jessica: Awhile back, I was working in the emergency department in a very small town where everybody knows each other. The hospital was very small. Our ambulance service was actually St. John's, so they weren't formally trained paramedics or the like. I was taking incoming calls as well as dispatch. I took a call from a gentleman who was reporting a major accident. I dispatched an ambulance and shortly thereafter received a call from the OPP requesting a second one, only this one was to be for bodies, not casualties. The doctor had arrived by this time and he instructed me to go with the second ambulance.

When we arrived at the scene, we found that the accident involved two, two-ton trucks. One truck with two brothers in it had pulled out to pass a transport, but it was extremely foggy and they hit the other two-ton truck head on. Sitting in the front of the truck that had been hit were a mother, father, a seven-year-old boy, and the family dog. Two other boys had been riding in the back, which was open like a pickup. None of these boys were over ten. Except for one survivor, everyone was dead at the scene — or at least as far as we knew. We directed our attention to the one survivor, preparing him for transport. There was a jacket near the victim, and thinking it was his, I picked it up and climbed into the ambulance with the patient. I was still holding this jacket when they started up the sirens preparing to leave the scene. Suddenly, I shouted at them to stop, stop! There is someone else here! They looked at me in confusion and denied that there could be anyone else at the scene. I was positive there was, all the while clutching this jacket. The police resumed their search, going out further this time. While one attendant stayed in the ambulance with the boy, I jumped out to help them search. Sure enough, there had been another boy in the back of the second truck. He had been thrown a distance away upon impact, but he was still alive.

Author: It's amazing how far you can be thrown in these accidents. You become like a human projectile. Did you say this was during the night?

Jessica: No. It was day but very dense with fog and was also in a secluded area where the surrounding foliage was high and overgrown. There were no houses around either, so I don't think this boy would have been found for days — if at all. The only clue I had to go on was this jacket that I now assume was his. The only thing I got from holding it was that we were missing someone. There was someone else here. After everything had calmed down a bit, one of the OPP officers whom I knew pretty well asked me how I could have known about the second victim. I couldn't explain. I held the jacket and just knew. Especially in a situation like that, it's not something you stop to question.

Author: Under emergency circumstances, you operate on instinct and training, almost like going on autopilot. That is not the time to analyze the probabilities and differentials involved in telepathy, psychometry, or even intuition.

Jessica: Exactly. There was another time — it would have been 1987 or '88 — when we had a fifteen-year-old girl brought in claiming to have been raped. I broke open the rape kit. It was procedure that the person who started the rape kit stayed with it until it was complete. Consequently, I was with her for some time and yet I got no impressions from her. I mean nothing. She identified the man who had allegedly done this to her. Because this was a small town, everyone knew him, and since he was not well liked, people would have no trouble believing he could have committed such a crime. The OPP officer whom I knew well brought him into the hospital and asked me for my impressions. (Through experiences he had long since come to trust me in these things.) I felt a bit awkward being in

152

this position, but nevertheless, I received an absolutely clear impression that this guy did not rape her and told the officer that. Shortly thereafter, the girl admitted that she had made the whole thing up. She was a frightened young girl who had gotten herself into some trouble.

Author: That wasn't the first time the police have used psychics to get a clearer picture of the circumstances.

Jessica: Well even with the case where that woman drowned her children and claimed they had been abducted, as soon as I saw her being interviewed on TV, I said to my husband, "She did it," and I saw water around the children.

Author: This was the Susan Smith case?

Jessica: Yes, the one down south. I didn't see a lake or anything, but the children were dead and they were surrounded by water. I get definite impressions like that. The OPP officer I mentioned earlier came to the point that he completely trusted my impressions on these matters. He would ask me about certain cases. For instance, they had a situation in which there was a man held up in his house. It was in an isolated location. They had heard a gunshot from within the house. They requested an ambulance and also asked me to accompany it in hopes of tuning into the situation in the house. They wanted everyone to stay in or behind their vehicles, but I explained to the OPP officer that I needed to walk around the house to gain a sense of it all. He allowed me to do this, coming with me, of course. Shortly thereafter, I told this cop that it was safe for them to enter the house; the armed man was no threat to them. He asked if the man was dead, to which I replied, no, but that there was something seriously wrong with him and added that there was no one else on the premises. Upon entering, they discovered that the man had tried to commit suicide but had placed the gun on the wrong angle and only succeeded in taking off his face. It had cauterized so he had not bled to death.

Author: The poor man. Did he die?

Jessica: I'm sure he's gone by now; the last I heard of him, he was in a psychiatric hospital up north.

Author: I've heard quite a bit about that place. [Name of hospital withheld by request of administration.] It was a very active haunted location.

Jessica: No kidding. It was my first job as a nurse. I was twenty years old. I would be there on a six-month contract and when the contract ran out, if they liked your work, they offered you a permanent position. It was all I could do to stick it out for the entire six months. I turned down the position when they offered it to me. The worst night of my life was the time I was there on the day shift. There was a horrendous snowstorm. This hospital is up on a steep hill that immediately iced up badly during these storms. There wasn't anything they could do about it. So naturally, we began getting calls from the next shift saying that they couldn't make it in. The day staff was going to have to stay on for the evening shift.

It was such a huge facility that some of the wards were not in active use. It was decided that cots would be set up in some of these wards so the staff could take turns sleeping. I knew immediately that there was no way I was laying my head down and sleeping anywhere in this place. It was simply one of the worst places I had ever been in. Even the land it occupied felt negative. At one point, I was asked to go to a particular room to get some IV poles. I took the keys and found my way to the room. As soon as I inserted the key into the lock, I got a chill and felt repulsed. I could not enter this room. I later found out that this was the room that had previously been used to administer shock treatments. Those poor patients would have been terrified. Psychiatric history is terrible. And this place was one of the worst. It was the only time I never looked upon my abilities as a gift or whatever. I could never believe that the patients could ever become well in such a place.

Postscript: At the time of this interview, Jessica was anxiously awaiting the arrival of her baby and an interesting event occurred while she was being interviewed that had never happened before. During the play-back of her interview, there was a background sound, which, upon further investigation, appeared to be the sound of a fetal heartbeat like one would expect to hear during an ultrasound examination. Of course no such examination was taking place; in fact the room was absolutely quiet. Whatever this anomaly may or may not be, I suspect, judging from the sound of a healthy heartbeat, which was listened to by a neonatal technician, Jessica will be having a very healthy baby.

After my interview with Jessica, I came across a psychiatrist who did part of his residency at this same facility. He has some experiences to share as well but wishes to remain anonymous, as he is still in practice in southwestern Ontario. He is yet another one of those who would never have entertained thoughts about this "spook stuff" as he jokingly refers to it. That was until his time at this hospital.

Author: This huge structure reminds me a bit of the Overlook Hotel in Stephen King's book *The Shining*. Did you read the book or see the movie?

Dr. M.:   Read the book [nodding and smiling]. I'm not sure if this place would quite fit into King's genre though. I have been to places that are gloomier and that have also had a reputation for unusual occurrences. Still, odd things did happen during the day, but it was mostly in the evening. Probably because it wasn't as hectic at night, so without the distractions of the day programs, you just noticed more things at night.

It was often interesting coming in some mornings and being told to check out the charts. It is hospital procedure that if an unusual occurrence takes place, it has to be written up. We would always rationalize it of course, putting down to some prankster patient, but really, we knew something else was going on. It was also problematic because we had patients who were psychotic, so when they complained of hearing voices [in the context of detailed conversation] or closet doors slamming shut, we didn't know if it was these strange phenomena or the patient hallucinating. With that said though, the events that the patients expressed concerns over were atypical of psychotic features. Also, we had patients complain who were not presenting with psychotic features. In fact, they had no history of psychosis and were not on any medications that could result in hallucinatory experience.

Author: What were some of their concerns?

Dr. M.:   Well, their sleep would be disturbed in the night by what they believed to be staff or patients talking near the bedrooms. The voices were not directed at the patients, nor did the patients express that it was they who were being talked about as would be typical with paranoid psychosis. They were just complaining that late-night conversations were disturbing their sleep. Of course when one or two of them would venture out of their rooms to complain or ask that they take the conversation elsewhere, there was nobody to be found near their rooms.

Mind you, there were many patients who were reluctant to come forth with their experiences out of fear that they would be evaluated as decompensating or, simply, declining in metal status, which is a reasonable concern. They did not want to be perceived as getting worse in case they were put on stronger meds or have a course of ECT ordered for them. In sessions, patients would reluctantly mention these events to me. Mind you, it wasn't a regular occurrence. I knew that the night staff did not hang about the patients' bedroom doors conversing, so I just did my best to assure the patients that in an old place like this, sound carried through the vents and such.

Bathroom and closet doors were harder to explain. The bathroom lights would often be turned on and the lights would get into the nearby bedrooms. A patient would get up to turn the light off and shortly thereafter, it would come back on. There were also numerous reports of taps being

156

turned on. The plumbers could find no cause for this. Things like that would often be complained about during morning rounds. That and the slamming of doors as well. It could be quite disruptive to the unit because people would become suspicious of each other.

Author: Do you think it contributed to destabilizing some patients?

Dr. M.:   I don't know if I could say that definitively. It was a bit of a gloomy place for some. I can see why the nurse you interviewed might have concerns about patients having difficulty becoming well in such an environment but I think that's true in most of these facilities, given the circumstances. I did dread having to be the one on call there though [laughing], but then again, you never like to be the one on call.

Author: Did you ever experience anything yourself?

Dr. M.:   Only once and it wasn't much, really. In fact, I heard about this sort of thing happening before. I had to come in to see two separate patients and was just making some quick notes in their charts. From down in the other end of the corridor, I heard footsteps, but a particular kind. They sounded like they were made by those old white nurses' shoes — the ones that had that distinctive squeak to them. The steps were slow and purposeful, like it was a nurse making her night rounds. In fact, at first I thought it was just that and simply continued on with my notes. Then it occurred to me that it was too early for the bed check and both night shift staff were with me at the nurses' station. I looked over at them to see if they were hearing this only to be met by their wide-eyed gazes, obviously wondering if I was hearing it too! I just chuckled and said, "Well, well. I've finally heard the infamous phantom footsteps. And all this time I thought you night staffers were just adding a little something extra to your coffee." Several other people heard these footsteps. They never did make it down as far as the nurses' station; they would stop several metres away outside of what is now a linen room. But as I said, they were quite deliberate. Step, step, step, step, stop for a few seconds and resume until they reached the linen room when they would just stop all together.

Author: Do you think it was a former nurse?

Dr. M.:   Who knows? Stories start to get around and before you know it, it's evolved into an urban legend. The story behind this one, which people swear to, is that it is a nurse. She was getting close to retirement after having devoted her entire life to nursing. She was put on permanent night shift out of concern that her skills were deteriorating and perhaps the less hectic pace of the night shift might be better for her. She had in fact been slipping up, like making errors in meds and so on. She was no dummy and suspected why she had been changed over to the night shift.

Anyway, that backfired because sometimes the night shift can be crazier than a well-structured day shift with a lot of support staff about. A patient suicided. It was this nurse that found her. She was only an eighteen-year-old girl. This nurse felt responsible, though, and was constantly reproaching herself with a barrage of "what if" scenarios. She retired shortly after that, though she wasn't required to do so. It's sad, really, because nursing was her life, so when she retired from that, especially ending it with that unnecessarily on her conscience, she just sort of retired from life. Suicides happen. You certainly don't merely shrug them off but you can't take it personally and internalize it, either, especially in this line of work.

Author: Sounds like she still sort of keeps a watch over things, though, if it's her. Theoretically, it is those who die by suicide or murder that most often become trapped. Are you aware of any reports of hauntings that maybe related to a suicide?

Dr. M.:   No. This is an old place. Patients and staff have died of numerous causes, and yes, suicide is a factor in some of those, but if everyone associated with this hospital, or any hospital, for that matter, who died under difficult circumstances came back, I'm afraid our hospitals would be overrun with ghosts.

Author: The nurse I spoke to mentioned negative impressions she received from a storage room that had been previously used to perform lobotomies.

Dr. M.: That wouldn't surprise me. I'm not sure which room she is referring to, though. We do have rooms where staff will come back frustrated that they couldn't get their keys to unlock a storage room. Once when I went down to try my key, it not only unlocked that door, but all the locks in the doors along the hall simultaneously clicked, too. The one I was trying to enter was formerly used for lobotomies.

The lobotomy era is scarier than any ghost story you could ever uncover. An American neurologist became its biggest cheerleader. He even took it on the road to demonstrate the procedure, as bizarre as that is. His name was Walter Freeman, and a neurosurgeon joined ranks with him. The neurosurgeon eventually broke away from Freeman, wanting nothing to do with him or his "procedure." Freeman was innovative in that he found a quick, efficient means to do this which would not only require only a bit of local anesthesia — if you so desired — but the "patient" would not even require a stay in hospital. Sort of a precursor to outpatient day surgery. I'm being sarcastic here, but this was not a shining time in the history of treatment of the mentally ill.

Basically what he did was replace a surgical instrument that the Italians had been using with a common ice pick and small hammer. The ice pick was inserted up the nose, and with a tap of the hammer, the pick would break through tissue, skin, and the meninges. He would then give the ice pick a sharp twist-like motion that severed the prefrontal lobe. How's that for a horror story? It was so gruesome that psychiatrists, students, and surgeons he was demonstrating this "technique" for would often vomit or pass out. Some patients died, and considering the state others were left in, the ones who died may have been the lucky ones. To make it all the more criminal, not one patient ever even benefited from this ice pick lobotomy. I guess if there was ever a reason to hang around and haunt a place or person, having that done to you would be better than most reasons.

Author: Do you think you had any of that at this hospital?

Dr. M.: Not that I'm aware of. I've heard the odd ghost story like the one I related earlier, but no one in particular has been identified. Even that nurse story is speculation. Like I said, we tried to rationalize most of what happened, but there were things that we just couldn't explain. Like a trolley being moved. In the long-term care, they used to take the p.m. meds around on a little trolley. The nurse would leave it just outside the room of the patient while she took the meds into the room. I was told by two nurses on more than one occasion that not only had the trolley been moved when they came out of the patient's bedroom, it had been stationed outside the bedroom where the next medication was to be dispensed, maybe three rooms down and on the opposite side of the hall. Needless to say, the first time this happened it was quite alarming. It was assumed a confused patient had been at the med tray. Rounds were suspended and a thorough drug inventory was taken of the trolley. Not one pill was missing or even out of place.

Author: That's a heart stopper, though. You might start to question your own sanity or memory.

Dr. M.: Yes, it was the one event that I think concerned people the most. It certainly concerned the nurse who had med duties. The other stuff I heard of was innocuous. The room that had been the morgue is now a storage room. It is kept locked, of course. A maintenance assistant would complain that his key would not unlock the door, so a supervisor would go down and find the door wide open. Because these events took place more than once and to more than one individual, a single person would not be blamed for something like leaving a door open. I guess it's true that there's safety in numbers.

Author: I interviewed a psychiatrist regarding the fear that if you experience such things, you've got a bit of problem that might require psychiatric assessment. Having worked in a place with this kind of activity, what would your response to that fear be?

Dr. M.: I really don't know much about the entire subject, of the parapsychology, I mean, not psychiatry [laughing]. I do know that the people I worked with were what you would call level headed and not prone to what they used to call flights of fancy. I certainly believed them and there were things happening that did not conform to any natural or standard modes of physical phenomenon. Was it psychic phenomenological? I think so, but when that sort of activity is better understood from a scientific point, we won't even refer to it as the supernatural anymore. I certainly don't believe that those who have such extraordinary experiences are of necessity in need of a psychiatric assessment. People have all kinds of experiences and beliefs that are unique to them as individuals. That's what makes the tapestry of life so rich. Humans have always ascribed meaning to events as well. Those who are overly fearful or prejudicial of ideas or experiences unfamiliar might want to explore why they are so with a counsellor. On the other hand, I'm not saying that people who have experiences of this kind are not also suffering from depression or anxiety disorder with or without psychotic features. That doesn't diminish the validity or meaning of the experience, though. I know that even having had a brief brush with this sort of thing left me a hell of a lot more open minded than I was before. It does raise a lot of wondrous questions and possibilities.

Although the following events did not occur within a hospital, the woman who experienced them is a nurse currently employed as the ward clerk of a hospital in Ontario, Canada. Her name is Kathy and she is fifty years old and originally from the United States. I interviewed her for this book in June 2001. She is a very practical, self-assured woman, as one might expect a nurse to be. Even in matters of the paranormal she displays a practicality in that what happened, happened, and so what if people think you're a little off the wall or don't believe you. What matters is what it means to you.

Kathy: The first thing that really made an impression on me was when I was about eight. We were in Washington, D.C. at the time, and I was crossing the street. I was going out between parked cars — just as I had been taught not to do — and, as I was about to come out from two cars, I reached my hand out and grabbed hold of one of these parked cars. This was back when the cars had those big tail fin rears so it was easy to get a good grip. For some reason, I would not let go of the back of this car. I was thinking, "Why am I standing here holding this car?" It wasn't as though I was caught on it or something. As I stood there, another car sped by, which really shook me up.

Author: If you had of let go, you would have stepped out into the path of a speeding car. You would have been killed.

Kathy: No doubt about that. As it was, the car couldn't have missed my foot by more than a couple of inches. It was years before I mentioned it to anyone. My grandmother said it served me right because I should have known better than to do that.

            The next I recall happening was when I was nine. We moved into a house just south of Baltimore [Maryland, U.S.A.]. This was back in 1960. It was a new house, so we were the only ones to have ever lived in it. From the day we moved into that place, I was uncomfortable. The house didn't bother my parents or brother and they just dismissed my concerns, you know, like an overactive imagination. I argued that they were wrong and that there was something in this house. I wouldn't leave my bedroom at night. If I had to go to the bathroom in the night, I would run there and then run right back to my room again. I couldn't put my finger on what it was.

When I was about fourteen or fifteen, my parents were out and my brother and I were outside. I came into the house for something. We had a basement that had exactly thirteen old wooden steps. They creaked. When you're that age you sneak out, so you have to know those kinds of things, including every part of the house that creaked. Anyway, I was in the house when I heard these footsteps coming up the cellar steps: one creak, two creak, three creak; I counted six in all before I called out, "Who's there?" At that, they stopped. But a few seconds later, they resumed: seven creak, eight creak, nine creak, and again I called, "Who's there?" Like the last time, the footsteps stopped for a few seconds and than started again. I knew there were only thirteen steps so by the time the footsteps reached twelve, I was out of there! I ran to tell my brother and friends that someone was in the house. We all went in and waited for someone to come out but no one did. When my parents returned, I told them what happened, but a thorough search of the house turned up nothing.

Author: You must have been getting chills as those footsteps got closer.

Kathy: You bet. It's funny that no one else in the house felt this. I could discuss these things with my mother. She was pretty down to earth but believed in the afterlife so she accepted such things. Some things you can attribute to an overactive imagination of a child, but not everything, and you don't simply outgrow it either.

For instance, back in the mid-seventies, I had been away from home to college and was married. Basically, I was feeling like I had outgrown all of that spooky stuff. Then I went home [to Baltimore] for a visit.

It was around two in the morning. My dad and brother were out and my mom had gone to bed. I was sitting in the kitchen having a snack. My mom is the type that when she goes to bed she is out for the night, a really sound sleeper. So I thought it odd when I heard this noise coming from down the hall. There is a bathroom a little ways down from her bedroom. I heard her bedroom door open followed by the sounds of her feet shuffling down the hallway toward the bathroom. It was very distinct. I could tell she had slippers on and even heard the floorboards creak. When she closed the bathroom door, it gave off this little ping noise that the latch on the lock always makes. Time passed and I didn't hear any other noises from the bathroom. I started getting that creepy feeling again, just as I experienced when I lived here as a kid. I started to remember some of the things that happened here and finally, I got up and went down the hall to see if my mom was okay. I called out to her but there was no answer. I knocked on the bathroom door and cracked it open; the lights were on but there was no one in there. I went down the hall to my mother's bedroom, opened the door and asked Mom if she had just been up to go to the bathroom. She said no and told me to let her go back to sleep. You can attribute some things to a house settling, but not something like that!

My dad died in 1999. I returned to the family home about three times after that to help take care of things and make various arrangements. The third time I was there, I slept in the living room on a sofa bed. My brother was home but working nights. I thought that there was no way I wanted to be alone in this house by myself at night. All I had with me was my brother's big goofy dog, named Gizmo. I had to laugh at the thought of Gizmo as my watchdog protector. After my brother left for work, I left all the lights on while feeling silly but strange. We had a fan on — Maryland is unbearably hot in the summer — and I went to sleep on the sofa. I heard voices whispering. I couldn't make out what they were saying. I thought it might be the fan so I got up to turn it off then went back to the sofa bed. Shortly thereafter, the whispering started up again. As soon as I got up, it would stop. I considered that it might be the angle I was lying on. Having a background in nursing and psychology, you look for all kinds of rational explanations, but nothing could explain these voices. They sounded like voices coming from a distant radio. That brought to mind the memory of my mom turning on the radio first thing when she got up in the morning. This happened two nights in a row.

One night when my brother and I were out for a drink, I told him about my experiences in the house and how I felt there. He said that although he had never felt any of that, the other night he had fallen asleep in the recliner and woke up when he heard the sound of voices whispering — just as I had heard. He suggested that maybe Mom was trying to get in touch with us. I tended to agree with that because at that time, I was looking around the house for Mom's wedding band. She never used to wear it; she just kept in one of her jewelry boxes. The morning after my brother and I had discussed the voices, I got the urge to have another look in the jewelry box where I knew she had kept the ring. We were going to sell the house and it was important for me to find the ring. This time I peeled back the cardboard cover overlaying the ring compartment. It came away easily as this was an old, well-worn kind of box. When I lifted the covering away, there was the ring. I was so happy and relieved. After finding the ring, neither my brother nor me heard the voices again, so we figured this confirmed our suspicions that it had been Mom trying to tell us something.

Another odd thing that happened to me was when I was in the West Nottingham Academy. I was fifteen at the time and I was there for a year. This is the second-oldest boarding school in the United States, dating back to 1744. It's in Maryland [Colora] and is an Irish Presbyterian school so there is a heavy Celtic feel and appearance to the place. Our dorm was an old frame house and there was a church with some very old gravestones facing our dorm. Our beds were on the second floor. I woke up one night and my eyes were drawn to this odd shape at the far end of the room. It was cloudy or misty but it had enough definition that I could make out a head and shoulders, about the height of an adult. It didn't change shape, but within it, it was watery, fluid-like, and that was altering (like water in gasoline). It wasn't frightening and didn't move any closer. All I could do was stare at it. I thought to myself that this couldn't be happening, so I closed my eyes, but when I reopened them, it was still there.

That reminds of something that happened to my best friend. She lives in Scotland now but at time of this incident, she was living in Cambridge [Ontario]. One afternoon, she was taking a nap on the living room sofa. She dreamt that her grandfather woke her up and complained that his feet were cold. She told him to take her slippers that were by the side of the sofa. He put them on and headed down the hall in them before stopping halfway, kicking them off and saying that they were no good because they didn't fit him. When she woke up, for real this time, her slippers were not by the sofa where she had left them; rather, they were halfway down the hall, precisely where her grandfather had kicked them off.

Author: Had you ever considered bringing someone in and doing an investigation of the Baltimore house?

Kathy: No, I never felt the need. I just accepted what was happening. My grandmother on my father's side was like that. She encountered the same sort of thing when she was living in Louisiana. It was just one of those facts of life that you learn to live with. It wasn't discussed a lot in our family but it was accepted.

Author: It sounds like this is almost a familial trait.

Kathy: Oh yes, and like I said, it wasn't discussed a lot, but it wasn't denied, either. Sometimes some of the things that happened would be put down to my imagination, but not in a ridiculing manner, like "don't be so stupid."

Author: Has anything happened to you since you moved to Canada?

Kathy: Not particularly. Ironically, when I'm on the look out for it, nothing happens. Still, I've always been open. I think a lot more people believe in it than are willing to admit. They're afraid that if they share their own experiences or beliefs, they'll be laughed at or thought of as crazy. That reaction has never worried me. If people want to call me crazy, fine; I've been called worse. As far as I'm concerned the entire subject is fascinating. For instance, just before my mom died, my dad called to say I should be prepared to come down in a moment's notice.

That day while my husband and I were driving to Hamilton, I said to him that my mom was going to die on one of the upcoming birthdays. (There were three birthdays coming up in September, including those of my two daughters.) Sure enough, the following weekend my dad called to say he had booked a flight for me and I had better get down right away. I saw my mom that Sunday morning. She died the following Monday, the birthday of one of my daughters. I felt she would pass away on someone's birthday so that the anniversary of her death would be a happy time with a celebration to distract people.

The oddest thing about my mom's passing, though, involved these little wallets and change purses she used to collect. After she died, my dad gave some of them to me as a keepsake, and I in turn gave a couple of them to my daughters. At this time in our lives, both my husband and I were still in university, and although I was working as well, we were pretty strapped for money. When I was looking at the change purses one day, I casually thought how nice it would be if I were to find a twenty-dollar bill in one of them. I opened one up and there was a twenty-dollar bill! It immediately reminded me of this story my mom told me about this really poor family that owned a certain teapot. Whenever the family was truly in need, they would find a bit of money in it. When times weren't so tough, it would remain empty.

Author: Did you think the money was from your mother?

Kathy: Possibly. It happened more than once, probably seven or eight times, and only when we were truly strapped for money. The first few times, I found the money in little pockets of those wallets. I figured that I must have somehow missed a pocket when I went through it. I mentioned it to my kids, suggesting that it may be from Grandma. They thought it was cool. They weren't frightened or anything. They just accepted it. Then one time when I was over at my mother-in-law's, one of my daughters called to say that she and her sister had been going through one of the change purses and found thirty-five dollars. This particular purse only had two pockets in it so there was no way I could have missed anything in it. Also, the money was folded the way my mom had always folded her money when she tucked it away.

Author: And it was always in American currency?

Kathy: Always.

Author: That makes sense, as your mother was an American. Throughout your nursing career, have you encountered any inexplicable incidents?

Kathy: Not a lot, really. There was one patient who was terrified of going to sleep. It turns out that in her family, whenever anyone was ill, if they dreamt of her mother, they would die soon after. I tried to calm her fears by explaining that maybe it was just the mother guiding people as a comfort. I also recall an elderly patient; she was 108 when I stared to work there. She was blind and bedridden. At the time of this event, her body was failing and we knew she wouldn't live much longer. I was working the three-to-eleven shift and one night on rounds, I asked her how she was doing. She said, "They're all over there in the light," pointing to the corner of the room. There was no light; the room was dark except for a bit of light coming in from the hallway. I asked her who was all over where. When I checked on her awhile later, I asked if "they" were still present. She said yes, they were all still there in the light. I told the other nurses about it and that I thought she would die very soon. I was off the next evening, which is when she passed away. She was 110 years old.

Dispatches From the Medical Front

The following interview was done with a woman who works in the housekeeping department of the same hospital as the interviewee in the previous segment. She came forward reluctantly after some friendly coaxing from a fellow staff member, for which I am grateful. She does, however, wish to remain anonymous. The wing of the hospital she is referring to is no longer used as a facility for patients. It is now used for administration and business operations. It has three levels. The third level is mainly used for storage. The second level is the one that houses the boardroom and the office of the CEO and other administrators. The ground floor is the location of the human resource centre and computer services. For the purposes of this book, we shall call it the Libra Building.

Author: For how long have you been employed at this hospital?

Cindy: For twenty-six years now.

Author: And the paranormal activity seems localized in the Libra Building of the hospital?

Cindy: Whatever it is, yes. I have worked on these units for the past five years now. It was during my first three years that most of the activity took place. It's been much quieter in the past two years. It mostly started out in the one staircase. The door has a lot of glass in it and you would see a shadowy figure move by it. At first I thought it was in my mind and I would go and see if there was a bat flying around or something. I was on a coffee break with two other people on the unit one night when one of them suddenly asked, "Did you see that?" I said, "What are you talking about?" She replied, "Out on the staircase! What is it?" I sort laughed and said, "Oh, you do not see anything." She insisted she did as if saying, how could you not see it, it's right there! The only thing I could say was that I had no idea what the [shadowy figure] movement was. The fellow we were with couldn't see it from where he was sitting, but when he got up to go to the washroom he swore he saw it too. I thought they were both joking, but they insisted that they were very serious. The thing is, I never mentioned the stuff that was going on to either of

169

these two people, but when they saw it too, I realized it wasn't my eyes or imagination. There really was something happening on these units.

So for three years, there was a lot of activity. It would call my name but it sounded as though it was right in my ear.

Author: Male or female?

Cindy: I just couldn't tell.

Author: Did you say you worked the night shift?

Cindy: Yes, three to eleven. I don't know if anything happens during the day or not. One night when I was in the boardroom on unit two, I saw these small flashes of light darting around. I thought it was might be specks of dust flying around. That still happens to this day. Six months ago I saw this television program where they had gone into investigate a house that was supposed to be haunted. They had these video cameras running and when they played the tape, there were these same flashes of light on the tape, just like the ones I see in the boardroom! They look a bit like falling stars, only tiny. The investigator said that this was a sign of activity. [Laughing] That scared me so I turned the television off.

I would also feel [something] touching me on the left shoulder. It's funny because these things always seem to happen when I'm not thinking about it at all, you know, really preoccupied with something else. If I go up to the unit wondering if something might happen, nothing does. So it seems to happen when I least expect it.

Author: Maybe it's feeling unnoticed and this is its way of getting your attention. Almost like saying, "Hey, you're ignoring me."

Cindy: I guess so. There is one place in particular where I will feel the tap on my shoulder or hear my name being called. It's in front of the human resource office across from the men's washroom. For some reason, that one part of the hallway is very active. The staircase with the shadows is way down the hall from this office, by the elevator. I haven't had anything happen in that stairwell for a couple of years now.

You're probably going to think I'm crazy when I tell you this but one night when I went into the unit, it was really a mess. I had to vacuum almost every square inch of the place. I was really mad about it. So there I am, angry, in a bad mood, and vacuuming away when I hear someone laugh. Like they were laughing at me. So I said out loud, "What the hell are you laughing at? You're dead!" Since that day, I have not had any experiences in that stairwell. I don't tell everyone that story, but I am getting better at not caring about what people think. For the first few years, I wouldn't mention any of this stuff to anyone. It's funny that when I'm off on vacation or sick leave, no one else in my department will work on these units. You can verify that with my boss. So I suspect others have felt or seen things there too, but they don't want admit it.

Author: That's probably true because I've heard a lot of rumors about these units but you're the only one who responded to my request for interviews. Do you have any sense of who or what it may be?

Cindy: I would love to know and why are they here? I'm not afraid of it, but how does it know my name? Is it someone in my family or does everyone who passes on know our names?

Author: These units are offices and boardrooms now, but do you know what they used to be?

Cindy: When I first came here, the units were used for older adults (geriatrics) who were more or less waiting to die, especially unit one where the patients would be bedridden. The top floor is where the staff used to live or stay. I don't know if that's related to the haunting or not. I know that when I'm in the boardroom, I'll often here keys jingling from above [the third floor]. That's why I suspected that [the haunting] was a previous staff, as staff always carry keys.

In the past couple of years, another staff member and myself have noticed that pictures in the hallway will move. Now I've never seen them move but I have heard them. [The pictures to which she is referring are very large portraits and landscapes with very heavy, ornate frames.] It sounded like they were being rattled or shaken against the wall, but gently. This other staff member and myself were chatting once when we heard a sound coming from the human resource centre. It sounded as though someone were kicking an empty box! We both looked at each other and asked, "What was that?" When I went in the resource centre an hour later to clean, there was this big empty box. These things make me very curious. (On the other hand) I have some definite religious beliefs. I'm a Christian and believe in the bible, but my religion or what it's taught me to believe doesn't address any of this stuff. Where does it all fit in with my faith?

Author: Do you feel conflicted by it? Are you concerned it may be from a negative force?

Cindy: Sometimes I feel conflicted. I'm not afraid of it. I do believe in the devil and evil spirits. There is certainly evil in this world. I don't believe this (hospital haunting) is evil. (Judging from what's happened to me) I don't believe it's trying to hurt or scare me but I do become scared sometimes. Especially in the first few years when I started working on those units, there were some nights when I felt so uncomfortable, I would just leave and do the work the next day. But that is very seldom now.

Author: Have you ever tried communicating with it?

Cindy: Well, that one time when I was angry. The only other time was when I had become fearful on a regular basis. I simply said to it, "Look, I have to work. This is my job. I have to be here, so stop it." It stopped for that night and for a little while after that. Maybe that's part of the reason it has been so quiet in the past couple of years.

Author: Perhaps it was a staff member just keeping on eye on things.

Cindy: That's what I suspected because of that unmistakable sound of keys. I mentioned this to the CEO once. I asked him if he had been working late last night because I heard someone walking around upstairs on unit two where his office is located. He just smiled and jokingly said it must have been the ghost. There is a portrait not far from his office that moves much more than the others. And the door leading into this unit rattles too, like someone is trying to get in, but after office hours, this whole unit is locked.

There was one thing that happened to me that was disconcerting. It was only the one time. It was outside the human resource centre. This was a Friday night and I will never forget it. I was about to clean the men's bathroom when I suddenly began to smell flowers. It was overpowering, like being in a funeral home in the days when they used to have wall-to-wall flower arrangements. I looked everywhere for the source of this smell. I checked the garbages and everything to see if someone had thrown out flowers or something but didn't find a thing. It was so strong; there was no escaping it. It kind of upset me, so I finished my work as fast as I could and left. The smell remained for the entire time I was cleaning that night.

Author: The odour of flowers is often associated with spirit manifestations. The sense of smell is a powerful memory trigger so it's an effective tool for spirit communication. Things like flowers, perfume, and pipes, but a foul odour is associated with a malevolent spirit. Has any of the staff on this unit said anything to you about experiencing such things?

Cindy: Just jokingly. The staff in housekeeping that refuse to work on those units never joke about it. If I even mention that there is another position becoming available in the hospital that I'm thinking of transferring to, the first thing they say is that no way are they replacing me on those units. So to them, it's no joking matter.

Author: Have you ever experienced any cold spots on the units?

Cindy: Oh, yeah! Especially within the first three years. I remember discussing this with Dr. Palmer, the CEO. I see him every Tuesday night when he works late into the evening. I asked him if they turn the heat way down in the night, but he didn't know. Some nights I would get so cold, I would have to go into the main hall and put my hands on the radiator to warm up. It was a terrible, unnatural cold. I'm the type who is always hot, and in this work you're always on the go so this was really weird. Some nights, it was so cold that I could hardly work. My hands were practically frozen. I haven't experienced that in a long time, though.

Author: So it wasn't localized. Did this happen often?

Cindy: It happened maybe once every couple of weeks. I checked with someone from environmental services and he confirmed that they did turn the heat down at nine o'clock. As I'm off at ten-thirty, I find it hard to believe that the temperature can drop that fast, especially considering the building had been heated throughout the day.

Author: It sounds more like the heat had been turned completely off, which they wouldn't do.

Cindy: No. I remember asking Dr. Palmer if his office was cold when he came in in the morning. He said no and that the first thing he did when he got into the office was open the window because it was too warm.

Author: Have you ever had anything like cleaning supplies tampered with?

Cindy: No. My job is so routine that if something like were to happen, it would be really noticeable.

Author: Well at least it doesn't sound like a mischievous poltergeist.

Cindy: No. Mostly there is just a kind of anxiety, you know, like, what's going to happen next. I should mention something that has happened to me outside of the hospital. It was a long time before I ever got up the nerve to mention this to anyone. Anytime I've lost someone, they appear as if to say goodbye. They come to my right side and it's usually when I'm doing something mundane like the dishes. For instance, my mother-in-law passed away last June and three days later, while my son and I were watching television, I felt her there, looked over, and there she was. There was a wonderful feeling of peace. I knew she had just come to say a final farewell to my son and me. I looked over at my son and he didn't notice anything. When I do lose people now, I've almost come to expect them, and when they don't come, I wonder why. I also wonder how common this is.

Author: You would be surprised at how common an experience that is. It's thought to be odd because it's simply not discussed. I just heard a case yesterday where the family had taken the grandmother into the home because the grandfather had been put in hospital and she was too ill to be left on her own. She dozed off in a rocking chair in the living room after dinner one evening while the family was quietly sitting around watching television. The grandmother woke with a start and said, "Ben? What are you doing here? When did they let you out? ... Oh, I see." Ben was the name of her husband. The family just looked at each other in confusion. A few seconds later, the phone rang; it was the hospital calling to inform the family of Ben's passing. They were very worried about how to break the news to the grandmother, as she was sick and they didn't want to exacerbate her condition. The grandmother walked in on them in the kitchen later that night. They were discussing this in hushed voices. The grandmother said they didn't have to worry. She knew her Ben had died because he came to her just that night to say goodbye and to tell her that she would be joining him soon. She was peaceful with his passing as he had come to her and she trusted that she would be with him again. She died within six months of congestive heart failure, but thanks to that visit, real or not, her final months were not burdened with grief and depression.

Postscript: I spoke with the CEO and a couple of the administrative staff who have their offices on the second floor of the unit. Although none of them have had any personal experiences, they had heard the stories and were quite open minded to it, except for one who was a bit taken aback by it. His office is on the second floor and is the site of a fair bit of activity, though he has never been privy to any phenomena (nor does he necessarily want to be). Nevertheless, he was told that in the days when this part of the hospital was a geriatric unit, his office was used as a temporary morgue until such time as an attendant could come and retrieve the body. Other members of the housecleaning staff have confirmed the stories but have little contact with the unit and declined to be interviewed.

Ever Vigilant

It would be remiss of me if I were not to mention St. Michael's, one of Toronto, Ontario's oldest hospitals, which opened its doors back in 1892 and is run by the Sisters of St. Joseph. The story will no doubt be recognizable to most ghost aficionados. I gratefully acknowledge the rendition of this account from the Ontario Ghost and Haunting Research Society.

"Ward 7B offers an interesting tradition of Sister Vincenza. 'Vinnie,' as she is called by the staff, turns lights on and off and can be seen occasionally making her rounds. There is only a little problem with 'Vinnie': she has been dead since the 1950s.

"The most eerie part of this, combined with the poltergeist and apparition haunting, is that when people see Sister Vincenza, her nun's cowl is circling a black chasm where her face should be. Devoted to the end and apparently beyond, 'Vinnie' is a definite fixture of this hospital.

The following was sent to us [Ontario Ghosts] in October of 2000:

'I am acquainted with one of the staff at [this hospital] on the seventh floor. Very recently [the fall of 2000], the night nurse, while on rounds, came around a corner and almost stumbled right into a figure dressed in a black robe from head to toe, slowly walking down the hallway from her. Scared, she turned and ran back to the nurses' station. Not long after, a code blue (cardiac arrest) rang out from the area in which the apparition was heading.

'Needless to say, the nurses did rounds in pairs for the rest of the shift.'

In other notes, Sister Vincenza has also been known to give patients blankets, and in general, care for them. Perhaps her devotion to the sick and suffering lives on in her even after death. In all accounts, her appearances have been of a helpful nature, even if it is helping one pass out of our world."

In April 2002, my friend Anita had the unfortunate need to be in St. Michael's as a result of an injury to one of her children. The medical situation was successfully resolved. Anita and her son also had an encounter with none other than Sister Vinnie. It began with a ride up the elevator that happed to stop on the seventh floor. No sooner had the doors opened than her son asked in a frightened voice, "Mom, do you feel something weird?" Anita felt it too and knew about the seventh-floor ghost, but her son had no way of knowing that they had stopped on the seventh floor because the gurney was facing the back of the elevator. Her son even had goose bumps (or more accurately in this case, ghost bumps). After her son was back in her room, Anita decided to do some investigating. She began to ask staff about the ghost of St. Mike's.

The first thing she discovered is that the ghost is not in fact confined to the seventh floor but roams about freely throughout the hospital, presumably keeping an eye on things. (The Sisters had a well-earned reputation for being vigilant and conscientious.)

Anita then spoke to some of the staff. Although she did not meet anyone who had actually seen Sister Vinnie, they all reported feeling her presence from time to time. It's a feeling that can't be denied or mistaken, just as you would feel the presence of a flesh and blood individual near by you. The staff also reported to Anita that sometimes people coming out of surgery would see the image of a nun by their bedside while in recovery. When they ask the staff about the mysterious nun, the stuff just tell the patients that it was probably the medication they were on. Other patients have asked the staff about who the nun was they see walking around the hallways, and the staff offers up the same explanation (not wanting to frighten patients). Apparently, Sister Vinnie remains a calming and positive presence in the hospital to this day.

Night Visitors

In this final dispatch from the medical front, a doctor who was visiting Canada from Portadown, south of Belfast, Ireland shares this fascinating phenomenon. Her name is Shannon Logan. She is forty (give or take a year or two) and works in a very busy emergency ward. She has long, reddish brown hair and very intense eyes. She is the mother of two girls and three boys. One of her children was lost to the conflict in Ireland, a conflict for which she has no patience.

"Since I was a wee one, we were always hearing stories based on a lot of Celtic folklore but I never remember hearing about this poltergeist. Me and my sister shared a room and there were sure enough odd things happening like hairbrushes out on the window ledge and waking up in the mornin' to find all the dresser drawers open with most of clothes hanging halfway out the drawers. There were also nights when — not many, thank Christ — but there were nights when I'd be woken by my bed covers being violently yanked off of me. I'd start crying out, 'Mary! Mary!' which would bring my mother in, too, but they thought I was just pulling a prank. Trying to get attention, that type of thing.

"My mother was very open to the spiritual side of life and she always used to give me strange side glances like she knew these were not pranks. She told me I took after her sister Katherine who drowned when she was twenty-one. Her sister was always foretelling things to come and even knew of her own ends yet to come. We lived in an old two-storey stone house and when the wind was kicking up and blowing through all the cracks in the place, you could sure enough believe in the tales of the banshees.

"The oddest and most frightening thing to happen to me though was these scratches. I was to later learn it was a mark of a poltergeist manifestation. It only occurs when something extreme happens, and I am so overwhelmed, I can't get my mind around it to react. I just sort of grow cold and numb. It happened when my son was murdered, and the last time it happened was last spring when we had victims of a bomb blast brought in. 'Tis certain this was not the first time we've had bomb blast victims in our emergency room, but this was my birthday, my mother had died recently, and one of the young male victims reminded me so much of my son Michael. The strange thing about these scratches is that they just appear out of nowhere and they don't bleed! That is truly amazing because they are so deep and vicious looking.

"On this day, I had just come back from the bathroom, so if there had been anything like scratches on my legs, I would have noticed. I was at the nurses' station barking out orders in my usual calm, polite manner when I felt a burning sensation on my lower right thigh, just above the knee. The emergency room was crazier that than usual on this day and we were trying to get patients stable, and while trying to get x-ray down and ORs booked I didn't have a chance to take a look at my leg. As time went by, it was becoming more painful and any time my scrubs, which were just light cotton, brushed against my leg, it burned like hell. I finally ducked into a supply room, lowered my pants and almost let out a yelp when I saw six scratches, four up and two across swelling up on my leg. They were a crimson red. I've never had the likes of these before. I've had the odd scratch appear just out of nowhere, but these! They took forever to heal, and I even used an antibiotic cream to be on the safe side. Like I said, that was last spring and they did leave scars. I guess I tend to be a little on the high-strung side but I only get these scratches when I don't let out what I'm feeling or can't react at all. I have seen and heard about these poltergeist scratches but I'm by no means convinced that they are of a supernatural etiology. They could be a somatic reaction to an extreme psychological state. That in itself is pretty amazing."

There have been other forms of poltergeist "assault" including slaps and pinches that also leave marks. Fortunately, this type of poltergeist manifestation is very rare, and, as Dr. Logan suggested, it most commonly occurs in extreme cases of psychological stress due to pain, threat, or long-repressed emotions. As has already been touched upon in this book, this type of phenomena can occur in persons who are emotionally blunted or who have had their emotional maturity stunted, but it can also occur in cases where it is not safe to express an outward reaction or the individual is so overwhelmed that an emotional response is impossible to formulate.

Before leaving the medical front, there is another strange and terrifying condition that is quite familiar to those in psychiatry and sleep disorder clinics. It is called sleep paralysis and occurs naturally to each of us every night. If our brain did not induce this temporary state of paralysis, we would, in all likelihood, become engaged in acting out our dreams, causing us serious physical harm. Sometimes, however, the paralytic state lingers as we are emerging from dreams (REM sleep), and we become briefly aware that we are unable to move or speak.

These episodes are known by different names, including hypnogogic and hypnopompic experiences (these two words refer to the state we are in just prior to entering or emerging from sleep), isolated sleep paralysis, the evocative old hag's syndrome, and in more recent times, the entity, so called by those interested in the paranormal as opposed to neurology. It is so named because the experiences one has during these episodes are so intense and vivid that some believe a supernatural entity is responsible. The individual undergoing this experience can have lucid hallucinations, including hearing doors open and close, footsteps, voices, and an undeniable sense that there is a person in the room, usually a threatening figure, and the sleeping person is unable to wake up and to defend him- or herself, locked in the twilight state between waking and dreams. These episodes are also accompanied by very intense emotions like fear, anger, or deep sadness. Michael Duffy shares his frightening encounter with this "entity":

"I was sleeping and thought I had been woken up by an intruder. I think it was male but it was definitely malevolent. I was sleeping on my stomach when I felt the weight of this large figure place itself on me. I felt like I was suffocating and was struggling like mad to shake it off me and get out of the bed. When I did manage to shake it off, it would only impose itself on me again. I can't describe how hard it was to move or call out for help, but I was finally able to do so only to be drawn down under again. When I did wake up for real, I not only turned the light on but I bloody well left it on for the rest of the night! In the morning, I felt a little silly at the thought of a forty-two-year-old man sleeping with the light on, but believe me, during the night, I was feeling anything but silly. It's funny how you keep getting pulled back under again, but there's a really heavy lethargy associated with this. You no sooner get close to the surface, thinking you've got to move and wake up, than bang, you're back in the netherworld."

Another individual reported that she felt like an ancient vampire was sucking the blood out of her. When she managed to wake up with a scream, she was actually covered in a thin layer of perspiration as a result of the struggle to break through into waking consciousness. Her story is reminiscent of the stringes, Greek vampires who not only suck the blood of sleeping victims but bring nightmares with them as well. There is also the myth of the succubus, in which legend has a female spirit preying upon unsuspecting males for sexual favours. One can appreciate why these episodes were tagged old hag's syndrome. So real and frightening are these experiences that they, along with catatonic states, were thought to have inspired the stories of premature burial by the master of the macabre, Edgar Ellen Poe. In fact, Poe's narrative of being buried alive, unable to move or call out to those entombing you that you are not dead, is a very apt description of sleep paralysis night terrors.

Although the cause of these episodes remains a mystery, they do seem more prevalent in persons within certain groups of individuals. These include those who suffer from panic attacks, bipolar disorder, and generalized anxiety disorder, as well as those who have interrupted sleep cycles or have sleep deprivation. Another suspected culprit is the use of anti-anxiety medications or sleep aids such as Valium or Restroil.

The best advice if you are experiencing sleep paralysis is to establish good sleep hygiene (go to bed and get up at the same time every day), ensure your bedroom is conducive to restful sleep, avoid prolonged use of prescription sleep aids, reduce stress in your life, and get enough exercise. That increases blood and glucose to the brain, which maintains healthy functioning. Avoid exercising too close to bedtime, as your adrenaline levels may remain too elevated to fall asleep or to obtain a restful sleep. If the episodes become frequent or too disruptive, have a word with your doctor. You may have to examine the circumstances in your life that may be causing them. You and your doctor can decide how best to address the problem, which may include attending a sleep disorders lab. It is also a good idea to keep a diary account of the night paralysis nightmares. They may offer clues as to what is happening and why. Who knows, maybe it's not sleep paralysis at all; it could very well be a supernatural night visitor. Good night from the medical front, and pleasant dreams.

Chapter Twelve
Interview with a Psychiatrist

"NEVER utter these words: 'I do not know this, therefore
it is false.' One must STUDY to know,
KNOW to understand,
UNDERSTAND to judge."
— Anonymous

Throughout the course of writing this book, indeed for many years
whenever the subject of the paranormal was broached, I would hear
the common refrain: "I would never tell this to anyone else because
they'd think I was crazy." Ironically enough, those who had undergone
counselling never dropped a hint that they had had any such experiences, usually out of fear that the psychiatrist would put them on drugs
or lock them away. In some cases their concerns are probably legitimate, but in psychology and psychiatry, it is of paramount importance
to maintain an open mind; such open-mindedness is an indication of
an adroit therapist. Many counsellors are open to such possibilities. In
fact I myself have met a few. However, they did not want to be identified for fear their colleagues would consider them crazy (and no one
makes referrals to a crazy psychiatrist)!

One psychiatrist, Dr. Ronald Pond, did agree to an interview. He has
been practicing medicine for forty-five years, his first twenty as a family
practitioner. The remainder of his career was dedicated to psychiatry; he
had a private practice and was a staff psychiatrist at the Homewood
Health Care Centre in Guelph, Ontario, where he would later become

medical director and CEO. He is currently semi-retired, though busier than ever. He is an affable, warm, and compassionate man, the type who would have no difficulty in establishing what is termed empathetic resonance in therapeutic vernacular with his patients. Not only intelligent, he possesses a sagacious and inquisitive scientific mind with somewhat of a Gestalt/Fritz Pearls attitude in that Pearls believed that reality was the sum of all awareness. He also shares R.D. Laing's supposition that even so-called hallucinations have significant meaning in the life of a patient and can be utilized as a therapeutic tool to gain insight. As you will read, he was practising hypnosis when it was still thought of as on par with using tarot cards in your practice. Interestingly, his wife is a professional astrologer, which undoubtedly has helped him to remain open to the possibilities, as has his experiences with his patients throughout his many years of practice. I'm sure this chapter will be quite insightful and I do so hope it will help people to feel less crazy about their experiences and suggest an alternative view for those inclined to form such a conclusion. Perhaps this chapter of the book will help to put to rest this persistent "crazy" prejudice once and for all. If people spoke of these experiences more often, they would come to know how frequently they occur in the lives of so many.

Interview with Dr. Ronald Pond, M.D. (FRCP); Psychiatrist. November 6, 2000.

Author: What first sparked your interest in the paranormal?

Dr. Pond: I guess my interest first started when I learned about hypnosis during a demonstration by Milton Erikson to a group of family doctors in St. Catharines. I was in family practice myself at that time. Not many people were doing hypnosis at that time. In fact I couldn't really discuss it with too many of my colleagues and yet I found it to be a really useful tool in many ways. Pain relief, relaxation, minor surgery, and I even delivered some babies with hypnosis as the anaesthetic. Hypnosis led to other things, such as exploring memory recall from early life experiences.

I guess it was around the time I became interested in psychiatry that my wife developed an interest in astrology.

Through that [astrology] we met some people in Toronto who were interested in other areas of parapsychology, so we attended a couple of workshops just to get an overview of the subject. One of the people doing a presentation on past life regressions led me to a greater interest in things that don't fit into our "normal" or our average notions of reality. I started to explore "past lives" while people were in a hypnotic state, and they described events and experiences from other times and places. It was very real to them, and I certainly don't believe they were putting me on, so I became even more intrigued with the subject.

Author: How do you as a psychiatrist differentiate between pathological states like psychosis where hallucinations can be present and genuine manifestations of the paranormal? Are there techniques you employ?

Dr. Pond: I have the attitude that whatever people tell me, unless they're obviously lying to me, if that is what seems real to them, then that is the way it is. Whether it's a hallucination or their perception of the world around them, I've come to realize that we can all perceive the same event in different ways, so perception is reality as far as I'm concerned. If you allow people to talk freely about their experiences and guide them in exploring the possible meaning or significance of those events, then to them, they are describing the way in which they experience the world around them. Are there elements in those experiences that might suggest an intervention like medication may be required? That's where my diagnostic skills are applied. But oftentimes the experiences people share with me don't really fit the criteria for a psychotic illness. Those features are not present so you work with what they have presented you with and see where it leads.

Author: Do you find your approach is unique or rare in that people presenting with such experiences might automatically be placed on medications?

Interview with a Psychiatrist

Dr. Pond: Yes. I think there are very few people in the establishment who accept these paranormal types of experiences as being anything other than symptoms of a mental illness. I can't prove it one way or the other. I do know that I get better results if I don't automatically label everything as an illness.

Author: Have you found over the years that even if a patient's paranormal experience cannot be substantiated you can still incorporate those experiences into the therapeutic process?

Dr. Pond: Oh, sure. I definitely wouldn't try to deny it or tell them that their experiences are silly or that they didn't happen. I accept it and try to help them put it into a different perspective, if that's possible. Or maybe I just help them to come to terms with it. There are some things we don't understand that we just have to learn to accept.

Author: There has been some controversy around the recovered and repressed memory. We still do not understand the mechanism of memory and thus the debate over recovered and false memory. Do you differentiate between recovered memories, false memory syndrome, and memories of past lives?

Dr. Pond: Yes and no. With memories that are recalled in the therapeutic setting or in the process of helping patients to understand themselves, the significance doesn't rest with whether the event is real or not. It's their inner self trying to communicate something that could enhance their life today. Where it gets into difficulty is when a well-intentioned therapist decides that they have to undo this thing that happened years ago and perhaps even punish someone for this deed that was maybe just in a person's mind. Certainly when I talk to people about memories of past lifetimes, I make it very clear that I don't know if this is real or not. On the other hand, when people are in a deep trance and they express something, they certainly believe it. They're not putting me on, and if it is a tool that helps them look at things differently today, I don't really care if it's real or not.

Author: So one litmus test is whether it is helping and healing.

Dr. Pond: Right, whether it's something early in this life or something from another life, it can often be helpful.

Author: Have you found that after someone has been in therapy for awhile and is perhaps stuck at an impasse that a paranormal event can act as a catalyst, instigating a breakthrough?

Dr. Pond: Yes, and our ego, which defends us against painful things, sometimes needs an excuse to let go, and whether it's a paranormal event or a breakthrough memory or whatever, that's not what really counts. In large part, that's what therapy is all about. Maybe that's what life is all about. It's not all therapy; it very often happens outside of a therapeutic relationship.

Author: What do you think the scientific explanation, if any, is for this activity? Do you think there is an actual soul in us that lives on?

Dr. Pond: I believe there is some energy, whether we call it the "soul," or the "entity," or the "life source." We're really talking about the same thing; it's just a matter of semantics. There is something there. I can theorize about it but I can't prove anything; personally I do believe in its existence.

Author: What do you think about employing tools like Ouija boards and automatic writing in a therapeutic environment?

Dr. Pond: It depends on the circumstances and the individual and what they're comfortable with. I don't think there's anything wrong with employing these techniques. I'm aware that there are some who are afraid of things like Ouija boards because they have the notion that there is some pure evil energy out there that can reach you through things like Ouija boards. I don't share in that belief myself. Energies can be manipulated to do many things for reasons we may not be consciously aware of. I also think there are dark sides to everything. If we can use the word God, I think the dark sides and the bright sides are both parts of "all there is," which is one description of God.

Author: I think people have personal experience with that through meditation or acupuncture and the like. In psychiatry I'm sure you've seen countless episodes of depression over the years. Have you observed a growing interest in the paranormal as well as people experiencing an existential crisis as opposed to the standard depressions?

Dr. Pond: I don't know if there really is or not. I think that there are lots of people who are curious about many of these things but would never talk about them within the profession [psychiatry] and who are a little afraid to go outside of the establishment line of discussion. As to the increased incidence of depression, I think that that has probably led to more of an interest in brain chemistry and the scientific stuff, which is very important, because when you're depressed, your chemistry is out of balance. But the missing piece is why does it get out of balance and why at this point in time and why to you and not to me. I'm not sure there's been a lot more thought put into those questions recently than there was before.

Author: I had one psychiatrist comment to me recently that the emphasis on neurochemistry in psychiatry has caused it to lose touch with the patients and that psychiatry has lost a bit of its soul or humanity. Would you agree with that?

Dr. Pond: Yes, especially in Canada. I think it is even more so here than in some of the countries where the psychoanalytic and the psychodynamic developments are still a more integral part of the training programs, although even there it is changing. It is my experience that in Canada, the educational focus is largely on neurochemistry and biology. There is very little if any training in the psychotherapies or psychodynamic overview.

Author: So you don't feel like you're connecting with humans any-more?

Dr. Pond: Professionally, yes. There are a lot of other people outside of the medical establishment who have a very different take on things. For example, I love going to an astrology conference because the people there are much more open to just being people. One way I can describe it is that at a psychiatric convention, when you get into an elevator, everyone just watches the numbers. At an astrology convention, you get into an elevator and everyone is hugging each other, asking each other what their signs are, just getting acquainted as fellow human beings. [Both laughing]

Author: You certainly wouldn't see that sort of thing at a psychiatric convention.

Dr. Pond: [Broadly smiling] No, not too often.

Author: Have you noticed the transcultural or Jungian archetypes in any paranormal experiences? For instance, with the near-death experiences, whether it's Arabs or Canadians or Swedes?

Dr. Pond: Yes, I don't think there are many differences, just some variations.

Author: So this might be an example of shared cultural collective unconscious?

Dr. Pond: Oh, absolutely, I think so. There is even research on the actual nature of memory. There is some scientific evidence that has suggested a theory that long-term memory resides outside of the brain/body and that ties in with the concept of the collective unconscious or the Akashic records. I wouldn't attempt to explain it but it doesn't seem so impossible to me as it does to other people.

Interview with a Psychiatrist

Author: Medicine is conservative by nature, but do you find that there are those in your profession who are open to this subject privately but [whom] you're not going to hear discuss it openly at, say, a medical convention?

Dr. Pond: Yeah. A good way to look at it is the growing acceptance and accommodation of alternative medicine, which up until a few years ago you wouldn't even dare talk about at a medical meeting. Now they've developed a division of alternative medicine because there are a number of people interested, but it's usually down the hall and at an out-of-the-way place that they have to meet [we laugh] rather than in the main stream. Nevertheless, it's there. It's a small opening and it's still a small part of the profession.

Author: Have you had any personal experiences yourself?

Dr. Pond: Not really, at least not something that I could give a definitive yes to.

Author: Have you ever witnessed anything paranormal while in a session with a patient?

Dr. Pond: [Hesitates] When you get into a very intense session with someone, for awhile you almost become one with them in a sense. It's almost as though your mind becomes in synch if you're really getting in deep and intense about something. You experience a sense that your energy is melding with that of the person you are working with. You get that healing or growth as a result. You don't get that kind of experience in a twenty-minute discussion about diagnosis and medications. It's a different kind of therapy. I've had that kind of experience.

Author: Do have any special interest in dreams? Can they link us to the collective unconscious or tender premonitions?

Dr. Pond: Yes, I think so. I don't really understand dreams very well. I certainly don't think that there is any absolute interpretation, e.g., if you dream this, it must mean that. There are dreams in which your inner self is trying to give you a message. I think people have to interpret their own dreams. You can maybe help them with the interpretation, but I don't think the equivalent dreams would necessarily hold the same meanings for you as it would to someone else.

Author: Given how common these experiences are, not so much the extreme phenomena but things like premonitions or subtle contact with a departed loved one, why do you think people are so reticent to discuss this topic? Where does this fear of being labelled "crazy" come from?

Dr. Pond: Well, throughout history, anything that gave the appearance of being "different from us" was perceived as being potentially bad, threatening, evil, or crazy because it is unknown and therefore feared. The fact that there's a great resistance to accept it is probably due to fear and ignorance. In small towns, for example, if someone were hallucinating vigorously on the street, people would be very upset by it. Whereas in New York, where it is more commonplace and people may be more accustomed to it, there is more of an inclination to just ignore it or not pay it any attention.

Sometimes I wonder exactly what is normal. We have generally accepted ideas of normality. [There is a line of thinking put forth first by R.D. Laing] that schizophrenia is just a normal person living in an abnormal world. I think you could make a case for that. I don't believe that is the explanation for schizophrenia but I think there is such a wide spectrum of "normality" that it is wrong of us to label as crazy or pathological everything we simply don't understand yet, though unfortunately that happens. Even with a more serious mental illness like a psychosis or severe depression that has a biological component [imbalance], people are reluctant to talk about it. It's one of those things you don't want anyone to know about. Many of us have heard of people in high office who have lost their positions because they suffered from depression at some time in their past. It's the thought in people's minds that it is deviant and somehow bad. It's the stigma of mental illness. Personally, I don't understand why the general public has such problems with it.

Author: There is a bit of a Catch-twenty-two in that if people were to discuss it openly, we would recognize what a fairly common experience it is, but because we hide it like some dirty little secret, it seems to be aberrant.

Dr. Pond: We do know that 20 percent of the population will have a mental illness in their family at some time in their lives. It is a fairly common problem.

Author: Do you find that people who are experiencing paranormal phenomena are more likely to have problems with their mental health just as are, say, the artistic or creative types?

Dr. Pond: I think there's a great range. Some of the people who seem to have a lot of paranormal experiences also seem to have a lot of creativity. There are many people who are considered to be normal in all ways except for this one [paranormal] experience. I find that people will come and talk to me about it simply because I have the reputation as [chuckling] believing in these "kooky" things, whereas they wouldn't go to a lot of my colleagues about it.

Author: That's interesting because you would think, especially in psychiatry, that an open mind is essential. But I guess as in medicine, it remains fairly conservative.

Dr. Pond: No, I don't believe the profession is open minded, at least not when it comes to "unscientific ideas."

Author: Are you seeing more of these types of experiences?

Dr. Pond: I could if I were able to put more time into it. There are certainly a lot of people who are very interested in psychic phenomena. Also, many people have wanted to experience a past life regression not for any specific concern; they're just sort of curious about it. Most people I have regressed to a past life were not Cleopatras or King Arthurs. They were just average people who lived usually sometime within the past century. They were, for example, pioneers, dull lives in a way. Because I believe there is a state in between lives where our higher self is able to examine that lifetime and learn from it, I always ask them, "What did you learn from that life?" and there's always been an interesting "Aha!" type of reaction. It's a feeling that they surface with from hypnosis. It's usually things like humility, love, forgiveness, and those types of things that had to be learned — not material things. Mostly experiences and feelings.

Author: Have you ever dealt with a near-death experience? It sounds similar in its transformative quality.

Dr. Pond: Not a lot. I've had a couple of people allude to it but nothing specific so I haven't been able to pursue it.

Author: Have you found that the past life work you have done, such as [examining] unfinished business, complements the work you do with people in therapy such as examining their current life and learning from those experiences?

Dr. Pond: Very much so, especially in relation to specific conditions. For instance, I think back to the mid centuries: poor people were treated very badly; they were often put in jail or even executed for what were minor transgressions. Oftentimes people in their current life will have a particular phobia to water or fire — maybe that's how they died in a previous life. I think hanging must have been a more prevalent practice than we are aware of, judging from all the people with throat problems that disappear after they relive that experience. Their symptoms simply dissolve. Why? I don't know. It works, though.

Author: So long as it works, that's the main thing.

Interview with a Psychiatrist

Dr. Pond: But even this bit of learning, e.g. "I had to learn about humility" or something, seems to make a difference in their lives. I would suspect that is similar to the near-death experience in that somehow a lot of things that we think of as being so important and so all-consuming at this particular time in life turn out to not be quite be so significant anymore. They can let go of some of those things. It provides a healing and closure.

Author: That reminds me of people who have survived death who come back saying that we must live our dying and make peace with our lives. Because we are, in a way, dying every day.

Dr. Pond: Most people are so afraid of death. We've made death into a bad thing, and yet it's the only sure thing in life. And in medicine, death is seen as something to be defeated and as personal failure. If you're a doctor and someone dies, you've failed, and that's too bad because we could make people's dying experience a lot better. The palliative care places are doing that now.

Author: If someone has had a horrific past-life experience that they can't seem to let go of and have not yet learned to forgive and move on, do you think they bring that baggage with them into this life?

Dr. Pond: Yes. Oftentimes, it's the same people we are tied to. The literature suggests that there are clusters of people that tend to go through their incarnations together though in different relationships towards one another. Sometimes you'll have what appears to be an irrational reaction towards someone, and it goes back to another life because you haven't let go of something. If we could learn to forgive and let go, it would make life a lot easier.

Author: Do you find we carry personality traits with us from previous lives, like the tendency to be generous or hold grudges?

Dr. Pond: Well, if in order to become one with God again we must complete our full life cycle, which could encompass many incarnations, so that we can learn from all there is to experience, then it is the time between incarnations that we probably set up the types of experiences we need to have. I don't know whether those decisions are coloured by our past life or whether there truly is a more heavenly state where we make those determinations. I really believe that we set up the kinds of experiences we need to have in this lifetime or that we choose to accept for the next go around [incarnation]; maybe with or without people who are familiar to us. Again, the literature indicates that there are groups or clusters of people who go through many incarnations together. We might make a decision in between lives that "these are the kind of experiences we need to have" as well as deciding on the roles such as mother, daughter, whatever. But how to generate the right settings and alignments for all that to happen is where I believe the forces of the cosmos come in. Maybe that's why astrology "works."

Author: Do you believe in a law of karma or something akin to it?

Dr. Pond: Yes, I do. I'm just not sure how to understand it. I don't think it's as simple a concept as say "doing this will have that effect." It's much more complicated than that. I do accept the concept; I just don't fully understand it.

Author: Do you think there is any danger, especially in working within the mental health field, that someone who has really been traumatized in this life, whether by abuse, rape, catastrophic loss, or whatever, that in believing in this philosophy of life, they may blame themselves by assuming they brought it all on themselves because they needed the experience or it was karma?

Dr. Pond: I think ultimately we all have to learn that we are responsible for ourselves but not for what happens to us; when other people do things to us we are responsible for how we react to it. And I'm not saying there is any simple way in which that happens. For example, can children react in any way differently to events than they do? [I.e., are there prescribed, correct, or conditioned reactions?] But even children, as they make their way through life, eventually have to take responsibility for how they are living today. That doesn't mean that to forgive someone who has done something horrible to us isn't very difficult. On the other hand, holding a grudge isn't going to undo it or change it. It only hurts the person holding the grudge. So if people could learn to accept responsibility for the way they handle things as well as forgiveness, they would make their own lives a lot better. But I don't think that someone who is now an adult and who suddenly begins to recall things in great detail and who feels compelled to have the world punish that person through the justice system, that doesn't solve anything. They just compound it. On the other hand, one can't say "I brought this on myself" because I don't think that's true. People have a responsibility for what they do to others. But terrible things happen to people and they seem able to cope with it okay. I think everyone, if they are basically mentally healthy people, comes to a point of acceptance where they say, "Yeah, that was done to me and it was really bad but I'm not going to let it spoil my life from here on." And maybe that's where the responsibility comes in. Sort of like in addiction recovery where they believe that you're not responsible for your disease but you are responsible for what you do about it. I think that's true. There's also the matter of prevention. We as a society need to do all we can to prevent these things from happening in the first place. But going after somebody decades after the fact doesn't help to heal at all.

Author: Have you had experiences with patients, especially while they were in a hypnotic state, where they seemed to be able to make contact with a higher consciousness or spirit guide?

Dr. Pond: Yes, I believe so. Some people seem to be able to achieve that more easily than others. They seem to have a closer connection, like psychics. Some people seem to be able to contact an alternate source of energy [consciousness], but I'm not sure if that's because they have something more highly developed or if it's just that other people have a lot of barriers that prevent them from doing that. We are all psychics if we would just let the barriers down. And I know that when you start to go with your intuition it becomes easier and more developed. [Chuckling] I'm not so great at that myself but I've seen my wife do that and the more she works with it, the more accurate she becomes. Pretty soon it evolves to a degree where you might say she is psychic. But it's just letting the forces of the universe [trusting them] guide you. I know there are occasions where [my wife] identifies her spirit guide and it seems to be there when it's needed. But I think most of us just don't listen to our intuition.

Author: Or trust in it. Do you think astrology could offer a similar kind of guidance, especially being that it's a bit more commonplace and accepted than psychic phenomena like telepathic links with spirits guides?

Dr. Pond: Well, that's interesting. Humans are used to thinking of themselves as being the centre of the universe. When really we are in this vast solar system that contains all these planets of which we know a fair bit about. We know they move with absolute precision through the heavens. We know a thousand years from now where each of the planets will be. Why is it so difficult to consider that they may exert some sort of influence on our lives? I can say that I don't understand it but it certainly doesn't bother me to seriously consider the possibility of there actually being an affect on us. Maybe that's all part of the plan by whoever or whatever set up this universe in the first place.

Author: Can your wife discern patterns in people's charts? You sometimes notice that people get into the same old messes because they can't see the patterns they're in.

Dr. Pond: Oh, absolutely. There are patterns. The Saturn and the Pluto cycles are huge ones that span many years. For instance, Saturn spans 27 years while Pluto is at 250. There are smaller ones too that happen on an annual basis, like the Mercury cycle.

Author: Can there be bursts of it every now and then? Sometimes things seem out of synch where nothing goes right, and that is often accompanied by an increase in poltergeist activity. It affects a lot of people.

Dr. Pond: Yes, and when these energies happen, it never fails that you hear comments like "it must be a full moon." The heavens are always moving, so you get these cycles and patterns. Freud talked about the repetition compulsion where we repeat behavioral patterns, which is sort of the same idea. If you look at it from the heavens it all seems to fit.

Author: I know that as Freud neared the end of his life he became much more amenable to the paranormal and the esoteric thesis that Carl Jung would put to him.

Dr. Pond: That's right, and Jung was quite the astrologer as well. Freud began as neurologist-scientist and part of his intent was to fit psyche into science. He never quite succeeded in that but his thinking did evolve and he began to see things differently. With Jung, he was much more inclined to look at things from a different viewpoint from the beginning. Jung and Freud had quite a falling out because Freud was pursuing the so-called scientific path whereas Jung was moving into a more unconventional direction which included the paranormal.

Author: Freud had seen Jung as a kind of heir before the big split. There were certainly some interesting psychodynamic elements in their relationship.

Dr. Pond: I think Freud was probably a little neurotic.

Author: [Both laughing] As we all probably are.

Dr. Pond: Well, we all have our own individual traits [idiosyncrasies] and sometimes they are labelled as neurotic. Maybe we can look at them as [individual characteristics] that we have to learn how to handle and use to our benefit.

Author: It can be consciousness expanding as well, even an illness.

Dr. Pond: Like obsessive-compulsive disorder. This is an obsessive, compulsive society. We throw clinical terms and medication at everything as if it were all negative, but it is what it is, and if we use it instead of letting it control us then we can achieve so much more in our lives.

Author: Have you ever met anyone that you experienced an immediate affinity for that may have been someone you had a connection to in a past life?

Dr. Pond: Oh, yes. We actually had an interesting experience. When one of my granddaughters was, oh, about two, at an age before we start to stifle these connections [memories] from the previous life, she asked her mother, "Don't you remember last time when I was the mommy and you were the little girl?" Well, that sort of blew us away.

Author: That's fascinating. What advice would you offer to parents if such a thing happened to them?

Dr. Pond: Certainly don't put them down or say that it's just silly. On the other hand, I'm not sure you want to say something like "let's pursue this" either. But don't criticize or ridicule them for it. Those kinds of memories tend to recede as the child nears four or five.

Author: It's intriguing and challenging because the more we learn, the more we discover how little we know or understand. We have a ways to go in our comprehension of life and consciousness.

Interview with a Psychiatrist

Dr. Pond: Even in psychiatry, I tend to see this profession currently where medicine was about two hundred years ago. We really knew very little about neurochemistry until the past few decades. That's relatively recent. And of course, we now have technology like CAT scans, PET scans, and functional MIRs that allow us to actually observe the living brain. So it is evolving.

Author: Of course being able to observe the brain doesn't automatically give us an understanding of it. That is where doctors such as you come in. Not just for an analysis of the hardware but for the compassion and understanding of the person attached to the brain. That is probably the more arduous and complex challenge, and maybe in the end, the more rewarding aspect of the work for all those involved.

Chapter Thirteen
Imagining the Rubicon: Some Scientific Theories on Psi

"The more we come to understand the universe, the less it looks like a great machine, the more it looks like a great thought."

— Sir Edward James

There are endless net of threads throughout the Universe.
The horizontal threads are in space; the vertical threads in time.
At every crossing of threads there is an individual, and every individual is a pearl.
The great light of Absolute Being illuminates and penetrates every pearl.
And also, every pearl reflects not only the light from every other pearl in the net,
But also every reflection of every reflection throughout the Universe.

— The Vedas

The study of parapsychology is a contentious and controversial issue within scientific circles, taken seriously by some and politely laughed off by others. Coupled with the fierce competition for research dollars, it is not surprising that there is little money available to advance research in this field. However, exciting research is being done. In this chapter I will present some of that current research as well as some of the hotly debated theories. The theories are diverse, ranging from physics to neurology. At times, the theories seem to stand in such contrast that few substantial insights or conclusions arise; however, they often do. The goal of this chapter is not to offer a crash course in physics or mathematics; even should I want to attempt such an undertaking, I am not qualified to do so. I am greatly indebted to those qualified persons who offered me their guidance and input in the composition of this chapter. Such sciences are marvellous subjects that can truly alter our perception of the time and space we inhabit.

The quest to uncover a possible scientific foundation and explanation for these mysterious events is far from a new endeavor. A few of Carl Jung's experiences with the paranormal were shared in the chapter "Chillers"; Jung was greatly interested in the scientific foundation for the relationship between inner states and their influence on outer reality. In his examinations of the psyche and the physical world, he collaborated with the Nobel prize-winning physicist Wolfgang Pauli on a paper entitled "Naturerklarung und Psyche," which was published in 1952. A scientific undertaking such as this would be natural for Jung given that even when he was a young professor at Polytechnic in Zurich in the 1930s, he was exposed to a great deal of innovative physics on the cusp of new and exciting discoveries. His interests would be further fuelled as he shared many dinners with Albert Einstein. As Jung once wrote, "It was Einstein who first started me thinking about a possible relativity of time as well as space, and their psychic conditionality. More than thirty years later this stimulus led to my relationship with the physicist Professor W. Pauli and my thesis of psychic synchronicity." (Unfortunately, Jung had a falling out with Einstein many years later, to the point of attacking him for being too one dimensional and analytical in his thinking. The real impetus for this turning on Einstein though might have been Einstein's correspondence with Freud regarding the Second World War. Jung never got over the split with Freud.)[1]

One scientific discipline that has been employed to research not only the mysteries of psi phenomena but to attempt to understand other inexplicable events that confound us is the chaos theory. Those researching chaos are attempting to discover a regularity hidden in a multitude of common processes and events; such events have the outward appearance of being random but possibly are the effects of complex systems and their interactions. The most frequent examples of chaos in action with random events include turbulence in fluids, weather patterns, predator-prey cycles, the spread of disease, and possibly even the onset of war. In essence, cause does not always equal the expected effect because there are too many unknown variables. Thus, when I do something to elicit a particular result and the opposite occurs, I am left wondering exactly how this result came about — what the heck happened? On the surface, chaos appears, well, chaotic in that it lacks any sequential order.

This is quite bothersome for a species that likes to believe it is virtually in control, even over such things as genetics. We are slaves to the manmade notion of cause and corresponding effect. As Carl Jung stated in a lecture, "Causality is the modern prejudice of the West." Jung saw clearly that physics supported parapsychology; he became aware that many of the events in life have no obvious cause. Our notion of cause and effect is like a pair of comfortable old slippers for the psyche; we are reluctant to give up such a concept.

Physics and mathematical theories clearly demonstrate that there are no absolute actions that result in a precise effect; there are only statistical probabilities. To further complicate matters, even statistical probabilities are not much to go on as there are too many hidden variables, as if the Fates, if you will, come along and blow the statistical probabilities right out of the water!

Those researching chaos, amongst other things, are attempting to render the interactions between complex systems predictable. One of the best examples of chaos in action is what is locked within your cranium — the human brain — for which there are specific regions believed to be conduits for psi. An example of our chaotic-neural system and potential for psi can be illustrated thus: The brain is a complex matter/energy system that has mini systems within its vast structure. Its cognitive centres are in constant flux. Consider that this biologic cognitive apparatus is composed of some 100 billion neurons. Each neuron can connect with up to 10,000 synapses. Within this vast neuronal network is the action potential of even the smallest cluster of neurons and the possible outcomes resulting from neurons and the quantum fields that are around them, but also the ones they generate. A completely random — or rather a seemingly random — event like a flux in the electromagnetic field that surrounds us elicits a resonant reply from within the brain. Let us say that the region of the brain responding to this was the parietal lobe, which could evoke in us an undeniable yet inexplicable sense of a presence such as an unseen spirit or angel or even an evil, threatening entity.

This is not to say such manifestations do not in fact occur. It merely suggests that our brains are sometimes more tuned in to sensing their presence because all the elements are in the right place at the right time. Without the external stimuli such as a certain smell or touch and the subsequent internal response, we might never become consciously tuned in to or resonant with a particular manifestation. In part, this is due to the RAS (reticular activating system), a part of the brain stem that filters out external stimuli or noise so that we do not become overwhelmed. There are particular areas of the brain thought to be significant in generating or receiving the energetic impulses of psi phenomena. Chief amongst these are the temporal lobes, located on either side of the head just above the ears and descending deep into the elegant folds of the brain. It is specifically the right temporal lobe that is thought to contain the psychic link. The temporal lobes have an intricate connection with the ancient part of our brains known as the limbic system, the region associated with our basic drives and emotions. It is sometimes referred to as the primitive brain in that basal survival instincts emerge from here. Some of those would be hunger, the drive to reproduce, and thirst, as well as emotional states like love, lust, hate, fear, and awe. Following is a brief synopsis of some of the functions that are partially mediated by or generated by the right temporal lobe. This will more clearly illustrate why this region of the brain is suspected as being a primary conduit of psi energy:

- extracorporeal sense: the feeling of being outside of one's own body;
- interpretation of the senses of smell, taste, and sound, especially as they pertain to meanings from past associations;
- vestibular sensations: uncommon orientation such as feeling as though one is leaning on a slant or that one is rushing through a tunnel or time and space;
- visual perceptions and interpretations: white lights or dancing

lights. The seeing of near photographic images of people or places (whether from the past, present, or "future");

- sense of a presence, whether a guardian angel, God, a ghost, or even the feeling that one is being watched;
- signs and synchronicity: the strong sense that things happening at a particular time and place have significant meaning such as a message or an omen;
- near-death experiences, mystical experiences, and most religious and spiritual/mystical experiences;
- feelings of déjà vu and jamais vu (the latter being the opposite of the former);
- religious fervour and obsessions, including stalking, jealous rages, murder or crimes of passion, and even crusades; and
- nirvana effect: those who slip into trances or meditate often have a sense of peace, contentment, and being at one with the universe. These experiences all generate out of the temporal lobe.

There is currently research being done to determine if our brains are in actuality wired for belief in a higher or supreme being (i.e., God) and, to a lesser extent, religious doctrine to bring structure and meaning to these unfathomable feelings and confusing events that sometimes plague us. There is a saying that if there were in fact no God, man would have to invent one. In a similar vein, the great Canadian neurosurgeon Wilder Penfield (who mapped out a great part of the human brain) came to the conclusion that if there were a physical location for the soul it would be the in right temporal lobe. There is scattered research that alludes to other specific regions of the brain but there is nothing substantive as yet.

It's more assumption than neuroscience to link the parietal lobes with clairvoyance or precognition; this is because of their role in the visual/spatial processing. Also, the occipital lobes, being the visual processing centre of the brain, are the target source for visualizing apparitions or other images. In fact, due to the complex nature of this phenomenon (and the brain for that matter), there are more than likely many areas of the brain involved in phantasmal encounters. One can perceive ghosts in more ways than simply "seeing" them.

There has been some work done on monitoring the electrical activity in the brain using EEGs with some interesting and potentially promising results. Not surprisingly, alpha waves are most prominent in telepathy and ESP. These are the waves that are steady and slow, indicative of a relaxed conjuncture. As stated in previous chapters, people often see apparitions when they are relaxed or doing something "mindlessly repetitive," which in all likelihood indicates they are in an alpha wave state. Beta waves are more rapid; you would be in beta status if you where writing a test, feeling threatened, or writing a book. The research is sparse in relation to beta and telekinesis, but that would seem to be the logical neuroelectrical wave state required to produce a telekinetic affect. Theta is the deepest relaxed wave state and is most likely the wavelength associated with the hypnogogic/hypnopontic experiences. Most of this is conjecture that needs much more careful research, including an examination of the neurochemicals radiated during or by these experiences. This is an area that has scarcely been touched on yet, just speculated upon.

Next is quantum mechanics, which is a theoretical branch of physics related to the makeup and conduct of energy in atomic systems. It actually dates back to the 1900s, spearheaded by physicist Max Plank, who won the Nobel Prize for his theories. Many others have since built on his work. One fascinating reading of the quantum theory is the concept of the many-worlds or multiverse model of the universe. To quote from a definition given by http://whatis.com:

> As soon as a potential exists for any object to be in any state, the universe of that object transmutes into a series of parallel universes equal to the number of possible states in which that object can exist, with each universe containing a unique single possible state of that object. Furthermore, *there is a mechanism for interaction between these universes that somehow permits all states to be accessible in some way and for all possible states to be affected in some manner.*

What this suggests, even though it sounds like an episode of the *Twilight Zone*, is that we exist in a multidimensional universe that contains within it parallel timelines. There may be four of us in different worlds but each one of us would be unique owing to our exclusive experiences. Nevertheless, these distinct states of existence occasionally overlap or make contact (perhaps via a chaotic reaction). We become consciously aware of some indefinable "something" or we experience an overpowering sense of presence or déjà vu, perhaps even being warned of something as in precognition. Even more rarely, we bump into our alternate selves, as in accounts of the doppelgänger. This is the sort of stuff that makes the "hard-core scientists" I interviewed roll their eyes; however, they do concede that if you subscribe to all these various theories, including the entire concept of parapsychology, then, yes indeed, the chaos and quantum theories offer possible explanations for many phenomena. Still, scientists such as Stephen Hawking and Ian Coavelle support the notion of multiverse and they are not exactly naïve or lacking in cognitive capacities. Albert Einstein did not share these views, however. According to Einstein, "God does not play dice with the Universe."

Quantum theory differs from classical or Newtonian physics in that quantum is *probabilistic* and Newtonian is *deterministic*. Quantum theory can be thought of as complex wave functions with each wave being related to the probability of an event taking place. All possible outcomes are in place. This collection is referred to as a state vector. In researching consciousness in relationship to quantum potentials and variables, it was noted that the act of passively observing had an impact on the outcome. Passive participation, if you will.

One of those who built upon quantum theory and its relationship to consciousness was Dr. Evan Walker Harris, who worked at NASA. Harris speculated on the degree to which consciousness with its complex electromagnetic fields influenced all these possible outcomes. He stated that consciousness is a nonphysical but real quantity that may influence the physical environment via a "quantum mechanical tunnelling" formula. Harris almost echoes the ancient sages when they spoke of the world as being made up from the stuff of mind.[2] Centuries following their proclamations, Harris wrote of consciousness influencing matter on the subatomic particle level and asserted that, "consciousness may be associated with all quantum mechanical process, since everything that occurs is ultimately the result of one or more quantum mechanical events."[3]

Anthony North summed it up nicely in his book *The Paranormal: A Guide to the Unexplained*: "When two particles collide — as happens millions of times every second in your fingernail — the mathematics of quantum physics state that there is an equal probability of them shooting off in any of the directions possible. Therefore, in its natural, uninterrupted state, quantum 'reality' is probabilistic, with every outcome of a specific event being as real as any other."[4] For Harris and others, the dynamic process by which consciousness influenced or shaped the physical was of key interest. (More on Harris, who was quite influential in this research, further ahead.)

This melds well with psychoenergenics, which, as the name suggests, studies the influence of mind/consciousness on the external and the internal environment. A current area of research is the potential healing effect of prayer or guided imagery/visualization on the outcome of the sick. Uri Geller with his metal bending skills is another example of psychoenergenics. What we are in essence speaking of is mind influencing the environment, which in turn influences mind. This possibly complements another theory put forth by Michael Persinger regarding electromagnetic fields.

I came across an eloquent and brilliantly arranged abridgement of these very complex theories written by Paul Stevens at the Koestler Parapsychology Unit in the psychology department at the University of Edinburgh. He has kindly given me permission to reproduce it for this book.[5]

Teleological Model of Psi

Helmudt Schimdt proposed a teleological (goal seeking) model that postulated psi as representing a modification of the probabilities for different world histories. That is, the psi agent need concentrate only on the desired outcome of an event. Psi would act to skew the probability of that event happening, or having happened in the case of retrospective telekinesis (retro PK). As such, this theory was not a theory of psi mechanism but one that looked at the way psi was experienced by the psi agent. It was one of the first parapsychological theories to include a unified psi: PK, ESP, precognition — all were aspects of one unified psi principle wherein reality was altered to match the expectation. This theory also meant that psi would be independent of space and time as when and where in the world history psi occurred would be irrelevant, and that psi is independent of task complexity as the psi agent aims only for the desired end point. As most human actions are essentially teleological — when we want to pick something up, we do not consider in detail which muscles we wish to move, and so on — this brought psi more into the realms of human experience. Feedback was considered to be vital: the psi agent can have an effect only if it is coupled to its environment in such a way that it may receive a stimulus. There was also what was called a "divergence problem." That is, all future psi agents could so have an effect on the present world history. In effect, this meant that for any experiment, the psi agent was not only the experimental participant but all future readers of the experimental paper!

Schmidt, H. (1975). "Towards a Mathematical Theory of Psi." *The Journal of the American Society for Psychical Research*, 69, (4), 301-320.

Quantum Mechanical Theory of Psi

Evan Harris Walker identified consciousness with quantum mechanical variables. In quantum theory, any system may be described in terms of a wave function — a complex superposition of waves, the squared amplitude of each being related to the probability of an individual event occurring. The complete wave function describes all possible outcomes to that system. Thus the wave function of a coin toss will describe the outcomes of heads or tails, with the amplitude of each being equal to the square root of the 50 percent probability of getting a head or a tail. The problem is that this wave function describes all the outcomes at once, whereas conscious experience tells us that we will observe only one outcome. This naturally led to the idea that conscious observation somehow affects the system, causing the wave function to collapse into a specific state — the one we experience. If this is indeed the case, then perhaps consciousness can actually choose, to some extent, which outcome actually occurs — a process which sounds very much like the concept of telekinesis.

Walker developed this theory by pointing out that the brain itself is also a physical system, and so it too develops probabilistically into a number of superposed potential states. That is, the collapse doesn't take place due to the physical act of observation, but is linked to an act of mind, consciousness taking on the role of a "hidden variable" of the wave function which describes the physical system. Schmidt also explicitly stated that PK was related to the collapse of the wave function in an extension to his original teleological model. An important feature of this theory is the unity of psi. PK, ESP, and precognition are all aspects of the observation process. In fact, the basic process may be seen as similar to the idea of retro-psychokinesis in that the observation of the system would appear to affect the outcome of the system, no matter at what time that outcome would be said to have been determined in a classical sense. For example, the collection of random number data at time t=0 could be affected at any subsequent time as long as it was not observed at t=0. ESP then becomes the selection of the system to correspond to the prediction. PSI is also seen as being independent of space and time. A requirement of hidden variables is that they must, according to the well-known tenet of quantum theory called Bell's Theorem, be non-local in nature. In real terms this would mean that the space-time location of the system to be affected is not important: only the feedback of the observer is. PSI is also independent of task complexity. Again, the important feature is the act of observation, so it is only the feedback that is important. This does mean that some form of true feedback to the observer is vital. However, this again brings up the divergence problem although in this model, while future psi agents can also have an effect, it is argued that they can act only to increase the variance of experimental results rather than change what has already been observed.

Walker, E.H. (1975). "Foundations of Paraphysical and Parapsychological Phenomena." In L. Oteri (Ed.), *Quantum Physics and Parapsychology*, Parapsychology Foundation.

Walker, E.H. (1984). "A Review of Criticisms of the Quantum Mechanical Theory of Psi Phenomena." *Journal of Parapsychology*, 48, 277-332.

Schmidt, H. (1984). "Comparison of a Teleological Model with a Quantum Collapse Model of Psi." *Journal of Parapsychology*, 48, (4), 261-276.

Thermal Fluctuation Model

Richard Mattuck presents an interesting variation of the quantum mechanical theory of psi based on the idea that the mind somehow utilizes the thermal energy of molecules to alter the outcome of an event. It is well known that there is a degree of uncertainty associated with any measurement, with the actual measured values showing small fluctuations around a mean value. These fluctuations are partially due to the agitation of the measured system by the random thermal energies of particles in the system (remember that an atom at a given temperature is equivalent to that atom having a certain kinetic energy in a random direction. The hotter the material, the more its atoms are "jiggling" about), and have shown to be related to the uncertainty principal in quantum theory. Mattuck relates a PK effect to the processing of information at a certain rate, and offers a detailed analysis of the rate of information change associated with a theoretical PK effect on various components of an example target system.

Mattuck, R.D. (1982). "Some Possible Thermal Quantum Fluctuation Models for Psychokinetic Influence on Light." *Psychoenergetics*, 4, 211-225.

The Model for Pragmatic Information

Walter von Lucadou utilizes a system-theoretic approach to psi rather than a quantum level approach. It does however assume that the description of any system will have a similar form to the axioms of quantum theory. Von Lucadou formulates a basic descriptive equation for the "pragmatic information," I, contained within a system, denoting the information which is meaningful to the observing organism, such that: $I=R*A=B*E=n*i$. The first term states that the pragmatic information will be determined by the readability, R, of the system (a change in the structure of the system). The second term states that the pragmatic information will also be determined by the novelty, E, of the information in the system coupled with the confirmatory value, B, of that information. The final term puts forward the idea that there is a minimum amount of pragmatic information, I (analogous to the idea of quanta in quantum theory). He then goes on to show how quantum theory axioms may, by analogy, be used to show the dynamics of inter-relationships between these concepts.

Von Lucadou also uses the system-theoretic concept of organiza-tional closure, an organizationally closed system defined as being one which dynamically defines its boundaries by the interaction of its con-stituent parts. Such a system will also be seen as a unified body when viewed from outside the system. A physical example would be an atom, which exists only through the interaction between a nucleus and its electron, but which has properties that exist only because of this inter-action. A psychological example would be a social group whose mem-bership share some common belief structure that is an amalgam of the individual beliefs, these individual beliefs also being influenced by the group belief. In a psi experiment, organizational closure is related to the interaction between the psi agent and the target system, and is described by the internal pragmatic information of the system. The experimenter is outside of this closure but wants to get external prag-matic information in the form of experimental results. A psi effect is then defined as a meaningful correlation between the psi agent and the target system, although the correlation is non-local — a property where the properties of one system are dependant on that of another, distant system but where there is assumed to be no causal connection.

Lucadou, W.v. (1987). The Model of Pragmatic Information, Proceedings of the 30th Parapsychological Association Convention, 236-254.

Lucadou, W.v. (1994). The Endo-Exo-Perspective-Heaven and Hell of Parapsychology, Proceedings of the 37th Parapsychological Association Convention, 242-252.

Psychically Mediated Instrumental Response (PMIR)

Another use of the systems theory approach to psi phenomena is that of Rex Stanford, who proposed a general model wherein an organism uses psi, as well as sensory means, to scan its environment for informa-tion related to its needs. This is often, but need not necessarily be, an unconscious process. In this model, cybernetic PK is viewed as being an instrumental response to this scanning. As the model is seen as an active scanning process by the organism, the use of psi would be governed by a variety of factors, both situational and psychological.

In this approach, PK and ESP are seen as being separate processes, although telepathy can be seen as involving both extrasensory scanning for information about another organism and mental/behavioral influence of that organism by PK. Psi events occur in relation to the needs of the organism, and depend on the closeness in time of the relevant object or event. One of the most interesting aspects of this model is that psi can occur without the need for conscious perception of the need-relevant circumstance, making this one of the few theories that does not explicitly imply a link between consciousness and psi. It also allows that explicit feedback is not necessary as ESP provides relevant information. Although the author only states that this role is filled by ESP, it at least allows for the more subtle forms of feedback due to the external interaction between the target system and its environment mention earlier.

Stanford later modified the theory into one of the conformational behaviour, removing the scanning component and saying that the organism merely reacted to relevant psi mediated stimuli in its environment. That is, conformance behaviour deals with "changes in the ordering of a relatively unordered system in relationship to a relatively ordered system," which allowed simpler organisms that would not normally be thought of as being capable of scanning their environment to utilize psi.

Standford, R.G. (1990). "An Experimentally Testable Model for Spontaneous Events." In Krippner, S. (Ed.), *Advances in Parapsychological Research* 6, (pp. 54-167). McFarland and Company.

Standford, R. G., Zenhausern Z., Taylor, A. and Dwyer, M. (1975). "Psychokinesis as Psi Mediated Instrumental Response." *Journal of the American Society for Psychical Research*, 69, (2), 127-134.

Decision Augmentation Theory

In this approach diametrically opposed to the OT's, this theory, which developed out of the Intuitive Data Sorting theory, posits that humans may have the ability to make decisions based on information gained precognitively.[6] Thus, rather than causing the desired outcome, they take advantage of natural fluctuations in the target system, selecting times and situations that will produce an outcome close to that which was desired. For example, in a "score high" PK protocol, the Random Event Generator (REG) might produce a binary data-stream of 01010010001011101011011011010001101101011100101000. If the data collection for a ten-bit sample was as for the first block (A), then the PK score would be 0.7 (seven ones and three zeros). For the second block (B) it would be 0.5 (five ones and five zeros). Sample A would then have would then have given an above chance PK score, where as sample B would be at chance level. DAT says that the psi agent could have received some sort of precognitive cue that would have enabled them to start data collection at the point where A begins rather than where B begins. If this biased selection process were continued, then we might conclude that the psi agent had influenced the data stream to be non-random when in fact it was still completely random overall. A further result of this process is that the final PK score will be inversely related to the sample length, and to the number of decision points available to the psi agent.

This model, being precognition based, requires psi independent to some extent although there is some debate as to whether it is an actuality precognitively perceived, or just a probabilistic future associated with a specific desired outcome. The main advantage of this approach according to the authors is that it removes the need to explain the two disparate active (PK) and passive (ESP) psi processes. It also allows for a PK effect in pseudo-random (and therefore deterministic) data, which would be difficult to explain by a causal influence model.

May, E.C., Utts, J.M., and Spottiswoode, S.J.P. (1995). "Decision Augmentation Theory: Towards a Model of Anomalous Phenomena." *Journal of Parapsychology*, 59, (3), 195-220.

May, E.C., Spottiswoode, S.J.P., Utts, J.M., and James, C.L. (1995). "Applications of Decision Augmentation Theory." *Journal of Parapsychology*, 59, (3), 221-250.

Dobyns, Y.H. (1993). "Selection Versus Influence in Remote REG Anomalies." *Journal of Scientific Exploration*, 7, (3), 259-269.

Dobyns, Y.H. (1996). "Selection Versus Influence Revisited: New Methods and Conclusions." *Journal of Scientific Exploration*, 10, (2), 253-268.

Electromagnetic Theories

The main electromagnetic theories tend to be split in two categories. The first is that there is a psi signal which is electromagnetic in nature, similar in nature to a radio signal. Advantages to this idea are that we know that organisms use electrical signals as part of their normal physiology, and we do indeed emit electromagnetic radiation which relates to physiological activity, and we understand the principals by which information may be encoded onto electromagnetic waves (this principle, called modulation, is how audio and video signals are transmitted by radio waves). The second category is that originally advocated by Michael Persinger. He proposed that psi involves the naturally occurring radiation that makes up the Earth's electromagnetic field. He proposed a simple synchronization effect wherein the conditions of this field affected two people simultaneously, causing both to have similar experience. When the two later compared notes, they might conclude that they had experienced a case of psi, erroneously supposing the experience was due to the transfer of a signal between them. This approach is essentially a classical case of "hidden variable." While this could possibly explain some simple experiences, it could not account for more complex experiences, or those where there did indeed appear to be a transfer of information. For such cases, Persinger goes on to propose that the naturally occurring wave might be used as a carrier wave in the same way as with the mental radio model, with the weak electromagnetic field of the psi agent imposing the desired information onto the stronger water.

Becker, R.O. (1992). "Electromagnetism and Psi Phenomena." *Journal of the American Society for Psychical Research*, 86, (1), 1-17.

Persinger, M.A. (1989). "Psi Phenomena and Temporal Lobe Activity: The Geometric Factor." *Research in Parapsychology*, The Scarecrow Press: 121-156.

Persinger, M.A. and Krippner, S. (1989). "Dream ESP Experiences and Geometric Activity." *Journal of the American Society for Psychical Research*, 83, 101-116.

Persinger has reviewed countless data on telepathy experiments and other types of spontaneous psi phenomena and summarized that positive test results and higher levels of activity correlated with geomagnetic fields. I am intrigued by much of Persinger's research but the more material I review, the more disturbed I become by what appears to me to be reductionism. One develops the impression that Michael Persinger believes that everything from God to ghosts to global warming can be explained by activity within the temporal lobes. He has also linked poltergeist as well as other paranormal activity with temporal lobe epilepsy (as did a pioneer of psychic research, William Roll).

It should be pointed out that most cases of spontaneous PSI have an external trigger, not an internal one. The majority of people I have encountered both directly and indirectly while doing research who had experiences of this nature do not have epilepsy of any type. Perhaps some do and have not as yet been diagnosed. Some also have depression, diabetes, hypertension, and even cancer. Most biological conditions have some affect on our neurochemistry as well as our perception and interpretation of the events of our life. We can easily fall into circular thinking under these circumstances. Are these sets of circumstances and their subsequent biological reactions the cause of extraordinary experiences, or do these circumstances somehow attune us to that to which we do not normally have access? There are also people who have no obvious triggers for phenomenal events and, as has often been repeated in this book, are the last people who would ever expect such things to happen to them. It is not yet known whether having one such experience conditions your brain in such a way that you become more sensitized to such phenomena, considering there are those who have repeated psychic events throughout their lives. Conversely, some have just one event.

Theories on near-death experience (NDE) include hypoxia and release of powerful endorphins (morphinelike neurochemicals, which tend to cause tranquility and euphoria, which begs the question why some NDEs, though rare, would be terrifying). Another rather simple interpretation, which is bereft of any substantial supporting evidence, is that of wish fulfillment. This may account for some hallucinations that have an NDE quality to them, but why are NDEs so common as to be universal? If they were crisis or dying fantasies, why do they all share an antimaterialistic theme? No one is rolling around naked in piles of money. Also they are non-sexual, so NDE do not reflect the fantasies and daydreams people acknowledge they have. The theory around drugs does not hold up because the visions are all fairly consistent, involving tunnels and life reviews. People have all kinds of drug-induced hallucinations, but they are not as uniform as are the NDEs.

The same applies to cerebral hypoxia. People have had near-death experiences with no oxygen deprivation to the brain. For a theory to be valid, it should be much more consistent than that which is being proposed to us in the drug and hypoxia hypothesis. The truth is that very little is known about the process of dying, as medicine does not study that process; its goal is to save life, or to at least resuscitate life when it can. (In December 2001, *The Lancet*, a respected British medical journal, published the results of a study on near-death experiences with a large group composed of 344 patients. It has raised a number of intriguing results and questions. For the author and others who study the various aspects of mind/body consciousness, one of the most startling findings was that the actual NDE experience involving the tunnel, seeing dead relatives, and the life review occurred when the patient's brain had actually flatlined; i.e., it was not demonstrating any electrical activity, a medical criteria for brain death. This puts a further challenge to the previously stated theories and also reiterates subject matter pertaining to the matter and location of mind/consciousness. What are the implications of a dead brain possessing consciousness and how does it fit with the quantum theories put forth in this chapter?)

Whatever the doctors hypothesize about the etiology of these experiences, one thing remains a certainty. *Something extraordinary is happening to these people who were, for a brief time, clinically dead.* Furthermore, their lives and attitudes are dramatically altered from their previous state of being and behaving. It is evident that the same cannot be said by those who artificially induce a pseudo near-death experience. Those who were clinically dead and came back are convinced, and remain so throughout their lives, that there is something beyond this corporeal existence. That is not to say that they know what it is in the traditional sense, i.e., heaven, Nirvana, purgatory, etc. But there is something beyond this life, a condition of essential being as well as peace and belonging, two conditions that seem very elusive but are much sought after in this life.

In spite of parapsychology not being taken all that seriously by the so-called "legitimate" sciences, this branch of science has pioneered studies that have later been incorporated into the mainstream of psychology and medicine. Dr. Ronald Pond mentioned two of these: hypnosis and other alternative treatments in medicine, i.e., healing. It is possible that these two areas alone instigated the now legitimate field of psychoneuroimmunology, which studies the impact our state of mind has on our physiological being. Various scientific fields have and continue to grapple with these mysteries, and each field brings its own unique perspective, offering us intriguing insights into the incredible world of the paranormal. Even if science cannot come to any definitive hard scientific conclusions, the implications of this continued research are far reaching for humanity. Princeton Engineering Anomalies Research (PEAR) eloquently states two important points:

> Basic Science: Accommodation of the observed anomalies within a functional scientific framework will require the explicit inclusion of consciousness as an active agent in the establishment of physical reality. This expansion of the scientific paradigm demands more courageous theoretical structures than exist at present, guided by more comprehensive empirical data than is now available, acquired via more co-operative interdisciplinary collaborations than are currently practiced.

> Cultural Implications: Beyond its scientific aspect and its technological applications, clear evidence of an active role of consciousness in the establishment of reality holds sweeping implications for our view of ourselves, our relationship to others, and to the cosmos in which we exist. These, in turn, must inevitably impact our values, our priorities, our sense of responsibility,

and our style of life. Integration of these changes
across the society can lead to a substantially superior
cultural ethic, wherein the long-estranged siblings of
science and spirit, of analysis and aesthetics, of intel-
lect and intuition, and of many other subjective and
objective aspects of human experience will be produc-
tively reunited.[7]

This phenomenon and the research surrounding it with its potential scientific and sociological gains has far-reaching implications.
Two of the difficulties are that it requires an open mind and adequate
funding. This subject seems to foster open minds, though many have
a genuine interest in it. Part of the difficulty is the prejudices individuals bring to bear on the matter, no doubt stemming from their
preconceived notions. For instance, the field of near-death experiences is wrought with preconceptions stemming from religious or scientific beliefs about death and the afterlife. Doctors dedicated to
conventional doctrine will proffer the various explanations based on
purely biological processes, and those who hold strong beliefs about
heaven and hell will frame their explanations to conform to their
belief system. In fact, negative near-death experiences have been
used as an encitement against suicide even though negative experiences are rare and not always associated with attempted suicide.
However, attempting to mould things into our belief system is human
nature, as is our tendency to disregard and ridicule those same things
when we fail to do so. It is also human nature to distrust and ridicule
what is new and foreign to us, especially when it challenges our conventional belief systems. And what a challenge it is in that we must
broaden our concepts on so many fronts, including the rigid scientific frontiers. Many people assume that if there is one group of profes-
sionals that by necessity must have open minds, it would be scientists. Oddly enough, this is not always the case. There exists in science an almost underlying dogmatic fundamentalism with unspoken
warnings to not stray too far from the conventional.[8]

To be sure, the study of anomalous events presents many difficulties and challenges. (I would like to point out that today's anomalous
events are tomorrow's commonplace events with perfectly rational and
logical explanations.) To be realistic, the testing, measuring, and eval-

uation of psychic phenomena can appear on the surface to be an almost impossible task to accomplish.

To begin with, the test subjects are generally not able to flick a switch and turn abilities like telepathy on and off. Some people known as psychics have developed a reasonable amount of control, but even for them, the stress of the lab environment often interferes with or blocks their abilities. Like those of us who experienced "brain lock" during exams in school even though we knew the material, psychics are only humans, not mechanical science projects.

One of the most challenging phenomena to investigate is also one of the most fascinating (at least to me, personally): the poltergeist. Poltergeists are notoriously unreliable, uncooperative, and unpredictable. They do not perform on demand or show up for lab appointments. It frustrates scientists and the individuals experiencing it, more so for the latter who feel they are being made a fool or a liar of. Keep in mind that a poltergeist is a psychic force emanating from within an individual while simultaneously interacting with the external electromagnetic (and emotionally charged) external/internal environment. The poltergeist activity is a psychologically complex dynamic, often involving more than the individual source of the poltergeist. In order to accomplish a thorough and accurate investigation, it must, by necessity, be long term and intrusive, i.e., continuous record cameras and sometimes other intrusive or inconvenient tests like EEGs. This may require months of continuous monitoring. Similar protocols are involved with the investigation of a purported haunting. Needless to say, this is not only disruptive and awkward for the person or persons involved, but it is also a costly expenditure for the investigating team or organization. As has been previously stated, the funds for such research are scarce to say the least.

There are some psi phenomena that are better suited to the lab, like standard telepathy/ESP test using either remote viewing or ESP cards (see glossary). Such tests have the advantage of being under the strictest of environmental controls. The PEAR lab is doing some incredible studies under very tight environmental controls.

There are many other challenges presented by the very nature of the phenomena. How does one study precognition under a laboratory setting? How does an individual even know that a vision or dream was a precognitive event? He or she would have to have made a note of it, placing it in a sealed envelope prior to the event. In fact, people who are prone to precognition often do just that with the twist being that the sealed, dated envelope must be handed over to another party for obvious reasons.

So many of these unique experiences are spontaneous and self-limiting; by that I mean that there may be once or even twice in a lifetime events, obviously impossible to study, but real, powerful, and quite common nonetheless.

Even with all our degrees and fancy equipment, I suspect that there are things we might never be able to explain. I also believe that is a good thing if it results in the human race appreciating the wondrous universe and our importance but insignificance in it. One of the main points I learned from those who died and were revived is that humanity needs to learn some serious humility, and perhaps that is one of the many benefits we will derive from the study of psychic phenomena.

Addendum: Following a meeting of doctors and scientists in 1998 in Athens, Greece, they tackled some of the obstacles in the way of in-depth and meaningful research into the nature of consciousness, reality, and anomalous phenomena. Some expressed concerns that our current scientific do not give us an adequate overview of reality and argued for "an extension of the existing paradigm to encompass consciousness" while others suggested that we should "recognize the limitations of [science's] approaches, confined as they are by measurement of events and processes in the physical world." It was pointed out that "a new paradigm would have to stake out appropriate epistemological boundaries, approaches (e.g. intuition, gnosis), methods, and procedures for verification." This is not the first time we have been presented with such challenges and it is exciting. Many are taking up that challenge, risking the derision of their peers and forging boldly ahead.

Appendix

Whether one believes that the experiences shared within this book are the result of supernatural elements, quantum waves, or an overstressed psyche, they have a profound effect on the lives of those experiencing them. Altering one's belief systems about life, death, and even self is just one way they burn holes through a person's life. For many, it offers a catharsis, healing, and growth. For others it is a frightening, distressing ordeal that leaves them feeling disorientated, isolated, and disconnected from what they once knew to be the "real world." As has been evidenced throughout this book, you are not alone. In fact you are in some very fine company indeed!

I would encourage those who have been so profoundly touched by these experiences to speak with someone, whether it be a friend, clergy, doctor, or counsellor, if for no other reason than to help you assimilate the experience into your life and psyche. If you are not comfortable with that, try writing it up as a short story; you will be surprised by the insights these experiences can give into your authentic self.

When it is necessary to seek external help depends on many factors, including the nature of the activity, the frequency of the events, the impact it is having on your personal or professional life, as well as your goal in seeking help; i.e., what do you want to achieve? Insight? Cessation of the activity? I recall a case of Hal Puthoff and Russell Targ that was presented Adams Smith's book *Powers of the Mind*.[1] A wife had learned that these two physicists were doing a study on the paranormal so she brought her husband in to see them. Apparently, he could hear the neighbours talking about him and had the ability to see what was going on in other rooms. They tested him and his scores were off the chart; he was brilliant and his abilities were genuine. Nevertheless, it was having a negative impact on his family and work life so the doctors put him on a medication called Thorazine, a powerful antipsychotic not without considerable side effects. On the medication, all the psychic abilities ceased! They would recur only if he went off the Thorazine. In spite of the side effects of the drug, he found his psychic abilities too disruptive to his ability to function in the world. That was his choice and it was the correct one for him.

There are other options that can be explored. Some people learn how to control these abilities to a great degree and successfully incorporate them into their lives. Some people have employed the technique known as automatic writing to redirect or suppress the energies. Others, such as Mathew Manning from England and Chris Howard from Sweden, went on to develop healing capabilities as a result of refocusing their psychic abilities. There are people and resources that can guide you in the techniques that may enable you to get control over what is happening. Why medication worked for this man is unknown. Drugs, including alcohol, certainly have an effect on these phenomena, but the mechanism by which this occurs is unknown, and for the person so affected, it does not really matter.

There are some people who are members of religious orders (in this book it happened to be those of the Christian faith) who expressed concern and confusion as a result of having had such experiences, as they felt it contradicted their beliefs or was a manifestation of evil. I spoke to representatives from three major religious denominations (a mullah, a rabbi, and a Jesuit Catholic priest). They were open to such experiences and did not interpret them as being "evil." In fact, most religions have many such mystical experiences interwoven into their rich history. There are some that most certainly would not share that view, of course. The way in which the people in this book found someone open minded to this subject within the religious community was to write or simply leave a message with the receptionist, giving a brief description of the nature of the problem directed to anyone open to addressing the issues. In all cases I am familiar with, the messages were responded to either directly or with a referral.

Appendix

In looking for more general or scientific assistance, the best place to start is your nearest university. Ask for the department of psychology. If the university has nothing pertaining to this subject taking place at their establishment, chances are they will be able to refer you to a university or researcher that can help you. If you have access to a computer, there are literally thousands of Web sites and chat rooms devoted to the topic. For practical reasons, I can only list a few. As of the writing of this, they are reputable, up to date, and especially useful. If you don't have a computer, your local library may provide Internet access should you feel the need to utilize that resource. The library is also an invaluable resource for books and magazines, of course.

Within the suggested readings section of this book you will find a variety of publications that have been of great help to many who have been touched by the paranormal. The list is varied but brief so I encourage you to visit your local libraries or bookstores to find something that may be more tailored to your individual circumstances and questions. Many I interviewed stated that they found biographies documenting personal experiences and the means in which individuals coped with them helpful, especially in making them feel less alone or "crazy." Some individuals even established a like-minded group in their community to share experiences and investigate other reported events.

One resource that is unique and of benefit to many who are having paranormal experiences or are having difficulty understanding and adjusting to them is the Spiritual Emergency Network (their book is listed in Suggested Readings). This is not a religious organization, though they do counsel people who have lost their faith or are having an existential crisis. Judy Tart wrote a fine essay regarding this group and its work and has kindly given me permission to reproduce a portion of it for this book:

> Many travelers on the spiritual path have found the going rough, or have suddenly found themselves at a level of awareness and/or energy transformation they were not prepared to handle. Perhaps others around them have also had difficulty in dealing with the enormous new levels of knowledge, insight, and energy their friends are experiencing. Even worse, many persons who do not consider themselves seekers or

spiritual wake up one morning to find their world suddenly changed, hearing voices, seeing visions, knowing the thoughts and secret feelings of those around
them. We know what usually happens to anyone in
our society who not only has these experiences but is
foolish enough to talk about them to others: a 72-
hour hold in the nearest "spiritual correction" center
and some massive doses of Thorazine to bring them
back to "normal."

In order to avoid this situation, and to help those
who are trying to figure out if they're becoming enlightened or going crazy, Stan and Christina Grof and Rita
Rohan several years ago established the Spiritual
Emergency Network (SEN). What does SEN do?
Anyone experiencing altered states of awareness, energy, insights, who needs some nurturing, reassurance, and
help while going through this transformation can call
SEN and hopefully find someone nearby who has had
similar experiences, or someone who is a therapist sensitive to and aware of spiritual dimensions of reality
whom they can contact for assistance. The network of
individuals and organizations in SEN numbers more
than 10,000 at present. By writing or phoning SEN you
can receive information and referral for yourself or others. There is also an educational program, including
articles, bibliographies, tapes, lectures, workshops, and
conferences on aspects of spiritual opening and crisis.

SEN's membership is open to anyone who is interested in the goals of spiritual awakening and what might
be called spiritual midwifery. ... Originally, the
Network's purpose was to deal with people having a crisis because of spiritual or psychic experiences happening
to them. They have found, however, that while this is an
important part of their functioning, a larger part is in
networking people and providing information to facili-
tate a more general emergence of spiritual potentials. For
many people, a little information to the effect that they
are not alone, that there are some words that describe

their experiences and books that can be read, is enough
to help them on the spiritual journey.

Many who have had brushes with the paranormal do not feel compelled to embark on a spiritual journey, but many others do feel a need
to examine the deeper or hidden meanings of life and our purpose for
being here. For those who feel they could benefit from SEN, it is a part
of the California Institute of Integral Studies. As of this writing, the
number for its information and referral services is 415-648-2610. The
society can also be contacted by mail at:

SEN California Institute if Integral Studies.
1453 Mission St. San Francisco, CA 94103, USA
General Inquiries: 415-575-6100
or at SEN@CIIS.

I would just add that, although paranormal experiences are common
and by no means indicate a problem of a psychiatric nature, there are
nonetheless psychiatric disorders that require assessment and possibly
treatment. It is tragically true that psychic manifestations have a history
of being pathologized with sometimes tragic results. Nevertheless, it
would be equally tragic if an individual who was clinically delusional and
could possibly suffer harm as a result were not to avail himself of assessment and treatment. These are extreme circumstances as most events
involving the paranormal are not very dramatic and are certainly non-
threatening. They also tend to be short-lived and are even described by
some as being boring, in the sense that they in no way resemble the spectacular events often portrayed in movies and books. They are certainly
never boring to those having such experiences.

Although these experiences are more common than is readily
acknowledged, they are unique to each individual. In the course of my
research, I encountered many poltergeist cases that shared almost iden-
tical elements. (In fact, amongst some researchers, there is an aphorism
that if you've seen one poltergeist you've seen them all.) Although the
phenomena can be similar in presentation, each case is unique pertaining to the individual involved and the effect it has upon them.
Some people are tempted to ignore (where possible) or shrug off these
experiences. I would strongly encourage you to take advantage of this

unique opportunity to explore not only your inner world but the external world as well, which is looking more fantastic than we could ever have imagined!

Following is a list of various groups and organizations that is varied to address any particular need. I have included in-depth mission statements to assist you in determining of which group can best address your situation.

Contacts:

Consciousness Research Laboratory
University of Nevada, Las Vegas
E-mail: info@PsiResearch.org

This is an invaluable research organization conducting important and intriguing work. Although it would make a referral, this is not the first group to contact for assistance with personal paranormal difficulties as it is primarily a research organization. The Consciousness Research Laboratory is a nonprofit scientific research organization established in 1993 at the University of Nevada, Las Vegas. In 1997, CRL became a private research institute in Northern California. CRL's mission is to perform scientific study of the role of consciousness in the physical world, with particular interest in those human experiences called "psychic."

Its director is Dean Radin, Ph.D., who became interested in psychic research as a result of conducting classified psychic research at SRI International in 1985. He and the CRL are associated with the Boundary Institute and the Institute of Noetic Science. Its Web site offers online psi tests for those with Internet access.

Institute of Noetic Sciences
101 San Antonio Rd.
Petaluma, CA, 94952. USA
E-mail: Webmaster@noetic.org

"We are a nonprofit membership organization that both conducts and sponsors research into the workings and powers of the mind, including perceptions, beliefs, attention, and intuition. We are bold enough to inquire about phenomena that don't fit in with the conventional scientific model. We educate the public about the latest findings through our publications, conferences, and Web site, and we support community building by providing ways for members and colleagues to share their experiences and ideas with one another through community groups, online discussion groups, and other networking opportunities."

Society for Psychical Research
49 Marloes Rd. Kensington, London, England, W8 6LA
Phone and fax: 020-7937-8984

The oldest of all the psychical research institutes, the Society for Psychical Reasearch was the model for many such organizations. It is highly regarded by scientists and laypersons alike. Its members undertake research and field investigations, carefully documenting and reporting on cases of purported psychic activity. Like other such organizations, it also supports research into the paranormal, including providing financial support to Ph.D. students in British universities. Its mission statement reads, in part:

> The principal areas of study of psychical research concerns exchanges between minds, or between minds and the environment, which are not dealt with by current orthodox science. This is a large area, incorporating such topics as extrasensory perception (telepathy, clairvoyance, precognition, and retrocognition), psychokinesis (paranormal effect on physical objects, including poltergeist phenomena), near-death and out-of-the-body experiences, apparitions, hauntings, hypnotic regression, and paranormal healing.

The society offers membership, which includes subscription to a quarterly journal, and holds regular conferences, lectures, and an annual international conference. Like its cousin in the United States, it has an extensive library, but a postal lending service is limited to the British Isles. There are also audio tapes of lectures given to the society.

American Society for Psychical Research
5 West 73rd Street. New York, NY, 10023, USA
Phone: 212-799-5050 Fax: 212-496-2749
E-mail: aspr@aspr.com Web site: www.aspr.com

This organization is well established and held in high regard by all who have any interest in parapsychology. They kindly sent me a recent edition of its mission statement:

> The American Society for Psychical Research, Inc. (ASPR) is the oldest psychical research organization in the United States. The ASPR was founded in 1885 by a distinguished group of scholars who shared the courage and vision to explore the uncharted realms of human consciousness, among them renowned Harvard psychologist and Professor of Philosophy William James. For more than a century the ASPR has supported the scientific investigation of exceptional human abilities.
>
> The ASPR headquarters is located in New York City. In addition to laboratories and offices, the ASPR maintains a one-of-a-kind library and archive. This international collection contains rare books, case reports, letters, and manuscripts that date back to the 1700s. The ASPR is a leading repository for an important part of American history.
>
> A pioneering organization with an international membership, the ASPR serves as a global information network for public and professional audiences. Through its publications and educational services it provides responsible information about relevant contemporary and historical research. *The Journal of the American Society for Psychical Research* is a peer-reviewed, academic journal that has been published by the Society since its inception.

Appendix

Koestler Parapsychology Unit
Department of Psychology, University of Edinburgh
7 George Square, Edinburgh, United Kingdom. EH8 9JZ
Phone: + 44-0-131-650-3348
Web site: http://moebius.psy.ed.ac.uk/

This research group is especially concerned with the science of the paranormal much along the lines of the information contained within
Chapter 13 of this book. A valuable resource tool with a variety of technical and non-technical information. Its mission statement reads, in part:
"We are part of the psychology department at Edinburgh University. Our
aim is to conduct systematic and responsible research into the capacity
attributed to some individuals to interact with their environment by
means other than the recognized sensorimotor channels."

Institut für Grenzgebiete der Pschologie und Pschohygiene (Institute
for Border Areas of Psychology and Mental Hygiene)
WilhelmstraBe 3a
D-79098 Freiburg i. Br. Germany
E-mail: igpp@igpp.de Web site: http://www.igpp.de

This is a unique institute and I am impressed with its research and
development of treatment modalities for those requiring assistance as a
result of paranormal activity. Unfortunately, most if not all of its literature is printed in German, so if you do not know the language or a good
translator, it will not be of much use to you. The staff are, however, in
touch with other institutes, so if they are unable to be of assistance they
should be able to make a referral (many of the staff are familiar with
English). The institute's mission statement reads as follows:

> The Institut für Grenzgebiete der Psychologie und
> Psychohygiene (IGPP) at Freiburg, Germany, was
> founded in 1950 by psychologist and physician Prof.
> Hans Bender (1907–1991). The Institute is a nonprof-
> it organization supported by a private foundation.
> Traditionally the Institute was engaged in interdis-
> ciplinary research concerning anomalous phenomena

(extrasensory perception, altered states of consciousness, psychokinesis, etc.). The current research mission is to achieve an improved understanding of the
humanities, social sciences, and natural sciences.

In addition, IGPP offers information and counsel-
ing services for people with extraordinary experiences
and entertains a research archive for parapsychology
and border areas of psychology.

The Institute maintains numerous scientific col-
laborations with universities and research institutes in
and outside of Germany.

Rhine Research Center
402 North, Buchanan Blvd. Durham, NC, 27701-1728, USA
Phone: 919-699-8241 Fax: 919-683-4338
E-mail: info@rhine.org

An old, well-established and respected organization, the Rhine
Research Center has engaged in serious research, including field investigations, for decades now. It has many resources as well as a newsletter and conferences. Following is a quote from its mission statement:

> [The Rhine Research Center] aims to improve the
> human condition by creating a scientific understand-
> ing of those abilities and sensitivities that appear to
> transcend the ordinary limits of space and time and by
> communicating that understanding in cogent and
> responsible ways. The Rhine Research Center will
> continue to achieve those goals through multidiscipli-
> nary research that meets the highest standards of rigor
> and integrity.

International Association for Near Death Studies
P.O. Box 502, East Windsor Hill, CT, 06028-0502, USA
Phone: 860-644-5216
E-mail: office@iands.org Web site: http://www.iands.org

Appendix

For those who have had or know someone who has had a near-death experience, or who simply want to learn more about the topic, an excellent resource is the International Association for Near Death Studies. Its stated goals are:

- To enrich our understanding of the nature and scope of human consciousness and its relationship to life and death;
- To encourage thoughtful exploration of all the facets of near-death and related experiences;
- To respond to people's needs to integrate the physical, mental, emotional, and spiritual aspects of the NDE into their daily living;
- To provide reliable information about near-death experiences to experiencers, researchers, and the public; and
- To serve as a contact point and community for people with particular interest in near-death and related experiences.

Center for Parapsychological Studies in Canada
Box 29091, 7001 Mumford Rd. Halifax, Nova Scotia, Canada, B3L 4T8
Phone: 1-902-453-1905 or 1-877-453-1905
Web site: http://www.cpsc.cjb.net

This is an organization under the leadership of David Walsh, Ph.D., who also teaches courses in parapsychology at the Nova Scotia Community College. It offers publications, referrals, and field investigations. The following is an excerpt from its mission statement:

> The mission of the Center for Parapsychological Studies in Canada is to add to the body of knowledge about our world, in particular, in areas commonly called the paranormal. The center was established in February of 1996. Its headquarters are in Halifax, Nova Scotia with chapters in New Brunswick, Prince Edward Island, Ontario, and British Columbia. We keep in touch with other official organizations and researchers, both local and international, and are building a web of researchers and resources to help us in our investigations.

Division of Personality Studies, University of Virginia Health Sciences Center
PO Box 800152, Charlottesville, VA, 22908-0152, USA
E-mail: DOPS@virginia.edu
Web site: http://www.med.virginia.edu/medicine/inter-dis/personality_studies

Anyone who has done much reading on the subject of reincarnation will have come across the name Dr. Ian Stevenson, who has accumulated a large body of research and case histories over the decades. Although Dr. Stevenson is retired now (but still heavily engaged with writing), the team at the Division of Personality Studies continues with their important and fascinating work under the direction of Dr. Bruce Greyson, who is also a psychiatrist and has been with the team for six years.

The Division's main purpose, and the raison d'être for its foundation, is the scientific investigation phenomena that *suggests that currently accepted scientific assumptions and theories about the nature of mind or consciousness, and its relationship to matter, may be erroneous* [italics mine]. Examples of such phenomena, sometimes called paranormal, include various types of extrasensory perception (such as telepathy), apparitions and deathbed visions (sometimes referred to as after death communications or ADCs), poltergeists, experiences of persons who come close to death and survive (usually called Near-Death Experiences or NDEs), out-of-body experiences (OBEs), and claimed memories of previous lives.

Despite widespread popular interest in paranormal phenomena, scientific research into their occurrence and processes remains extremely meager.

DOPS is one of only five university-based research units in the world that are investigating similar paranormal phenomena. The other four are Princeton University, the University of Edinburgh, the University of Amsterdam, and the University of Freiburg in Germany. The University of Virginia's unit is the only one of the five whose staff have a special interest in studying the evidence for survival after death. ...

From the Division's research, eleven books and a large number of articles published in scientific journals have been produced. Other articles and books are in various stages of preparation. The staff presents papers based on their research at scientific meetings when opportunities arise. The [Web] site includes lists of the books and articles published by the Division's staff; the lists can also be obtained by writing to the Division.

Because of public interest in paranormal phenomena and the tendency of some members of the public media to sensationalize the subject, members of the staff believe they have an obligation to disseminate accurate information to the public. Accordingly, as time permits, they make themselves available for interviews and as consultants to representatives of the media, *provided they can receive assurance that the subject will be treated in a serious manner.*

The devision welcomes accounts of experiences that may be of a paranormal nature, whether your own or someone else's. They ask accounts be typed, sent via regular mail, and be of a reasonable length. Please do not send audiocassette format. They advise that people who submit accounts should be "willing to participate in research, which often involves questionnaires and sometimes interviews. Identities of persons sharing experiences with us will be carefully concealed in any published report." They regret, however, that the small size of their staff sometimes makes it impossible for them to investigate every case brought to their attention.

The Behavioural Neuroscience Program, Department of Psychology, Laurentian University
Ramsey Lake Rd. Sudbury, ON, Canada, P3E 2C6
Phone: 705-675-4824 Fax: 705-671-3844
Neuropsychology Lab: 705-675-1151

Dr. Michael Persinger and his team are well known for their research in anomalous activity and its potential relationship to temporal lobe epilepsy and electromagnetic fields to name just two theories they have researched. If you are having particularly disturbing experiences and even feel threatened by them, this team would be a good starting point as a contact or referral source.

Society for Scientific Exploration
Office of the Secretary, Laurene W. Fredrick
University Station, P.O. Box 3818 Charlottesville, Virginia, 22903-0818

This group is located at the University of Virginia and investigates various anomalies including UFOs and crop circles. Its mission statement reads:

> The primary goal of the international Society for Scientific Exploration (SSE) is to provide a professional forum for presentations, criticism, and debate concerning topics which are for various reasons ignored or studied inadequately within mainstream science. A secondary goal is to promote improved understanding of those factors that unnecessarily limit the scope of scientific inquiry, such as sociological constraints, restrictive worldview, hidden theoretical assumptions, and the temptation to concert prevailing theory into prevailing dogma. ...
>
> The society encourages such investigations for several reasons that may appeal to different communities:
>
> - To the research scientist, we commend the intellectual challenge of explaining away an apparent anomaly or seizing the new knowledge presented by a new one.
> - To the student scientist, we point out that science does not begin with textbooks: it begins with the unknown and ends with the textbooks.
> - To the nonscientists, we acknowledge that deep

public interest in some of these topics calls for unprejudiced evaluation based on objective research.

- To the policy maker, we point out that today's anomaly may become tomorrow's technology.

The Boundary Institute
P.O. Box 3580, Los Altos, California, 94024, USA
Phone: 650-941-0778
E-mail: info@boundaryinstitute.org

For the scientifically minded amongst you or for those who had an interest science and psi activity tweaked by Chapter 13 of this book, this important and exciting research institute will be of particular interest to you. It has online experiments (and has posted a paper summarizing the first year results of these experiments). The institute was founded in February 2000 and receives its financial support through individuals and organizations.

With the permission of its president, Richard Shoup, I reproduce its mission statement:

> The Boundary Institute is a nonprofit scientific research organization dedicated to the advancement of twenty-first century science. Our research activities include the development and exploration of new approaches in physics and mathematics, testing of new theory by experiment, and investigations of certain anomalous phenomena. The Institute's experimental program has focused primarily on certain poorly understood phenomena usually called "psychic" or "psi." Extensive evidence suggests that these well-established but enigmatic effects are real physical phenomena, despite their sometimes peculiar and elusive character. We believe that psi phenomena, while currently poorly understood, are amongst the most provocative and important challenges facing science today.

Our theoretical program is well grounded in existing knowledge, building on established quantum theory and other physical laws and principles. However, we are exploring a particular new approach to physical structure and processes called *Link Physics* that shows exceptional promise as an extension and clarification of existing quantum theory, including possible explanations of psi phenomena and much more. In particular, we can now show how core laws of quantum mechanics really belong to pure mathematics, not physical reality. And we are beginning to see how to understand and explain psi phenomena — without contradicting existing, well-established physical laws.

The questions we ask at the Boundary Institute concern the fundamentals of physics, the phenomena associated with consciousness, and ultimately the nature of reality itself. Our tools of inquiry are the standard ones of science, including grounded theoretical development, carefully controlled experiments, statistical analyses and replication, collaboration with other researchers across a variety of fields, and peer reviewed publication.

Through these activities and with these tools, we look to broaden science to include the whole of human experience, and to bring about a better partnership between science and the whole of nature.

Parapsychology Foundation
228 East 71st Street, New York, NY, 10021,USA
Phone: (212) 628-1550.
E-mail: info@parapsychology.org
Web site: http://www.parapsychology.org

Founded in 1951, this organization sponsors research and distributes academic grants to study the many areas of psychic phenomena. It has an extensive library and many publications, including *The International Journal of Parapsychology*. The foundation is not only dedicated to the study of the paranormal but also actively engaged in the dispersal of research results to further the knowledge and awareness of psi to the scientific community and the public in general.

Haunted Hamilton
Web site: http://www.hauntedhamilton.com

Large organizations are sometimes an impractical source of help. More and more, smaller groups are forming to reflect the particular needs of individual communities. Haunted Hamilton is one such group. It was started by Daniel Cumerlato and Stephanie Lechiak, who are dedicated to the research and investigation of history and hauntings around the world. One of the group's goals in the investigation of paranormal activity is to call attention to the preservation of historic sites and buildings. Physically, they are located in the Hamilton/Niagara region in Ontario, Canada. The group is currently about 80 percent online and can only be contacted through the Internet. If you need assistance, but you don't have a computer, you may be able to access the Internet at your local library, or perhaps with a friend's computer. In that case, you can leave a name and phone number where you can be reached with a brief description of your problem. The group's investigation services are free of charge. It has monthly meetings at the historic Museum of Steam and Technology and also holds public events. (Information on such events can be obtained from the Web site.)

The group has a monthly newsletter that includes updates, stories, and lists upcoming events. Currently the newsletter is only available through the Web site. Daniel, Stephanie, and the group's two psychics undertake frequent investigations of paranormal activity, however, most of these are private. As they state: "We take our research very seriously and don't intend on exploiting or minimizing anyone's ghostly experiences." They document the investigation, pointing out some of the more interesting elements and include any photos or EVPs (sound recordings). Some are put on the group's Web site along with other personal experiences contributed by others who wish to share their stories. Daniel and Stephanie carefully monitor the Web site to protect its integrity and the contributors so no one's experiences are put down or questioned.

If you reside in the Hamilton, Niagara, or Toronto, the group is looking for field consultants to write articles on the history and hauntings that represent the city they live in.

Ontario Paranormal Research Coalition
Web site: http://www.pararesearchers.org

As the name suggests, this group is a coalition composed of groups that research various inexplicable phenomena, including ghosts and hauntings. Its mission statement outlines its goals as follows:

- To actively pursue and encourage research, investigations, and documentation of stories, legends, myths, and first-hand accounts of the paranormal;
- To freely provide access to information relating to the studies of the paranormal within Ontario and Canada;
- To maintain the highest standards of professionalism in regards to our activities; and
- To promote a healthy respect and attitude towards all belief systems in regards to the paranormal.

The Academy of Religion and Psychical Research
PO Box 614, Bloomfield, CT, 06002-0614
Phone: (860) 242-4593
E-mail: bateyb@infi.net

For those with an interest in the spiritual or even religious dimensions of psi phenomena, the ARPR is a unique and invaluable organization doing much-needed work.

The Academy of Religion and Psychical Research was formed in October, 1972 as an academic affiliate of Spiritual Fronteirs Fellowship International. Its purpose is threefold:

First, to encourage dialogue, exchange of ideas, and cooperation between clergy and academics of religion and philosophy and scientists, researchers, and academics of all scientific and humanistic disciplines in the fields of psychical research and new disciplines as well as the historic sciences.

Second, to conduct an education program for these scholars, the Spiritual Frontiers Fellowship membership, and the general public, blending data already available in the area of their common interest with the interchange of views stimulated in these scholars, to the end that both the scientific and religion communities may be better informed about such facts and views and their propriety value and respectability.

Third, to work closely with, and offer good offices to all reputable organizations having related interests in the fields of education, religion, science, and psychical research.

The Academy will endeavor to sponsor conferences and symposia for the presentation of scholarly data, points of view, and interchange of ideas in the area where religion and psychical research interface; publish papers resulting from such meetings and other appropriate materials on this area that will be of interest to academics, scientists and the clergy; and monitor, evaluate, explain, and report the significant data in this area for the benefit of scholars.

The Academy of Religion and Psychical Research sponsors an annual conference at which academically significant presentations that combine aspects of both psychical research and religion are given.

Some of its annual conferences have covered such topics as personal survival of bodily death, frontiers of consciousness in the new millenium, implications for artificial intelligence for religion and psychical research, and their 2002 mediumship: a gateway to higher dimensions of existence. Its conferences are taped and available on cassette and in published form. The academy also awards a prize of five hundred dollars for the best paper.

The Ghost Research Society
PO Box 205. Oak Lawn, Illinois, 60454-0205, USA
Web site: http://www.ghostresearch.org

"The Ghost Research Society was formed as a clearing house for reports of ghosts, hauntings, poltergeists, and life after death encounters. The society members actively research and investigate all reports that come their way, including private homes and business. The society also analyzes alleged spirit photographs, video and audio tapes that they come across from ordinary people or society members. The society employs a number of specialized devices to detect the presence of ghosts."

Anyone is welcome to become a member; the costs are broken down in three categories: sustaining member, $25.00 ($35.00 foreign); patron membership, $50.00; and lifetime membership, $175.00. The society has a publication entitled *Ghost Trackers*.

Magazines:

Magazines are difficult to come by on this subject, but one that is often accessible in larger or specialty bookstores is entitled *Fate Magazine*, which publishes a wide variety of material on psychic experiences. It also accepts articles and personal accounts of the paranormal for consideration for publication. If you have trouble locating a copy, contact P.O. Box 64383, St Paul, MN, 55163-0383, USA.

There is also *X-Project Magazine*, which can be reached at P.O. Box 1042, Burlington, VT, 05402, USA or by E-mail at Editor@xproject.net.

Another journal is entitled *The Electronic Journal for Anomalous Phenomena*. As the name suggest, it is published on the Internet. It can be reached at eJAP@psy.uva.nl.

As previously stated, most of the groups and organizations listed here have publications available to both members and nonmembers. There are also various newsletters published on the Internet, the majority of which are available free of charge.

Notes and Sources

Introduction:

1   Broughton, R.S. (1991). *Parapsychology: The Controversial Science.*
    New York: Ballantine Books.

Chapter 1

1   The street name was changed for obvious reasons. To my knowl-
    edge, there is no Highgate Street in Guelph, Ontario.

Chapter 5

1   Styron, William. (1990). *Darkness Visible: A Memoir of Madness.*
    New York: Vintage Books, p. 65.

2   An interesting side note: In spite of our many efforts and various
    cameras, from digital to Polaroid, we were unable to produce a pic-
    ture of the piano cited in this chapter. The results were either solid
    black or bright white.

Chapter 6

1   Levine, Stephen. (1997). *A Year to Live: How to Live This Year As
    If It Were Your Last.* New York: Bell Tower. pp. 125 and 127.

Chapter 8

1 "Dawn" (1973). Lyrics by Jackson, Emerson, Davison. Performed by The Nice.

2 Rogo, D. Scott, and Bayless, Raymond. (1979). *Phone calls From the Dead*. New York: Berkley Books. pp. 21-22.

3 Jung, Carl. (1963). *Memories, Dreams, Reflections*. New York: Pantheon Books. pp. 155-156.

4 The Freud/Jung Letters. The correspondence between Sigmund Freud and C.G. Jung. (Abridged ed.) Edited and with intro by William McGuire. 1994.

5 Jung, Carl. (1920/1948)."The Psychological Foundations of Belief in Spirits." *The Structure and Dynamics of the Psyche*, 8, 301-318.

Chapter 9

1 There are materials that hold and emit more radiation and have stronger electromagnetic fields than others. Granite and sandstone are two such materials. This may explain why some psychics and mystics employ specific minerals as a psychic conduit in their rituals. There is also a theory being explored that considers the effect seismicity and tectonic stain have on the manifestations of anomalous events including UFO sightings and increases in poltergeist activity.

People have often speculated that perhaps it is not the given structure that is haunted but the ground it is built on. This has caused some scientists to closely examine the geophysical elements that could be causing or interacting with anomalous phenomena. Although the science being applied toward this activity may be new, the notion of land being "good" or "evil" is certainly not new. There are Native American tribes that talk about land that can go "bad" or that has become "spoiled." The questions are, how does one spoil land (some means become immediately apparent) and can one recover the land once it has been spoiled. There are purification rituals, but the legends suggest time and isolation has to purify the environment. In Native and other legends, fire is also purifying, and in some cases where the cause of the fire cannot be revealed in an investigation, the legends do mention such places "combusting" and consuming themselves.

These Native legends complement other cultural and religious beliefs about hallowed or sanctified ground. Popular culture adopts the same idea when it locates its haunted mansions on burial grounds; ironically, a former graveyard is probably the best place to build a house if the goal is to avoid things that go bump in the night. If it were feasible, it would be interesting to determine the history of the residents in the surrounding houses. Did an inordinate amount "bad luck" visit their households as well, or is the negativity isolated to this house? We can only wish the next inhabitants better luck.

2   In order to obtain an accurate analysis of an environment, ideally one would like continuous access to the location. Otherwise it is difficult to say with any certainty what is or is not normal for any given location with the exception of highly irregular readings. In this case, the hydro was not hooked up to the house and there were artificial generators of radiation or magnetic fields such as microwaves, pagers, or cell phones. Where the electric field is measured in standard units of kV/meter, with a sensitivity of about 1 volt/meter, the field's strength throughout the house ranged from normal to above average with the lowest ebb in the kitchen registering at 2 volts/meter. The highest intensity field was within the master bedroom at a spot just beyond the bedroom door. We have been unable to ascertain any physical cause for localized manifestation. This was also the location of one of the two fixed cold spots with the house, although we do not know if the two are related.

Bearing in mind that there is natural ionizing radiation all about us and that everything from cellphones to sun spots can instigate fluctuations within the mean count of ionizing particles, the radiation levels within this house tended to be on the high side, with a peak of 4.1 millisieverts in the basement. Normally occurring background radiation can range from 1.5 to 3.5 millisieverts/yr but can be much higher in some places.

3   The only sound on the audio tape was interjections of static as though a candy wrapper were being crumbled. Otherwise it was simply the white noise of a blank tape.

Chapter 13

1   McLynn, Frank. (1996). *Carl Gustav Jung*. New York: St. Martin's Press. pp. 467-468.

2   For further reading on this theory, refer to the following. Although old, it lays a good groundwork for a fundamental understanding, especially for the novice of quantum physics:

Harris, Evan Walker. (1974). "Consciousness and Quantum Theory." In Edgar Mitchell (Ed.), *Psychic Exploration: A Challenge for Science* (Chapter 23). New York: GP Putnam & Sons.

3   Harris, Evan Walker. (1970). "The Nature of Consciousness." *Mathematical Biosciences*, 7, 138-197.

4   North, Anthony. (1998). *The Paranormal: A Guide to the Unexplained*. London: Blandford Press.

5   Stevens, Paul. (1997). "Theories on the Physical Basis of Psi." Retrieved November 5, 2001, from University of Edinburgh, Department of Psychology, Koestler Parapsychology Unit Web site: http://moebius.psy.ed.ac.uk/Text/Physical.html

6   OT stands for Operating Thetan, where thetan is jargon for "soul" and operating is supposed to mean "knowing and willing cause over life, thought, matter, energy, space, and time."

7   Princeton Engineering Anomalies Research Lab. Implications and applications for anomalous research.

8   Let us recall that the no one could imagine why any scientists would be devoting time and money into this thing called a laser. What in heaven's name could you ever use it for? And the

Notes and Sources

Canadians responsible for the development of insulin were thought at the time to be completely crazy.

Appendix

1   Smith, Adam. (1975). *Powers of the Mind.* New York: Ballantine Books. p. 338.

Glossary

Akashic Records: The term for the permanent record of all thoughts and deeds throughout history that is believed to be recorded in the Universal Mind, Cosmic Consciousness, or Mind of God. It is believed that in altered states of consciousness, one is able to gain access to portions of this universal consciousness. It has also been suggested that this is the means by which artists or scientists get their ingenious inspirations. There are similar ideas in world religions and mysticism; e.g., the Christian God is thought (though not literally) to have a book of records on each individual which you will encounter on the Day of Judgement.

Anomalous Events: The technical term used in reference to unexplained phenomena of undetermined etiology; e.g., someone could be seeing the apparition of a deceased relative or they could be having a seizure of the temporal lobe.

Aport: An object that has materialized, e.g., a book an individual wanted to read, or stones falling from the ceiling, a piece of jewelry, etc. It was thought at one time that mediums could conjure up such objects, but most instances were later discovered to be trickery. Some objects can disappear never to found again, or they might turn up in an unlikely place. In some instances, the object of the recipient's desire materializes "out of nowhere," such as a record or even garbage bags, as had happened to an individual cited in this book.

Glossary

Astral Projection: The projection of the ethereal/psychic self and consciousness beyond the physical body to another location. When seen or perceived by other persons at the location, the astral form is known as an apparition of the living.

Aura: An energy field radiating from animate and inanimate objects, especially around the human body, which gives off different colours at various times and various degrees, indicative of the physical, pshychic, and mental state of the person or object. Can be seen by most psychics but is most often felt even by those who cannot see the actual field.

Automatic Writing: Writing not under the conscious directive of the individual holding the pen. It is spontaneous and its appearance is often different from the handwriting of the individual. Can also be in a language unknown to the writer or manifest in a drawing. A common deviation of this is doodling. A tool often employed by psychics, researchers, and some psychiatrists.

Biolocation: The appearance of a person in two locations at the same time; believed to be an astral projection or an apparition of the living.

Cryptomnesia: A forgotten memory. In broader psychic terms, this includes memories of a past incarnation or memories derived from a collective unconscious.

Déjà vu: A sense that a new experience has happened before. From the French meaning "already seen."

Dematerialization: The disappearance of an object, partially or completely, by spontaneous psychic means.

Doppelgänger: A real or ghostly double of a living person. In legend, if one meets up with one's Doppelgänger, death is imminent.

Ecosomatic State: The sense that one is outside of one's own body.

Ectoplasm: A white, foamlike substance that has been observed oozing from the bodies of mediums in deep trance states. This material, which is accompanied by the odour of ozone, can take the shape of an object or the bust of the person the medium is trying to contact. It was often revealed as a parlour trick, though not in all cases.

Ganzfeld: A type of sensory deprivation developed by psychologists and employed in some psi tests, i.e., telepathy, remote viewing.

Guide: A benevolent spirit that guides and protects a living individual. Does not have to be related to the person. Commonly thought of as angels, though the two are dissimilar.

Hypnogogic: The altered state of consciousness that resides between wakefulness and sleep, what some have described as a twilight state. Persons in this state are open to suggestion and receptive to telepathic messages, including those from their guides.

Incendiary Effect: Most commonly associated with poltergeist phenomena in which objects that have been bent, moved, or thrown are warm or hot to the touch. For unknown reasons, some objects have even combusted. This usually occurs only at the time when the poltergeist activity is extreme to begin with and further escalates. Water spots are a more common (and safer) manifestation of the poltergeist. There are also documented cases of spontaneous human combustion, but there is no concrete link with this frightening event and poltergeists.

Metaphysics: The scientific philosophy concerned with the elucidation of ultimate causes and their interconnectedness.

Materialization: The emergence or manifestation of a psychical object by psychic means (see aport).

Noetics: The study of various states of consciousness. A more rigid variation is known as cognitive neurobiology.

Out-of-Body Experience: As the name suggests, this is the experience of being outside of one's physical body, sometimes floating above it looking down at oneself. Some people are able to travel to locations and observe activity; i.e., one man described popping out of his body just as he was falling off to sleep and observed himself lying in bed but did not see his wife. As soon as he wondered where his wife had gotten to, he found himself in the family room and saw his wife sitting quietly reading a book. Within a flash, he was back in his body. He told her of the experience the following morning and she was amazed, explaining that she could not sleep and, not wanting to disturb him, went to the family room to read. OBEs should not be confused with the psychological phenomena experienced by people who have suffered a shock or trauma and feel unreal and disconnected from their bodies. These are not psychic OBEs but rather a response to severe stress.

Parapsychology: A branch of science that studies such phenomena as hauntings, telekinesis, ESP, telepathy, etc.

Poltergeist: From German meaning noisy spirit. Determined to be random, spontaneous psychokinetic activity emanating from a particular person who is normally unaware that they are the source of the phenomena. Most commonly occurs to young people, emotionally immature people, or individuals that are natural but undeveloped psychics experiencing serious unresolved emotional issues. Commonly involves displacement, disfiguration, or breaking of objects, unexplained noises, flushing of toilets, banging of doors, etc. Generally a nuisance, but can on rare occasions become quite destructive, violent, and expensive.

Psychic Photography: Also referred to as thoughtotography. The purported ability by some to project mental images onto an unexposed film. Ted Sheros was probably the most studied and well known for this anomaly, though there were others.

Psychometry: The ability by some persons to determine the history, circumstances, or the knowledge of the owner of an object simply by holding it. It is an ability often employed in forensic cases such as missing persons or other police investigations.

Psychokinesis: Also telekinesis. The ability to manipulate physical objects with the mind alone.

Pyrokinesis: The ability to instigate or manipulate fire.

Remote Viewing: The ability to see people, places, or objects in places from remote locations. For instance, in one experiment, the target person went to the parking lot of a university and was holding a painting of a landscape. The other person was in another city and, after performing some relaxation exercises, wrote down that he saw the target person in a parking lot, standing next to a red car and holding a painting which she could not make out, only that is had a dark brown wooden frame. The target was in fact standing near a red car but was not even aware of it until it was mentioned when the experiment was reviewed. The target was sending only impressions of the parking lot and the picture (which was in fact in a dark wooden frame. Remote viewing is a popular test in lab studies because it can be strictly controlled. It can be thought of as a form of telepathy or general ESP. The use of Zender or ESP cards are often employed in the lab as well. These are cards with specific symbols such as stars, waves, square, circle. The hit-miss ratio is analyzed to determine the statistical probabilities of lucky guesses or actual correct ESP hits.

Revenant: One who returns from the dead.

Quantum Field Theory: A physical field considered as a collection of particles and forces and observable properties of an interacting system which are expressed as finite quantities rather than as state vectors. (A vector is a physical quantity that has both magnitude and direction.)

Quantum Vacuum: Being devoid of any form of matter. The space housing an infinite sea of electrons having negative energy, which is observed as being empty space.

Glossary

Scry: To see into the future or into other dimensions such as the after-life by gazing into a crystal or specially designed mirror.

Subjective Anomalous Experience: Any personal occurrence of a psychic nature (see anomalous events).

Synchronicity: A theory developed by Carl Jung to explain the principle of meaningful coincidences which also takes into account ESP and telepathy.

Teleportation: The unexplained and mysterious movement of an object from one location to another.

Trance: A deep meditative state in which the individual is able to access realms of consciousness not normally accessible in regular conscious states. It is employed by some psychics to communicate with the dead. It is also considered to be an altered state of consciousness, and while in such a mental state, many receive creative inspiration or guidance.

Vertical Dream: A dream whose content centres around true life events of which the dreamer has no knowledge, whether it be centred on the past, present, or future.

Vertical Impression: Knowledge that is imparted on an individual without their conscious awareness.

Xenoglossy: The expression of strange or foreign communication previously unknown to the experient.

Suggested Reading

Auerback, Loyd. (1986). *ESP, Hauntings, and Poltergeists: A Parapsychological Handbook.* New York: Warner Books.

Bardens, Dennis. (1965). *Ghosts and Hauntings.* New York: Taplinger Pub. Co.

Broughton, Richard S. (1991). *The Controversial Science.* New York: Ballantine Books.

Bucke, Richard. (1972). *Cosmic Consciousness: A Study in the Evolution of the Human Mind.* New York/London: Olympia Press.

Clery, Val. (1985). *Ghost Stories of Canada.* Toronto: Hounslow Press.

Colombo, John Robert. (2000). *Ghost Stories of Canada.* Toronto: Dundurn Press.

Denning, Hazel. (1996). *True Hauntings: Spirits with a Purpose.* Llewellyn Publications.

Doyle, David. (1985). *The Sphinx and the Rainbow.* Boulder/New York: New Science Library/ Random House.

Eisenberg, Howard. (1977). *Inner Spaces: Parapsychological Explorations of the Mind*. Don Mills: Musson Books.

Fanthorpe, Lionel and Fanthorpe, Patricia. (2000). *Death: The Final Mystery*. Toronto: Dundurn Press.

Frankl, Viktor. (1995). *The Doctor and the Soul: From Psychotherapy to Logotherapy*. New York: Vintage Books.

Frankl, Viktor. (1959). *Man's Search for Meaning: An Introduction to Logotherapy*. New York: Pocket Books.

Gersten, Dennis. (1997). *Are You Getting Enlightened or Losing Your Mind?: A Spiritual Program for Mental Illness*. New York: Harmony Books.

Grof, Stanislov and Grof, Christina. (Eds.), (1989). *Spiritual Emergency: When Personal Transformation Becomes a Crisis*. New York: JP Tarcher Inc.

Guiley, Ellen. (1987). *Tales of Reincarnation*. New York: Pocket Books.

Jung, Carl. (1963). *Memories, Dreams, Reflections*. New York: Pantheon Books.

Jung, Carl. (1933). *Modern Man In Search of Soul*. New York and London: Harvest/Harcourt Brace Jovanovich.

Lenz, Frederick. (1979). *Lifetimes: A true Account of Reincarnation*. New York: Fawcelt Crest.

McLynn, Frank. (1996). *Carl Gustav Jung*. New York: St Martins Press.

Manning, Mathew. (1974). *The Link: The Extraordinary Gifts of a Teenage Psychic*. Buckinghamshire: Colin Smythe Ltd.

(Marinoff, Lou. (1999). *Plato Not Prozac: Applying Philosophy to Everyday Life*. New York: HarperCollins.

Mindell, Arnold. (1988). *City of Shadows: Psychological Interventions in Psychiatry*. Boston: Routledge.

Mitchell, Edgar D. (1974). *Psychic Exploration: A Challenge for Science*. New York: GP Putnam & Sons.

Moody, Raymond Jr. (1975). *Life after Life*. New York: Bantam Books.

Moody, Raymond Jr. (1977). *Reflection on Life after Life*. New York: Bantam Books.

North, Anthony. (1996). *The Paranormal: A Guide to the Unexplained*. London: Blandford.

Pearce, Joseph Chilton. (1971). *Crack in the Cosmic Egg: Challenging Constructs of Mind and*
Reality. New York: Pocket Books.

Pinker, Steven. (1997). *How the Mind Works*. New York: WW Norton & Company Inc.

Rogo, Scott. (1978). *Mind Beyond the Body: the Mystery of ESP Projection*. New York: Penguin.

Schick, Theodore, and Vaughn, Lewis. (1995). *How to Think about Weird Things: Critical Thinking for a New Age*. California: Mayfield Publishing.

Talbot, Michael. (1981). *Mysticism and the New Physics*. New York: Bantam Books.

The Tibetan Book of the Dead

Also refer to the appendix of this book for organizations and groups that have newsletters, journals, research papers, and special publications.